Organizational Dynamics of Creative Destruction

Organizational Dynamics of Creative Destruction

Entrepreneurship and the Emergence of Industries

Stephen J. Mezias and Elizabeth Boyle

Published 2002 by
PALGRAVE MACMILLAN
Houndmills, Basingstoke, Hampshire RG21 6XS and
175 Fifth Avenue, New York, N. Y. 10010
Companies and representatives throughout the world

PALGRAVE MACMILLAN is the global academic imprint of the Palgrave Macmillan division of St. Martin's Press, LLC and of Palgrave Macmillan Ltd. Macmillan® is a registered trademark in the United States, United Kingdom and other countries. Palgrave is a registered trademark in the European Union and other countries.

ISBN 0–333–99862–6

This book is printed on paper suitable for recycling and made from fully managed and sustained forest sources.

A catalogue record for this book is available from the British Library.

A catalog record for this book is available from the Library of Congress.

10   9   8   7   6   5   4   3   2   1
11   10   09   08   07   06   05   04   03   02

Printed and bound in Great Britain by
Antony Rowe Ltd, Chippenham and Eastbourne

Contents

List of Tables vii

List of Figures viii

Acknowledgements ix

1 Introduction 1

Part I Ecologies of Learning and Intrapreneurship 15

2 The Three Faces of Corporate Renewal: Institution,
Revolution and Evolution 17
Reprint of Mezias and Glynn, 1993

3 Mimetic Learning and the Evolution of Organizational
Populations 53
Reprint of Mezias and Lant, 1994

**Part II The Evolutionary Dynamics of New Industry
Creation 81**

4 Resource Partitionng, the Founding of Specialist Firms and
Innovation: the American Feature Film Industry, 1912–1929 83
Reprint of Mezias and Mexias, 2000

5 The Community Dynamics of Entrepreneurship: the Birth
of the American Film Industry, 1895–1929 111
Reprint of Mezias and Kuperman, 2001

**Part III The Role of Institutions in New Industry
Emergence 143**

6 Legal Environments and the Population Dynamics of
Entrepreneurship: Litigation and Foundings in the Early
American Film Industry, 1897–1918 145

7 Industry Creation, Legitimacy and Foundings: the Case of
the American Film Industry, 1896–1928 159

Part IV   Conclusion   **187**

8   Organizational Dynamics of Creative Destruction:
   Entrepreneurship and the Emergence of New Industries   189

Notes   195

Bibliography   197

Index   211

List of Tables

1.1 Refereed journals publishing articles related to entrepreneurship
2.1 How resources devoted to search are changed in response to experience
3.1 The effects of organizational and environmental characteristics on the proportion of mimetic firms in a population
3.2 The effects of organizational and environmental characteristics on the proportion of mimetic firms in a population
4.1 Descriptive statistics
4.2 Correlation matrix
4.3 Regression results for specialist foundings
4.4 New genre production and distribution by generalists and specialists
4.5 Specialist poportions in genre amd population
5.1 Key innovations in the emergence of the film industry
5.2 Four categories of entrepreneurial behavior
7.1 The coding of cognitive legitimacy and sample headlines
7.2 The coding of sociopolitical legitimacy and sample headlines
7.3 Coding of the effect of headlines on cognitive legitimacy
7.4 Coding of the effect of headlines on sociopolitical legitimacy
7.5 Distribution of *New York Times* articles

List of Figures

1.1 Number of articles taking a supply and/or demand perspective
2.1 Flow chart of search decisions
2.2 Flow chart for determining performance
2.3 Flow chart for determination of change
2.4 Mean total innovative changes in the four conditions
2.5 Mean refinements to current technology in the four conditions
2.6 Mean resources in the four conditions
2.7 The learning curve assuming no innovation and a maximum of 50
3.1 Mean proportion of surviving firms of each type as a function of time
3.2 Effect of the probability of environmental change on the mean proportion of mimetic firms
3.3 Effect of the magnitude of environmental change on the mean proportion of mimetic firms
4.1 Proportion of films produced and distributed by generalist firms
7.1 Cumulative headline count

Acknowledgements

The authors are grateful to the American Film Institute and to ICP/Proquest for expediting their work immeasurably by making available the American Film Institute's Catalog of Films Produced in the United States in CD-ROM form. They would also like to thank their colleagues for their helpful insights and support. The research assistance of Michael Barnett, Mikelle Calhoun, Alan Eisner, Jerry Kuperman, and John Mezias is acknowledged.

1
Introduction

The words 'organizational dynamics' begin the title of our book because the major thesis of this book is that organization theory provides a set of useful frameworks and questions for the study of entrepreneurship. The creative destruction borrows Schumpeter's colorful language to signal the specific focus within the broader field of entrepreneurship that will be highlighted by perspectives from organization theory and throughout our book: the emergence of new industries. The good news is that recent research, including the studies reported in the remaining chapters of this book, has made important progress in developing the application of frameworks from organization theory to study the issue of the emergence of new industries. At the very least, this work also has provided the beginnings of the answers to key questions. The less good news is that there is still a long way to go. Hitt, Ireland, Camp, and Sexton (2001: 488) provided a recent summary of the state of theory development in entrepreneurship: 'Although entrepreneurship has existed as a practice and field of study for quite some, there is no commonly accepted and well-developed paradigm for research in the field.' While there is still considerable truth to this summary, we believe both that there has been progress and that organization theory provides useful frameworks for understanding and conceptualizing this progress. Perhaps the most fundamental contribution of organization theory to the study of entrepreneurship has been research attention to higher levels of analysis. This work has moved not just beyond the great man, but beyond the boundaries of entrepreneurial firms as well. In the remainder of this chapter we will discuss implications of this expansion of the scope of entrepreneurship.

We proceed as follows. We begin by exploring how organization theory has redefined the phenomenon of interest to students of entrepreneurship, particularly in suggesting the need to study higher levels of analysis.

Chasing entrepreneurship: redefining an elusive phenomenon

What is entrepreneurship, and how can we understand it as social scientists?The order of the questions here was intentional, and we will begin with the issue of defining entrepreneurship. In reviewing approaches to defining entrepreneurship, however, we remain attentive to the second question. We assume that students of organizations have provided some useful insights into entrepreneurship as an object of social science. At the same time, we want to remain conscious of the larger context of a huge increase in studies of entrepreneurship (Thornton, 1999). As a consequence, we begin our study of entrepreneurship by examining the place of a diverse group of researchers that we call organization theorists in the context of the larger phenomenon of an increase in attention to the topic of entrepreneurship. We start with the observation that despite the increasing popularity of entrepreneurial research since the late 1980s, there is still a struggle over the proper focus for the study of entrepreneurship. Our fundamental claim is that a comprehensive definition of entrepreneurship must include an organizational perspective.

According to Thornton (1999: 34), the '... knowledge base of entrepreneurship research has been generated by three founding disciplines: psychology (McClelland, 1961), economics (Schumpeter, 1934), and sociology (Weber, 1904).'Landstrom and Sexton (2000: 437) described the beginnings of the recent wave of attention to entrepreneurship: 'In 1982, when the entrepreneurship field was beginning to emerge, the major topics were financing, growth, the process of entrepreneurship and research methodology.'As these topics suggest, psychology and economics, which tend to be individual in their orientation, were first on the scene. Sociology, for the most part, arrived late to the party, where each discipline has tended to speak mostly to its own. As a result, dialog in the field of entrepreneurship has been, according to Thornton (1999: 20), '... organized by camps, where the lack of cross-level and cross-disciplinary interaction tends to obscure the overall picture of what gives rise to entrepreneurship.'

We believe that a sociological perspective on entrepreneurship offers the opportunity to enhance cross-level and cross-disciplinary interaction by suggesting an integration. We begin by reviewing the recent attention to entrepreneurship among students of organizations. The distinction between supply and demand sides, we argue, clarifies how recent increased attention to entrepreneurship has refined the scope of entrepreneurship research. We summarize this change in scope in terms of the issue of levels of analysis and focus on the subfield of organizational sociology (Scott, 1998). Our conclusion is that work in this area has developed an approach focused on understanding the phenomenon of new industry emergence. We close with a model of the organizational approaches to the emergence of new industries that links with the remaining chapters of this book.

Levels of analysis in entrepreneurship research

Supply and demand perspectives on entrepreneurship

We begin with the observation by Thornton (1999) that the recent increase in sociological attention to entrepreneurship has resulted in a shift from largely supply side perspectives to more inclusion of demand side perspectives. According to her framework, the supply focuses on the individual traits of entrepreneur that are seen as the primary drivers of the supply of entrepreneurs. Until fairly recently, this had been the dominant focus of entrepreneurship scholars, epitomized by the great man theory of entrepreneurship. Thornton (1999: 19) contrasted this approach with a supply side approach as follows: 'Newer work from the demand-side perspective has focused on rates, or the context in which entrepreneurship occurs. 'We begin by examining the rise of demand side perspectives, verifying that it did and is occurring. Our motivation for doing this is summarized well by Nodoushani & Nodoushani (1999), who argued that entrepreneurship knowledge is inseparable from the language that gives it expression. Our evidence for the rise of demand side perspectives is a language-based study of the extent to which there is a shift in levels of analysis in entrepreneurship work.

Supply-side and demand-side abstracts analysis

In this study we used articles published in peer-reviewed journals identified by (Shane 1997) and MacMillan (1992) as high quality entrepreneurship research outlets. In doing this our intent was to examine only those publications in peer-reviewed journals that would be generally recognized as scholarly in their orientation. Thus, we did not include articles appearing in *Entrepreneurship Theory & Practice* because the journal is not peer reviewed. The final list of journals included in our search is given in Table 1.1. The time period covered is January 1994 to March 2002; we think this time frame is the most relevant for the analysis because many authors have commented on the dominance of articles taking a supply-side perspective in the prior years (Woo, Dallenbach, & Nicholls-Nixon, 1994; Thornton, 1999). We collected a sample of articles by searching the ABI/Inform database looking for article abstracts containing any of the following words or phrases: entrepreneurship, entrepreneur, venture capital. This returned a total of 304 articles in the journals that we had designated. We removed articles that did not have abstracts. Given that our focus was on entrepreneurship as an object of study, we removed any article focusing on entrepreneurship education, franchising, general business strategy, technology, innovation, and networks, along with those with the primary purpose of giving 'How To' advice. We performed our analysis of abstract content on the 241 articles that remained after these exclusions.

Table 1.1   Refereed journals publishing articles related to entrepreneurship

Academy of Management Executive
Academy of Management Journal
Academy of Management Review
Administrative Science Quarterly
American Journal of Sociology
American Sociological Review
California Management Review
Harvard Business Review
Journal of Business Venturing
Journal of High Technology Management Research
Journal of Management
Journal of Management Studies
Management Science
Organization Science
Organization Studies
Sloan Management Review
Strategic Management Journal

In order to determine the presence of demand and supply side perspectives on entrepreneurship, we looked for the presence of key words and phrases in the abstracts. The following classifications guided our coding:

Phrases Indicating Supply-Side View – from the psychological literature: attributes, individual, confidence, psychological, ethnic, backgrounds, achievement, locus, propensity, style, values, personality, personal, characteristic, women, female, ability, social, trust, skill, qualities, cognitive, empowerment, affective, and psychometric. From the sociological literature: supply, class, group, ethnic, immigrant, and community.

Phrases Indicating Demand-Side View – environment, embeddedness, social capital context, ecological, institutional, resources, economic, structure, spin-off, niche, agency, privatization, industrial organization (IO), contingency, system, network, cyclical, opportunity, climate, market attractiveness, and privatized/privatization.

Abstracts that contained phrases from both categories were counted as taking both a supply and a demand side perspective and are counted separately.

The results of our analysis are presented in Figure 1.1. Two trends are the most relevant to this chapter and book. First, there is an upsurge in scholarly interest in entrepreneurship, particularly from 1999 onward. Although we did not include the data, the first three months of 2002 annualized suggest the trend is not only continuing but also accelerating. This is particularly true of the new trend for more articles to take a demand side as opposed to a supply side perspective. We conclude that the number of articles with entrepreneurship as their main focus has surged since 1999 and that this increase appears to be driven by interest in demand-side related questions. Second, though the number is small, there has been some effort to integrate these two perspectives. We salute this development; however, we will not focus on it here. Our object in the remainder of this paper is to explore the implications of the emerging demand side perspective using the lens of organization theory.

Ecologies of learning entrepreneurship

One notable feature of this expansion of scope has been its implications for the definition of both what constitutes entrepreneurship as well as the kinds of behaviors and processes that must be encompassed

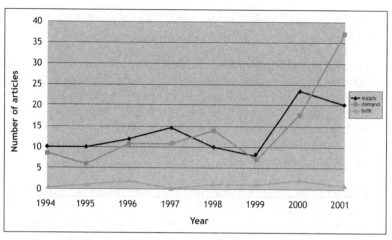

Figure 1.1   Number of articles taking a supply and/or demand perspective

to understand it fully. A first class of broader definitions of entrepreneurship has been those that emphasize search. This work takes its cue directly from theories of administrative rationality (Simon, 1947; March and Simon, 1958) and the behavioral theory of the firm (Cyert and March, 1963). It marries the observation that search for alternatives and discovering their costs and benefits is an important part of understanding outcomes in organizations with the traditional concerns of entrepreneurship: innovation, the foundings of firms, and the creation of new industries. This work has also borrowed from economic perspectives on search (Nelson and Winter, 1982) and entrepreneurship (Kirzner, 1979), emphasizing constraints on entrepreneurial choice from search costs and rules (Lant and Mezias, 1992).

A second class of broader definitions is related to the kinds of behaviors that are included in the meaning of entrepreneurship. A common extension of the meaning of entrepreneurship is to encompass innovative behavior by existing organizations (Ginsberg and Guth, 1990); what Pinchot (1985) called intrapreneuring. A major strain of these arguments is directly related to the level of analysis issue: Networks, alliances, joint ventures have become integral to the creation of new firms and new industries (Powell, Koput and Smith-Doerr, 1996). Indeed, this is an essential point of the systems model of entrepreneurship (Van de Ven, 1993b). Mezias and Kuperman (2001) characterize these ideas in terms of the community dynamics of entrepreneurship, suggesting a two by two typology of entrepreneurship based on whether a behavior produces economic innovation and whether the founding of a new firm is involved. The point of these typologies as well as others that have been derived from studies of entrepreneurship is that the definition of phenomenon is broader than would be suggested by the traditional great man approach. One of the most important implications of these broader definitions is that change by existing organizations can be important participants in entrepreneurial activity, particularly the emergence of new industries.

In the feature film industry, Mezias and Mezias (2000) found that small specialist firms were proportionately more likely to participate in the creation of new film genres. This points to the relevance of organizational learning as a framework for understanding two important aspects of entrepreneurship: innovativeness and search. A framework in which organizations are modeled as systems that learn from experience has a long tradition in organization theory (March and Simon, 1958; Cyert and March, 1964; Levinthal and March, 1981). Much of the research based on this perspective that we report in this book illustrates the usefulness of this perspective for understanding intrapreneuring: the process of making existing organizations more entrepre-neurial. From a Schumpeterian (1942) perspective, entrepreneurship can be understood as process of 'creative destruction.' One historic meaning of this label has been to emphasize that the emergence of new industries and the transformation of existing industries have occurred largely as the result of small, innovative firms displacing older, larger, previously dominant firms (Tushman and Anderson, 1986). At the same time, work on entrepreneurship from an organization theory perspective has reminded us that new industry creation, especially in more recent times, cannot be understood without examining the role of existing firms. Both Wade's (1995) work on the microprocessor and the work of Powell, Koput, and Smith-Doerr (1996) on biotechnology illustrate this point in detail. This work suggests that the issue of how to make existing firms more innovative is important to general research on entrepreneurship, not just from the perspective of understanding intrapreneurship.

The second section of the book summarizes literature that uses an organizational learning perspective to understand the level of innovativeness at firms modeled as systems that learn from experience. Lant and Mezias (1990) suggest that search is the key to understanding entrepreneurship and relate different search rules to key perspectives in organizational theory, including an adaptive perspective, an institutional perspective, and population ecology. They show how different propensities to search might evolve over time in a population of firms characterized by different search rules, adaptation, and selection in a changing environment. They provide examples of impediments to innovation that may result from a learning process. Lant and Mezias (1992) address the issue of convergence and reorientation, arguing that the same learning processes that produce convergence can also produce occasional surprises like reorientation. They model this in terms of routine responses to perceptions of the relationship between firm characteristics and performance, which changes over time. Mezias and Glynn (1993) take up the question of why it has been so difficult for existing firms to remain innovative. They develop a model of firms as experiential learning systems to explain why attempts to increase innovation by devoting more resources to it often fail, which they term the paradox of institution. They go on to address why attempts at radical innovation often fail, which they term the paradox of revolution. Finally, they suggest an approach that involves loosening the level of bureaucratic control in organizations, which they term the value of variance. Mezias and Lant (1994) develop the concept of an ecology of learning: A population of firms characterized by competition for resources and the potential for change based on interpretations of past experience. They show that despite the claims of some ecologists to the contrary (Freeman and Hannan, 1984), core change in organizations can survive under a wide range of conditions. Thus, the topic of how change affects population demographics, one variant of the broad issue of intrapreneuring, can be seen as relevant even from an ecological perspective.

The evolutionary dynamics of new industry creation

The contributions of organization theory to understanding entrepreneurship go beyond merely redefining the phenomenon. Most importantly, organization theory has provided frameworks for the empirical study of entrepreneurship that have produced systematic evidence to enhance our understanding of the phenomenon. Perhaps the most established of these is derived from the population ecology approach (Hannan and Freeman, 1977) and addresses the population dynamics of the founding of new firms. The density dependence model predicts that foundings will have a curvilinear relationship with the founding of firms. When the total number of firms in a population is small, increases in the number of rims will enhance the founding of firms. This is argued to be a result of the increasing legitimacy that each additional firm provides when the population is small. As the number of firms in the population continues to increase, however, competition begins to occur. After this point, increases in the number of firms increase the competition, which decreases the founding of new firms. Mass dependence (Barnett & Amburgey, 1990) is suggested as a further measure of competition, with the prediction that the greater the mass of the population, the more likely is a reduction in foundings. Lagged foundings have also been found to have a similar effect, with their number enhancing subsequent foundings at low levels and suppressing them at higher levels.

All of these models, however, tend to focus on mature populations and long time spans. The questions that motivate much entrepreneurial research tend to be more about the creation of new industries and shorter times spans, especially those that are characterized by the rapid founding of large numbers of firms in a fairly short period of time, such as during the rapid emergence of a new industry. In fact, the predictions from population ecology discussed so far depend on the size of the population hitting the carrying capacity in order to hold; yet, many of the populations most appropriate for the study of questions of interest to students of entrepreneurship may not arrive at this point during the periods under study. For example, in their work on the early American feature film industry, included as Chapter 4 of this book, Mezias and Mezias (2000) did not find support for any of the predictions concerning when competition would suppress foundings. It is not our claim, however, that this means that taking the population as the unit of analysis or using an ecological perspective is not relevant. Again, the findings of Mezias and Mezias (2000) are instructive: They did find that the feature film industry became concentrated rather quickly in its history. Based on this, they examined predictions of the resource-partitioning model (Carroll, 1985), another ecological approach. They found that higher concentration among large generalist firms, those that both produced and distributed films, led to an increase in foundings of specialist firms, those that only produced or only distributed films. Thus, even a population that has not yet approached carrying capacity can be studied using an ecological perspective; we believe that focusing on the population dynamics of foundings is an important contribution to the study of entrepreneurship.

Another useful application of an ecological perspective has developed from consideration of the community dynamics of new industries. Expanding on the social context perspective (Van de Ven, 1993b),

Mezias and Kuperman (2001) suggested that a focus on the community of populations of firms that comprise a new industry can be useful. They used the value chain of the early film industry to suggest that three populations of firms that were relevant to understanding entrepreneurship in that case. Two concepts from the technological literature (Wade, 1995) are applied to understand the development of the American film industry; both are relevant to the claim that successful entrepreneurship requires understanding far more than single founders or single firms. The first concept is second sourcing, which refers to entrepreneurial behaviors that lead to the creation of additional sources in the same function of the value chain. An example from the discussion in the chapter would be additional sources of short films, which together guaranteed that there was a supply of films adequate to support the emerging demand for films. The second concept is related sourcing, which refers to entrepreneurial behaviors that lead to the creation of additional sources in a function in another part of the value chain. This would suggest that the creation of additional sources of short films would benefit nickelodeons, the primary location for exhibition during the latter part of the short film era.

Creating legitimacy for new industries

The institutional perspective has had as a core tenet that the legitimacy of organizational arrangements is defined externally (Meyer and Rowan, 1977; DiMaggio and Powell; 1983; 1991). Recent empirical work on the legal environment (Edelman, 1992) has refined our understanding of how this proceeds, clarifying that firms are not simply passive recipients of the dictates from above (Oliver, 1990; Edelman, Uggen, and Erlanger, 1999; Mezias, 2001; Rindova & Fombrun, 2001). Baron, Dobbin, and Jennings (1986), Edelman (1992; 1990), Mezias (1990), Edelman and Suchman (1997), Sutton and Dobbin (1996), Kelly and Dobbin (1999), Dobbin, Sutton, Meyer, and Scott (1993), Dobbin and Sutton (1998) among others have presented well-documented examples of how firms, professions, and the state interact to define legitimate organizational governance. Yet, this deepened understanding of how legitimacy is defined by legal environments has not been put to use to build on the ecological claim that foundings will increase. We attempt a partial remedy of this deficit in Chapter 6. Specifically, we focus on how litigation became an instrument for industry control, affecting the evolution of the industry, during the early history of the American film industry.

As we discuss in this chapter, this was driven by at least two forms of litigation. The first and more important of these concerned patents. It had long been a strategy of Edison to use patent litigation as a tool of market control, a pattern he continued in the film industry. This litigation went on for approximately twenty years and involved hundreds of cases. Various decisions, overturning of decisions, and the changing alliances that evolved around the control of patents created significant uncertainty about the future course of the industry during this period. For example, from July 1901 until March 1902, an Edison legal victory made his firm the only legal producer of films in the country. Edison and Biograph were bitter rivals in the patents war from 1902 until 1908, when they entered into an alliance with their respective groups of firms. This alliance, called the Motion Pictures Patents Company, used litigation as well as less savory tactics in its attempts to control the industry before it was finally declared illegal under the Sherman Anti-Trust Act in 1918. A second form of litigation concerned the copy-righting of films. The main reason why this litigation is less important is that the central question: whether films could be copyrighted and how, was resolved in about two years. Nonetheless, there was signifi-cant uncertainty regarding the protection of films between 1901 and 1903; in fact, Edison ceases all production during the early months of 1903 rather than have his films copied by others. However, in April 1903, a ruling that films could be copyrighted and the establishment of well-defined procedures for doing so largely resolved the issue.

The focus of Chapter 6 is on explaining how these uncertainties in the legal environment affected foundings. Our central claim is that the uncer-tainty associated with both types of litigation and the alliances that grew up around the Edison and Biograph patent claims resulted in the sup-pression of the foundings of firms. We also argue that the legal environ-ment was tied with the growth of Hollywood. First, newly founded firms located there to escape the thugs hired as enforcers by Edison, Biograph, and their allies, which were largely based on the East Coast. This trend was further aided by the efforts of the Los Angeles Chamber of Commerce and city government to create incentives for moving to the area; we argue that this represents another aspect of the legal environment.

The final topic for entrepreneurship research that has been suggested by organization theory is the creation of legitimacy for new industries. Lounsbury and Glynn (2001) provide a good summary of this literature as well as some propositions about entrepreneurship that are suggested by it. These arguments are well illustrated by the quest for cognitive and sociopolitical legitimacy among key stakeholders during the early days of the film industry. We develop this argument in great detail in Chapter 7 with a focus on the empirical measurement of legitimacy. Of course this topic is not independent of the others we have examined; we review the role of both second and related sourcing in helping to create cognitive legitimacy for the industry. The focus of this analysis, however, is on the creation of film as a source of entertainment. We view this as an enormous undertaking that involved the activities of many persons and firms operating in all functions of the value chain. An important aspect of this undertaking was creating and training the audience. Film began as a novelty, with individuals peering into a peephole kinetoscope to see animate objects first captured in motion. Even up to the point where nickelodeons first became widespread, simple subjects – a horse jumping or a hot air balloon flying – were sufficient to fill theaters. The attraction of these 'galloping tintypes' diminished quickly, however, and audiences began demanding more interesting subject matter; initially, this was met with newsreels and extremely short narratives.

Subsequently, efforts to attract audiences with sensationalism created much negative publicity for the nascent industry; quick action had to be taken to contain the damage and avert tight censorship. This resulted in extensive efforts to link film with legitimate theater and high culture rather than lowbrow entertainment and immigrant audiences. This began with bringing in theater talent of all kinds, acting, production, and writing, continued with the move from nickelodeons to theater palaces, and culminated with the creation of Hollywood. The trappings of the movie industry as we know it today, from the star system to the studios to the Academy Awards, all had their beginnings at this time. This sociopolitical and cognitive legitimacy was crucial to obtaining resources such as Wall Street financing and the political capital to avoid tight governmental regulation. As important as these resources were, however, we would claim that the most important result of these early efforts was the creation of the magic of the movies: the mass experience that makes Hollywood the world cultural capital that it is today.

On to the dynamics of organizations

The remainder of this book consists of three sections and a brief conclusion. The next section is animated by the insight from the emerging literature linking organizations and entrepreneurship that understanding the emergence of new industries requires comprehending the role of change at existing organizations. The two chapters in this section explore the framework of ecologies of learning, illustrating how this framework can be applied to understand change at existing organizations. This is followed by a section with two chapters applying ecological models to understand the emergence of new industries. Chapter 4 focuses on the population dynamics of foundings in the emerging film industry of the US. Chapter 5 focuses on the community dynamics of new industry emergence, again using the example of the early film industry in the US. The final section of the book has two chapters that apply an institutional perspective to understand the issue of new industry emergence. Chapter 6 focuses on legal environments and how they impact foundings in the early American film industry. In Chapter 7 we again take up the example of the early film industry and analyzes how legitimacy challenges to that new industry were overcome. We then close with a brief conclusion focusing on issues for future research. We believe that the creation of the American film industry is best understood by using a variety of perspectives from organization theory and hope to convince our readers of this in the remainder of this book.

Part I
Ecologies of Learning and Intrapreneurship

Given our presumption that existing firms have a role to play in the entrepreneurial behaviors that result in the emergence of new industries, we now turn our attention to the role that these firms play. We use the term intrapreneurship as a label for these activities to highlight that these behaviors are both linked with and distinct from the traditional construct of entrepreneurship. The term entered the popular lexicon with the publication of the book *Intrapreneuring* (Pinchot, 1985). As the literature on this general topic has evolved, there have come to be at least three types of activities that have been studied. Covin & Miles (1999:48) described these activities as occurring when: '... 1) an established organization enters a new business; 2) an individual or individuals champion new product ideas within a corporate context; and 3) an "entrepreneurial" philosophy permeates an entire organization's outlook and operations.' By grouping these different activities together, we do not mean to imply that corporate venturing, intrapreneurship, and management with an entrepreneurial philosophy are interchangeable in all contexts. Rather, we do this because, for our purposes, the distinction that we wish to highlight is on the level of analysis used to explain these phenomena, not differences among them. Our point is simple and directly related to the distinction between supply and demand side perspectives on entrepreneurship more generally (Thornton, 1999). While the intrapreneuring literature is extensive, it tends to focus on individual attributes, e.g., creativity (Amabile, 1989), or organizational attributes, e.g., large size (Kanter, 1983).

We have argued that the emerging demand side perspective on entrepreneurship (Thornton, 1999) has focused research on higher levels of analysis. In fact, we have argued that existing firms become relevant to entrepreneurship once we try to understand the emergence of new industries using the community level of analysis. As Mezias and Kuperman (2000) argued, innovation and imitation by existing firms is a fundamental part of the creation of new industries. In keeping with this movement to the community level of analysis, our chapters on intrapreneurship will focus on ecologies of learning. Chapter 3 is a reprint of Mezias and Lant, (1994), which does two important things in terms of the themes of this book. First, it explains the concept of ecology of learning, a framework that integrates an organizational learning perspective with an ecological perspective. This framework models firms as systems that learn from experience in stylized ecologies where outcomes of the systems are interdependent. Second, having established this framework for analysis, the analysis in the chapter focuses on the question of whether organizational level change can persist in the face of selection pressures (Freeman and Hannan, 1984). Clearly, it is only where organizational level change persists that it can play a role in the emergence of new industries.

Having established that organization level change can persist, we next turn our attention to various impediments to intrapreneurship that may arise among organizations that learn from experience and evolve in an ecology characterized by competition and selection pressures. This is the topic taken up in Chapter 2, a reprint of Mezias and Glynn (1993). In this chapter, the authors use a model of firms as systems that learn from experience and create an ecology where incumbent firms identify and choose between opportunities for innovation or refinement. The authors find that these firms experience two paradoxes: the paradox of institution and the paradox of revolution. Both result in resources intended for innovation resulting only in refinement of existing technologies. Their findings also point to the value of variance, suggesting that loosening controls is a better route for producing innovation in routine based systems that learn from experience.

2
The Three Faces of Corporate Renewal: Institution, Revolution and Evolution

Stephen J. Mezias and Mary Ann Glynn

Introduction

In this paper we explore corporate change and renewal in large, established organizations by examining how different types of innovation strategies affect organizational outcomes. We start from one of the hallmarks of the management literature: a concern with the trade-off between the flexibility and efficiency of large bureaucratic organizations (March and Simon, 1958; March, 1991). In a classic discussion of this trade-off, Thompson (1967: 148–150) termed its management the paradox of administration. In almost all discussions of this paradox, there is virtual agreement that at least some innovation, change, and corporate renewal is vital; Kanter (1983: 23) argues that organizations cannot survive without innovating. Despite this often espoused critical need for innovation, analysts from March and Simon (1958) to the present (e.g., Tushman and Nelson, 1990; March, 1991) have observed that executing rapid, radical change in large organizations is more difficult and less frequent than executing routine, incremental change. Traditionally, organizational size, formalization, and complexity have been viewed as obstacles to innovation (Burns and Stalker, 1961; Thompson, 1965; Aiken and Hage, 1971; Pierce and Delbecq, 1977; Kanter, 1983; Rogers, 1983; Nadler and Tushman, 1989; Brown, 1991); Kanter (1985: 54) epitomizes this argument in her claim that when it comes to innovation, small is beautiful.

Two types of organizational change, incremental convergence and radical reorientation (Tushman and Romanelli, 1985), have been differentiated in the literature. Various terms have been used to describe this distinction, including persistence and change (March, 1981), frame bending versus frame-breaking change (Tushman, Newman and

Romanelli, 1986), and incremental versus radical innovation (Dewar and Dutton, 1986; Ettlie, Bridges, and O'Keefe; 1984; Nord and Tucker, 1987). Thus, there seems to be an emerging consensus that large bureaucratic organizations experience short bursts of intense, discontinuous change followed by longer periods of convergence and incremental change.[1] Much of the literature on change and renewal has focused on the question of how to make organizations innovate more effectively; given the relative infrequency of radical change, this has often meant a focus on how to make organizations innovate more. Thus, our focus in discussing corporate renewal is on strategies that enhance the ability of large, bureaucratic organizations to make radical change to existing practices, routines, and structures. We will associate corporate renewal with the process of innovation, defined as non-routine, significant, and discontinuous organizational change. We sharply differentiate the process of innovation from that of instrumentalism or refinement to existing systems, structures, and technology (Kanter, 1983). Innovation embodies a new idea that is not consistent with the current concept of the organization's business (Galbraith, 1982: 6); as March and Simon (1958: 175) argued, it cannot be accomplished '...by a simple application of programmed switching rules.' Damanpour (1991: 561) points out that radical innovations '...produce fundamental changes in the activities of an organization and represent clear departures from existing practices;' in contrast, incremental changes '...result in little departure from existing practices.'

In our analysis, we focus on innovation broadly as a managerial process rather than narrowly as a purely technological process for two reasons. First, for any type of innovation to be implemented, management must be able to recognize and support opportunities for change; most innovations involve both technical and administrative components (Leavitt, 1965; Van de Ven, 1986). Second, as Arrow (1971), Chandler (1977), Cole (1968), and Williamson (1983) argued, we have largely overlooked the contributions of administrative innovations because they are not as easily identified, protected, or patented as their technological or mechanical counterparts. Based on the assumption that innovation is an administrative process, we examine how different types of routine practices and strategies affect the amount and type of innovation that an organization experiences. As radical an outcome as innovation might be, we believe that it can be understood only in the context of routine organizational functioning. As March (1981: 564) observed: 'Most change in organizations results neither from extraordinary organizational processes nor forces, nor from uncommon imagination, persistence or skill, but from relatively stable, routine processes that relate organizations to their environments.' Examining routine practices as a source of innovation is particularly important for large organizations because of the ways in which fundamental organizational practices, especially the rationality and rules associated with bureaucracy; affect innovation (Howell and Higgins, 1990). We are less optimistic about the plasticity of the structure of large organizations, an assumption inherent in work that suggests making bureaucratic organizations more entrepreneurial (Kanter, 1983; Pinchot, 1985). Instead, our approach is to examine the structure itself and its effect on innovation; consequently, we focus on the organizational rather than the individual level of analysis. While we acknowledge that individuals can significantly affect bureaucratic innovation (e.g., Amabile, 1988; Downs, 1976), we have chosen to focus instead on organizational level variables because they have been the most widely studied and are recognized as primary determinants of innovation (Damanpour, 1991).

In examining innovation in established organizations, we adopt a view of organizations as experiential learning systems (March and Olsen, 1976; Levinthal and March, 1981; Levitt and March, 1988; Lant and Mezias, 1990; 1992). The themes of organizational learning and innovation have been intertwined previously, both in conceptual work (e.g., Angle and Van de Ven, 1989; Brewer, 1980; Stata, 1989; Tushman and Nadler, 1986; Tushman and Nelson, 1990; Brown, 1991) and in empirical research (e.g., Henderson and Clark, 1990; Cohen and Levinthal 1990; Sahal, 1981). The principal contribution of a learning framework lays in the formalization of the insight that organizational change and innovation can be modeled as an experiential learning process. A learning model seems particularly appropriate because it takes into account the effects of history, and in particular, how the organization's past may affect its future capabilities for renewal and change (Lant and Mezias, 1990; 1992). We attempt to make two primary contributions in this study. First, by integrating the literatures on organizational learning and innovation, we offer a more complete theoretical framework for thinking about the problem of corporate renewal. The framework organizes the literature on change and innovation with three strategies that we label as institutional, revolutional and evolutional. While none of these individual strategies is unique to our paper, integrating them into a single framework is. Second, by using a simulation methodology, we can perform the explicitly dynamic assessments suggested by this theoretical framework. Our contribution is to offer a model that produces results consistent with real world observations. Earlier work on the management of innovation has tended to rely primarily on rich, descriptive case studies (e.g., Howell and Higgins, 1990; Jelinek and Schoonhoven, 1990) or on broad, empirical studies across a number of different types of organizations (e.g., Tushman and Anderson, 1986); little work has been directed towards the routine processes that support the management of renewal, in spite of the recognized need for such work (e.g., Van de Ven, 1986). With our simulation analysis, we can assess the effectiveness of alternate renewal strategies for an organization adapting to an ambiguous environment.

Theoretical framework

The three faces of innovation

Following Kanter (1983), we define innovation to be the process of bringing any new, problem solving idea into use in an organization. Like Kimberly (1981), Marcus (1988), and Rogers and Shoemaker (1971), our central criterion for defining innovation is that it must be perceived as new to the adopting organization. Innovation thus represents discontinuous or 'frame-breaking' change that involves change in the underlying technology so that existing organizational skills and competence are rendered obsolete. In contrast, incremental change or refinement improves the performance of current technology by building on existing organizational know-how and competence (Tushman and Anderson, 1986). We recognize that the distinction between radical innovation and incremental refinement may not be quite so clear as these definitions seem to suggest; indeed, refinements sometimes lead to major innovations. For example, to develop new products, GE uses a 'multigenerational plan' by first introducing a version that embodies 'tried-and-true technologies;' only later does GE introduce versions based on newer, untried technologies (Stewart, 1991). However, because the distinction between refinement and innovation is one of the central notions in the literature on organizational innovation (Damanpour, 1991; Henderson and Clark, 1990) and for purposes of illustration, we make a sharp distinction between incremental refinement and radical innovation.

The emerging consensus concerning the need to manage innovation and corporate renewal has not been accompanied by agreement on the most appropriate strategy for managing innovation and renewal. Angle and Van de Ven (1989: 676) made this point: '[J]ust as we learned many years ago that there is no best way to manage, we expect that we will never find one best way to innovate.' However, while there may not be a single best way, it is important to delineate the costs and benefits, as well as the intended and unintended effects of different types of innovation strategies. Our review of the literature on the management of innovation identified three broad themes that represent fundamentally different strategies for managing organizational innovation: the institutional, revolutional, and evolutional approaches. Organizations following the first two approaches employ intentional strategies to facilitate innovation, either within the current organizational paradigm (institutionalizing procedures to encourage innovation) or outside the paradigm (revolting against or ignoring institutional procedures). The third path, the evolutional approach, models innovation as a chaotic or probabilistic process not easily amenable to conscious attempts to increase its occurrence.

Previous work on innovation implementation uses categorization schemes that can be susbumed within our framework. For example, Kimberly (1981) recognizes two approaches, revolutional and evolutional approaches to implementing managerial innovation, while Marcus (1988) details differences between a rule-bound, centrally authorized approach and an autonomous, evolutionary approach. The classifications used by Howell and Higgins (1990) in describing how 'champions' bring about technological innovation included categories analogous to the institutional and revolutional approaches, but did not include a category corresponding to the evolutional approach. We believe that the three part typology we propose is especially useful in facilitating a comparison of the trade-offs inherent in each approach; illustrating how these trade-offs might unfold over time is the focus of our simulation model.

Institutionalizing innovation

Much of the literature on innovation emphasizes the theme of rational, functional, planned innovation (Howell and Higgins, 1990). Successful innovation is seen as the outcome of an organized, purposeful, and systematic process (Drucker, 1985); innovation occurs by design and as a result of an organization's rules and procedures. In their study of high technology organizations, Jelinek and Schoonhoven (1990) found that innovation was an integral part of on-going operations. The institutional approach is illustrated by the case of David E., reported by Howell and Higgins (1990: 45–46). As vice-president of national accounts for a large financial institution, David became convinced of the need for an integrated office system. He followed the standard corporate approval process, carefully detailing the costs and benefits of the system and presenting an in-depth business case to the executive committee. David succeeded in selling the innovation to an entrenched bureaucracy by preparing a carefully documented business plan that promoted the benefits of the new technology on a financial basis. As David's story suggests, institutionalizing innovation involves manipulating bureaucratic rules so that learning new ways of doing things at the organization is facilitated (March and Simon, 1958; 184–188). The basic ideas of the institutional approach have been to devote more resources to innovation and highlight its importance. While there has been some refinement of these standard notions (e.g., Tushman, 1977; Burgelman, 1984), they remain an essential, albeit occasionally overlooked (Howell and Higgins, 1990), part of conventional wisdom about innovation at organizations.

Much of the literature argues, however, that an institutional approach to innovation results not in the discovery of radical, frame-breaking innovation but in refinements to existing systems and technologies (March and Simon, 1958). Both Galbraith (1982) and Quinn (1985) argued that a linear process of devoting additional resources to innovation tends to result in minor, incremental changes rather than major, radical innovation. This idea has been one of the hallmarks of organization theory, harkening back to March and Simon (1958: 173) who wrote: 'Individuals and organizations give preferred treatment to alternatives that represent continuation of present programs over those that represent change.' Managerial concerns about the assimilation of a new technology often contribute to this tendency to maintain the status quo. Kotter and Schlesinger (1979: 107) describe this reluctance: 'More than a few organizations have not even tried to initiate needed changes because the managers involved were afraid that they were simply incapable of successfully implementing them.' As Brown (1991: 103) points out, concerns about implementation tend to shift the research focus '...away from radical breakthroughs toward incremental innovation.' To overcome this limit, two other perspectives on managing innovation have been advanced. The revolutional approach assumes that problems in innovating are due to the organization's rules and procedures; consequently, change is introduced by disregarding or breaking the institutionalized rules. By contrast, the evolutional approach suggests that changing the rules or processes of the system may not be feasible or fruitful. Rather, encouraging innovation requires changing the inputs to the system, typically by allowing the simultaneous development of multiple and varied projects, often at different levels of risk.

Revolution and innovation

The revolutional approach to innovation involves conscious efforts to move away from the current organizational paradigm. Such intentional strategies to move beyond the status quo are designed to overcome two problems with the institutionalization of innovation. First, revolutional strategies recognize explicitly that important changes sometimes cannot be discovered by operating within the status quo (March, 1976); a change of paradigm (Brown, 1978; Pfeffer, 1981) or organizational theory-in-use (Argyris and Schon, 1978) may be necessary. Second, revolutional strategies assume that resistance to change will block successful implementation of innovations produced by an institutionalized process (e.g., Kimberly, 1981; Rogers, 1983; Van de Ven, 1986). As Brewer (1980: 339) cogently puts it: 'One person's innovation is ordinarily another's destruction.' In the extreme, a revolutional approach argues, as does Galbraith (1982: 14), that '...innovating and operating are fundamentally opposing logics.' As a result, organizations need to distinguish between structures designed for efficiency or production and those designed for innovation (Thompson, 1965; Delbecq and Mills, 1985; Galbraith, 1982; Kanter, 1983). Typically, operating organizations have structures that are mechanistic (Burns and Stalker, 1961) or segmentalist (Kanter, 1983), while innovating organizations are organic (Burns and Stalker, 1961) or integrative (Kanter, 1983). Revolutional strategies advocate spin-offs, skunkworks, special ad hoc teams or autonomous work groups that operate outside the existing organizational structure (Kidder, 1981; Burgelman, 1984; Kanter, 1985). The rationale is that the dominant culture in established organizations is centered on rules that stifle innovation (Kanter, 1983). Organizational learning takes place only by breaking habitual and routine ways of thinking and acting (Senge, 1990). Much of this work has pointed to the importance of individuals who fight for particular change, the innovation champions who operate as revolutionaries or renegades, deliberately violating bureaucratic rules and management directives. A good example is given in Howell and Higgin's (1990: 50) discussion of Jeffrey, a director of systems engineering for a major telecommunications company. He had become frustrated with bureaucratic resistance to a new technology and described how he overcame this opposition: 'What we were doing wasn't part of standard operating procedure ... so I simply went out and bought the technology. I didn't bother fighting the traditionalism and the b.s.'

Examples of revolutional strategies include temporarily relaxing rules and rational analysis (March, 1976), learning from hypothetical histories (Levitt and March, 1988; March, Sproull, and Tamuz, 1991), and questioning the norms and assumptions inherent in everyday organizational activities (Argyris and Schon, 1978). A revolutional approach is embodied in what Brown (1991: 103) called pioneering research, which seeks to redefine corporate problems so as to discover new, radical solutions. The common thread in these revolutional approaches is that they encourage playfulness (Glynn and Webster, 1992) so as to allow unusual and innovative behavior to emerge. In describing the technology of foolishness, March (1976: 81) argued that these strategies encourage innovation by offering '...temporary relief from control, coordination, and communication.'

In overcoming institutional barriers to innovation, however, the revolutional approach is vulnerable in its dependence upon individual innovation champions. By assuming that individuals will shoulder most of the risks associated with innovation, the approach hinges primarily on what Sahal (1981: 32) terms the 'heroic entrepreneur' theory of innovation. What innovations are eventually adopted may depend less upon the quality of the idea or technology and more on the individual innovator's ability to persist and amass necessary resources and support. Furthermore, as Tushman and Nadler (1986: 82) note: 'Because organizational learning and innovation is a group and intergroup phenomena, individual contributors rarely produce the creative ideas or solutions required for complex or discontinuous innovation.' Finally, with the chaos that can ensue under the onslaught of questioning goals, violating rules, and breaking traditions, organizational efficiency may suffer. When innovations originate in separate centers or skunkwork teams, they are often difficult to implement; integrating across the organization's innovating and operating units is potentially problematic. This problem may be exacerbated when innovating units explicitly adopt structures that are viewed as being in opposition to the structures of the parent organization.

The evolution of innovation

Evolutional strategies to enhance innovation are less intentional than either the institutional or revolutional approaches. Strategies that encourage the evolution of innovation are designed to allow the organization to move beyond its current capabilities by making boundaries unclear. They embody the important idea that innovation is a chaotic, probabilistic process. After studying several of the world's most innovative large companies, Quinn (1985: 83) concluded: '[I]nnovation tends to be individually motivated, opportunistic, customer responsive, tumultuous, nonlinear, and interactive in its development.' There is an increasing awareness that theoretical development of this perspective is essential if we are to give appropriate attention to the role of chance in most organizational innovation (Angle and Van de Ven, 1989: 652). At the same time, the relative newness and underdeveloped state of the literature on the evolution of innovation may render such strategies difficult to recognize. For example, Quinn (1985: 78–79) noted that companies often permit redundancies or encourage several programs to proceed in parallel. Nadler and Tushman (1989) observed that managers often pursue alternative options or small-scale side bets. The evolutional perspective suggests that despite their espoused intentions or true genesis, the effect of evolutional strategies is to encourage innovation by a process of imperfect routine maintenance (Levitt and March, 1988).

These strategies are termed evolutional because they often seem emergent or unintentional for an individual organization; nonetheless, they need not be wholly accidental. Systematic attempts to encourage the evolution of innovation include using and experimenting with slack resources as a buffer against organizational controls (Cyert and March, 1963; Bourgeois, 1981), the promotion of those who take risks (March, 1981; 1988), glorification of organizational change as a managerial imperative (March, 1981), and loose coupling (Weick, 1979). In general, an evolutional approach involves making routines, performance measurement, and control less precise. As Angle and Van de Ven (1989: 679) suggested: 'It may be necessary, in order that the innovation have a chance to succeed, to relax traditional notions of managerial control.' Kanter (1985: 46) describes this as a portfolio approach, which involves '... seeding many diverse projects and many diverse experiments ... with an expectation that some will fail, but some will pay off.' Evolutional approaches to innovation are often characteristic of research linking individual creativity and organizational innovation. For example, one research and development scientist interviewed by Amabile (1988: 125) offered this observation: 'Quite often I will be tinkering in something that management will have no interest in, yet when I start to develop it into something, there will be a lot of interest. If they had close reins on me, they would have killed a lot of projects at an early stage and nothing would have resulted.'

The organizational learning perspective

Levitt and March (1988: 319) describe organizations as experiential learning systems that are '...routine-based, history-dependent, and target-oriented.' Unpacking this description is an excellent way to summarize the key points of the organizational learning perspective as we use it in this study. First, it is important to emphasize the view of organizations as routine-based systems that respond to experience. This model of organizations as experiential learning systems typically have three categories of routines: search, performance, and change.

1. **Search:** Modeling of search routines focuses on the process by which organizations attempt to discover adaptive opportunities in an ambiguous world via a costly and routinized process of search (Simon, 1957; March and Simon, 1958; March and Olsen, 1976; March, 1981; Sahal, 1981; Nelson and Winter, 1982). Cyert and March (1963) make the distinction between search that is focused on improving and refining current practices, i.e. problemistic search, and search that is focused on changing the practices used by the organization, i.e. innovative search. They argue that it is innovative search that leads to fundamental organizational change. Levinthal and March (1981) translate this into the distinction between refinement search and innovative search.

2. **Performance:** Performance routines typically underscore the argument that organizations compare actual outcomes against a moving target: an aspired level of performance that changes over time in response to experience. Several functional forms guiding the adaptation of aspiration levels have been proposed (e.g., Levinthal and March, 1981; Herriott, Levinthal, and March, 1985); we rely on a general form of aspiration level adaptation that has been supported in empirical work (Glynn, Lant, and Mezias, 1991; Lant, 1992).

3. **Change:** Change routines underscore the notion that organizational change, whether an attempt to refine current capabilities or to implement new and different capabilities, is a stochastic response to experience. Organizations are more likely to persist in activities associated with success and desist activities associated with failure (March and Simon, 1958; Cyert and March, 1963).

Second, it is important to emphasize that the learning process is history dependent; there are no unique equilibria or closed form solutions in this process. Two aspects of history dependence are particularly important in this study. First, following Amburgey, Kelly, and Barnett (1990), we assume that organizations have change clocks that are reset each time there is an innovation. For some time following a significant innovation, the effort and resources that normally would be devoted to search and change are devoted instead to getting the organization to function using the innovation that has just been adopted. Thus, there is a small window of time when there is no search or change following each innovation. If the organization is within this window of inertia, it will not search or change in the current period. The second consideration highlighted by a history dependent learning model is increasing competence: the well-known learning curve. It is well established that over time organizations improve their performance with new technology, but at a decreasing rate (Yelle, 1979; Argote, Beckman, and Epple, 1990; Argote and Epple, 1990; Epple, Argote, and Devadas, 1991). Thus, we see an immediate reason why organizations may be reluctant to innovate: They will lose the competencies they have built using the status quo. Indeed, this notion is at the heart of Tushman and Anderson's (1986) distinction between competence-enhancing and competence-destroying technological change. Thus, when organizations innovate, they do not perform as close to the true underlying potential of the new practices as they did with the old practices. The results are organizational myopia (Radner, 1975) and competency traps (Lave and March, 1975; Levinthal and March, 1981; Levitt and March, 1988). Inferior alternatives with which the organization has competence are preferred to superior alternatives with which the organization lacks competence.

Finally, the argument that organizational learning is target oriented highlights the importance of aspiration levels (March and Simon, 1958; Cyert and March, 1963; Mezias, 1988; Glynn et al. 1991; Lant, 1992) in mediating the execution of change routines. The assumption that change is more likely when performance is below aspiration level has been a central tenet in the organizational learning literature. When performance meets or exceeds the aspiration level, change is less likely (March and Simon, 1958; Cyert and March, 1963); if change does occur under conditions of success, it is a largely serendipitous grab at an opportunity that is perceived as extraordinary (Levinthal and March, 1981; Harrison and March, 1984; Marcus, 1988). In addition, once it has been admitted that aspirations adapt to performance (March, 1981; Levitt and March, 1988; Glynn et al. 1991; Lant, 1992), the picture is complicated considerably. The questions of how quickly aspirations adapt to performance, the pattern of subjective success and failure this generates, as well as the association of particular routines with this pattern of success and failure become crucial to understanding organizational outcomes (Levinthal and March, 1981).

Learning and innovation

The three innovation strategies we have outlined can be understood more completely when placed in the context of a learning model. The learning model directs attention to how an organization's routine-based strategies for encouraging innovation may have intended and unintended results under conditions of environmental ambiguity. Our contribution in this paper is to demonstrate how the three different innovation strategies suggest paradoxes and sometimes lead to unanticipated outcomes concerning both the type and the amount of innovation activity. We discuss three implications of the learning model for organizational innovation. First, we have interpreted an institutional approach to managing organizational innovation as consistent with the strategy of devoting more resources to search within current organizational routines and structures. Two plausible assumptions about the context in which organizational search takes place suggest that institutional strategies will result in a skew towards refinement. First, if the adoption of a new innovation replenishes the pool of refinement opportunities (Levinthal and March, 1981), then immediately after adopting an innovation, refinement search will be especially productive. Second, if innovation opportunities improve as a function of time since the last innovation was adopted (Tushman and Anderson, 1986), then immediately after adopting an innovation, innovative search will be relatively unlikely to lead to discovery of good opportunities. This description is consistent with a cyclical pattern of technological innovation argued by Sahal (1981) and empirically demonstrated by Anderson and Tushman (1990); periods of technological ferment and high innovation are followed by periods of incremental modifications to the dominant design. Taken together, these two assumptions imply that, in the periods following adoption of an innovation, the organization will tend to associate refinement search with better performance and innovative search with poorer performance. *Ceteris paribus*, this leads to more resources being devoted to refinement search and less to innovative search. This will tend to delay the discovery of new innovations. An additional problem exacerbates this anti-innovation tendency further: Routine comparisons of an innovation and existing practices do not adjust sufficiently for the fact that competence has been built with existing practices. This evaluation bias tends to result in a 'competency trap' (Levitt and March, 1988) or reliance on the 'old winning formula' (Tushman and Nadler, 1986: 75) that precludes innovation. For all of these reasons, increases in total resources devoted to search will not increase the amount of innovation. We call this the paradox of institution:

> **The paradox of institution:** Devoting more resources to search in the context of routine organizational functioning will not increase innovation.

Second, suing the learning model, we have interpreted revolutional approaches to managing innovation as being consistent with the strategy of devoting more resources to search for those technologies that depart radically from current organizational competencies. In terms of the distinction between refinement and innovative search (Cyert and March, 1963; Levinthal and March, 1981), we assume that revolutional approaches involve devoting more resources to innovative search. We have assumed that the distribution of innovation opportunities improves with the time since the last innovation adopted by the organization (Levinthal and March, 1981; Sahal, 1981; Tushman and Anderson, 1986). This implies that, in the periods immediately following the adoption of an innovation, devoting more resources to innovative search can only result in extensive search through a relatively sparse pool of innovations. A few organizations will find improvements, but the majority are not likely to find an innovation worth adopting. At the same time, the additional expenditures on innovative search are lowering the performance of the organization. Consequently, the majority of organizations will come to associate innovative search with poorer performance; this will tend to result in a reduction in the amount of resources devoted to innovative search. Taken together, these assumptions suggest a pattern of results that we call the paradox of revolution: Increasing the resources devoted to innovative search will not increase the amount of innovation. Initially, there may be an increase in the amount of innovation as a few organizations find innovations as a result of the additional resources devoted to innovative search. However, the majority of organizations will not find a useful innovation. The additional expenditures on search will lower their performance, and they will enter a cycle of reductions of expenditures on innovative search. As a result, the revolutional approach will not increase innovation above the level that would have been observed in the absence of additional expenditures on innovative search.

The paradox of revolution: Devoting more resources to innovative search in the context of routine organizational functioning will not increase innovation.

Third, with respect to evolutional approaches to managing innovation, the learning perspective offers the following observations. Levinthal and March (1981) modeled both innovative and refinement search as drawn from a distribution of alternatives to current practices. They argue that the amount of improvement to be gained from these alternatives is symmetric around zero and that the variance of innovative search is greater than that of refinement search. They assume that there is some error in the evaluation of alternatives, but, on average, organizations tend to reject alternatives that do not offer an improvement to current practices and accept those that do. In such a model of search, variance is an unmitigated good: An increase in the variance of the pool of search opportunities will increase the expected improvement to current practices to be realized by search (Kohn and Shavell, 1974; Levinthal and March, 1981). Learning models have also characterized organizational control systems as improving mean performance at a decreasing rate, but at the cost of reducing variance (March, 1981; 1988). If reduced variance translates into a narrowing of the pool of opportunities examined in search, this decreases the expected value of organizational performance in the long run (Levinthal and March, 1981). This is why the evolutional approach to managing innovation often endorses the loosening of organizational control. These observations translate into the value of variance, which is at the heart of the recommendations of evolutional approaches to managing innovation.

The value of variance: Increasing the variance of innovative search, ceteris paribus, will lead to more innovation.

Simulation analysis

We have argued that organizations learn via a longitudinal process of considerable complexity; deriving the implications of this theoretical framework is quite complicated. It is difficult to predict how the processes will develop over time in different contexts to yield various organizational outcomes. The unfolding of these processes can be observed, however, in a computer simulation. A computer simulation can take a complex set of assumptions, simulate a set of organizational processes, and represent the implications of these processes for organizational outcomes (Cyert and March, 1963; Levinthal and March, 1981; Morecroft, 1984; Herriott et al. 1985; March, 1988; 1991; Lant and Mezias, 1990; 1992; Levinthal, 1990). In this paper, we use simulation methodology to study the strategic management issues of corporate renewal, change, and innovation. The basic rules that govern the behavior of the simulated organizations are described in the following sections; technical details of how these rules were operationalized are described in a separate Appendix. In keeping with our administrative perspective on innovation, our use of technology follows the broad definition proposed by Levinthal and March (1981: 187): 'By technology we mean any semi-stable specification of the way in which an organization deals with its environment, functions, and prospers.'

Our simulation model will be used to demonstrate how certain assumptions about organizational functioning lead to different predictions regarding organizational performance, resources, and innovation activity. Morecroft (1985) argued that simulations that address issues of organizational strategy should be careful to describe their premises and present partial tests of the simulation models. Following this advice, we carefully outline the assumptions of our model. To the extent that these assumptions are based on empirical evidence or are intuitively appealing, concerns about generalizability are mitigated. With respect to partial tests, the skeleton of our simulation program uses the decision rules described by Levinthal and March (1981). While our study goes beyond this skeleton to address a different set of issues, many of the decision rules are identical. Not only does this help to accumulate knowledge by explicit comparison with past work, it also allows us to rely on the partial model tests that they conducted. The purpose of our simulation is to clarify ideas about innovation and how they may lead to intended and unintended outcomes. The ability of a model to demonstrate the linkage between assumptions and outcomes is gained at the cost of imposing precision that can threaten the external validity of the analysis. Along these lines, the construction of the simulation model required a key assumption: The innovations we model are of a single type adopted by one cohesive unit in an organization. While most organizations are innovating on multiple fronts simultaneously and innovations of different organizational units may impact each other over time, we restrict the simulation to an examination of the behaviors of one independent business unit over time. For the sake of clarity, we use the word 'unit' to capture this idea in our analyses.

Search routines

Search is modeled as the execution of a series of steps in the simulation program as depicted in Figure 2.1. The steps are as follows:

1. The possibility of search is checked against the unit's change clock (Amburgey, Kelly, and Barnett, 1990). If change occurred recently, the resources normally devoted to search are instead devoted to getting new routines running; thus, there is no search in the current period.

2. The cost of search for the unit is determined as a function of the amount of search done by the unit in the recent past. If there has been some search, the cost of search decreases with each search but at a decreasing rate; this is equivalent to assuming that there is a learning curve for search (Yelle, 1979; Levinthal and March, 1981). When there has been no search, the ability of the unit to conduct search decays; we assume that the cost of search increases at a decreasing rate with each period that the unit does not search.

3. The unit assesses whether search has been associated with success or failure in the recent past; based on this decision, resources devoted to search are increased or decreased. The rules by which this decision are made are presented in Table 2.1; the basic rationale is that when search is associated with success it is increased, and when it is associated with failure it is decreased. We follow Levinthal and March (1981) in having the unit make three separate decisions based on these rules in each period: The first concerns overall resources devoted to search, the second concerns resources devoted to innovative search, and the third concerns resources devoted to refinement search.

4. The unit determines if performance was above or below aspiration level in the last period. Following Cyert and March (1963) and Levinthal and March (1981), we impose the following rules: If performance meets or exceeds the aspiration level, then the unit devotes more resources to innovative search. Conversely, if performance is below aspiration level, then the unit devotes more resources to refinement search. The number of searches of each type are determined by dividing the resources that have been allocated for each type of search by the cost of each type of search. Each search is a draw from a distribution of opportunities. Innovative opportunities are

new technologies with values that are uniform on a symmetric interval around zero; the range of this interval increases with the value of current technology and time since the last innovation. The value of refinement opportunities are multiples of the value of current technology uniform over a symmetric interval around one; the range of these multiples decreases with the number of refinements already made to current technology.

5. The variance of search processes is updated. We assume that the variance of innovative search increases with the time since the last innovation. This implies that the probability that an organization will discover worthwhile innovations increases as a function of time since the last innovation. We also assume that the variance of refinement search decreases with the total number of refinements already made to current practices; this is equivalent to assuming that there are decreasing returns to refinement (Levinthal and March, 1981). The time path of this decrement resembles the 'S-curve' function of technological progress described by Foster (1986: 32): 'Ships don't sail much faster, cash registers don't work much better, and clothes don't get much cleaner.' As more resources are put into the refinement of dominant designs, it becomes increasingly difficult to make progress because of the limitations inherent in the technology.[2]

6. The program exits the search routines.

Table 2.1 How resources devoted to search are changed in response to experience

	Performance relative to target	
	Meets or exceeds 'success'	Falls below 'failure'
Search resources increased in the last period	Increase	Decrease
Search resources decreased in the last period	Decrease	Increase

Based on the rules in this table, each unit makes three separate decisions in each period. The first involves total search resources, the second innovative search resources and the third refinement search resources.

The determination of performance

The determination of the unit's performance in the simulation is depicted in Figure 2.2. The steps in the program are described as follows:

Figure 2.1   Flow chart of search decisions

1. The main source of ambiguity, the exogenous drift in the value of the underlying technology, is determined. Basically, this involves the determination of two random quantities: the magnitude of drift, depicted on the left, and the direction of drift, depicted on the right. Absent any action by the unit, a random walk on the potential value of the underlying technology is created. This complicates the unit's experiential learning by introducing variation in performance that is unrelated to the actions of the unit. This operationalization of environmental ambiguity follows Levinthal and March (1981), and the values of these quantities are set to correspond to the mean value of drift in their model.

2. The actual value the unit derives from its current practices is a function of where it is on the learning curve. If this is a period in which it has adopted an innovation, it moves to the bottom of the learning curve.[3] For analytical convenience in this study, units move toward a maximum potential level of performance with a technology as they gain experience with it; hence, we describe units as moving up

the learning curve. In periods subsequent to the first period after adoption, it moves up the learning curve; in keeping with empirical data, we assume that as the unit gains experience, its performance increases at a decreasing rate.

3. The performance of the unit is determined by taking the value of how well it did with current routines and subtracting the resources spent on search in the current period.

4. The adaptive aspiration level is computed; as we model it, the aspiration level changes over time in a process that is both incremental, i.e. anchored on the aspiration level in the previous period, and adaptive, i.e. responsive to experience (Glynn et al. 1991; Lant, 1992).

5. The program exits the routines for determining performance.

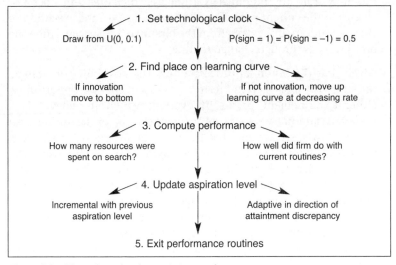

Figure 2.2   Flow chart for determining performance

Change Routines

The determination of change in the program is depicted in Figure 2.3 and is outlined below.

1. The possibility of change is checked against the unit's change clock. As with search, if the unit has only recently changed, then a subsequent change is not permitted.

2. Performance is compared with the aspiration level. If performance meets or exceeds aspiration level, then the probability of change is a function of the value of options the unit has found in executing its search routines. If performance is below aspiration level, then the probability of change is an increasing function of the amount by which the unit has fallen below aspiration level. The difference between performance and aspiration level is called the attainment discrepancy (Glynn et al. 1991; Lant, 1992); hence, the notation in the figure is meant to convey that the probability of change is a function of the attainment discrepancy.

3. In keeping with our probabilistic model of organizational processes, we model the change decision as a random variable. Whether the unit will actually change in this period is a binomial random variable with the probability of success equal to the probability of change. If the draw from the binomial is a 'failure,' then the unit does not change in the current period, and the program exits the execution of change routines. If the draw from the binomial is a 'success,' then the unit proceeds through change routines.

4. Given that the binomial process allows the possibility of change, the unit still must determine if it has discovered an opportunity, either a refinement or an innovation, which it believes is a preferred alternative to current practice. As in Levinthal and March (1981), we assume that the value of alternatives to current practices is known with some error. Based on this comparison, the unit may decide that there is some preferred alternative and adopt it. If the preferred alternative is an innovation, then the unit has undergone a major change; if it is a refinement, then the unit has undergone an incremental change. Conversely, the unit could decide that none of the opportunities discovered through search are preferable to current practices and exits the change routines.

5. The program now exits the change routines.

Simulating the behavior of organizational units

The three categories of routines are executed for fifty business units over fifty time periods. Each unit is initialized as if it had innovated, i.e. adopted a new technology, in period 0; all parameters are set to the same values as in Levinthal and March (1981). Three outcome measures are reported by the program:

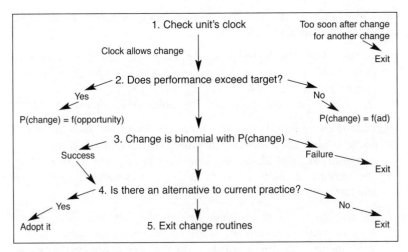

Figure 2.3 Flow chart for determination of change

- First, we observe the mean total innovative changes (subsequent to the period 0 change) made by units in the population. This measure gives an idea of how many units have adopted a new technology as the program progresses through fifty periods.

- Second, we observe the mean total refinements to current technology made by units in the population. Each time an innovation is adopted by a unit, the mean of refinements to current technology is reset to zero. This measure gives an idea of the propensity of an average unit in the population to refine current technology.

- Third, we observe mean total resources of a unit in the population. In each period, the performance of the unit with its technology is added to total resources, and the total cost of searches conducted by the unit is deducted from total resources. This measure allows assessment of search in light of its effect on unit growth.

Operationalizing the innovation strategies

To operationalize the innovation strategies, we ran the program under four conditions. These represented a baseline model and three variants created to examine the paradoxes of institution and revolution as well as the value of variance. We contrast the four different conditions to determine the effects on the performance, resources, and innovation record of units when we vary the model as described below.

- The Baseline Condition: The program operates exactly as described in the flow charts.

- Variant One, The Institutional Approach: To test the paradox of institution, we made one alteration to the baseline program: As each unit executed its standard operating procedure for determining total resources to be devoted to search, the amount was increased by 25%.

- Variant Two, The Revolutional Approach: To test the paradox of revolution, we made a different alteration to the baseline program: As each unit executed its standard operating procedure for determining the amount of resources to be devoted to innovative search, the amount was increased by 25%.

- Variant Three, The Evolutional Approach: To test the value of variance, we made a different alteration to the baseline program: As each unit executed innovative searches, the variance of the distribution of the outcomes of these searches was increased by 25%.

While these operationalizations are precise and parsimonious so as to make clear the link between existing theory and our results, there are some inherent limitations. Obviously, the model does not capture fully the richness or complexities of each of the innovation strategies. Moreover, it assumes that each unit follows only one strategy and does not change that strategy during the period of the simulation. Finally, the model does not take into account intra- or inter-organizational factors that may influence the innovation process; our models are intended to depict the behaviors of an independent business unit operating within a large, bureaucratic organization.

Sensitivity analysis

To assess the sensitivity of our results to the choice of parameters and structural equations that govern decision making by units, we ran six variations on the main model.[4]

1. Low ambiguity variation: Levinthal and March (1981) termed the level of exogenous drift in technology a measure of ambiguity. We adopted the level of drift from their model for our main model; to test the sensitivity of our results to this choice, we also ran a variation with lower ambiguity.

2. High ambiguity variation: To further test the sensitivity of the model to this choice, we also ran a variation with higher ambiguity.

3. High inertia variation: Drawing on recent empirical work (Amburgey et al. 1990), we posited that units would not search or change for some period of time following adoption of an innovation. In operationalizing the main model, we chose a value of two periods for this waiting time. To test the sensitivity of the results to this parameter, we chose a value that we believed represented a high level of inertia, ten periods.

4. Slow increase variation: In consonance with much theoretical and empirical work, we posited that the value of innovation increased with the time since the adoption of the last innovation. To test the sensitivity of our results to the particular functional form of the relation between time since adoption and the value of innovation, we ran a variation that had a slower increase than our main model.

5. Fast increase variation: To further test sensitivity to this parameter, we also ran a variation where the value of innovation increased more quickly than our main model.

6. Additive variation: Following Levinthal and March (1981), we specified a multiplicative relationship among the quantities used by the unit to determine search expenditures. To test the sensitivity of the results to this specification, we ran a final variation that specified an additive relationship among these quantities.

Results

The baseline model and its three variants are examined in a series of figures comparing effects for the four conditions: baseline, institutional, revolutional, and evolutional. The figures compare the means of units in the four innovation conditions on three outcomes: innovative change, refinements to current technology, and resources. Given uncertainty about the distributions of these variables, we used non-parametric comparisons to assess whether the conditions differed significantly. Thus, the comparisons we report are robust to violations of the distributional assumptions of a comparison like the t-test. In addition, these tests offer more conservative assessments of the significance of results than parametric tests.[5]

Results supporting the paradox of institution can be seen in several figures. First, Figure 2.4 depicts mean innovative changes by condition over time. During the first 18 periods following initialization of the simulation, there are no innovative changes in any of the conditions.[6]

This combination yields a period of no innovation following initialization of the simulation. The baseline condition produces its first innovations in period 22, while the institution condition does not produce its first innovation until period 25. However, from that point onward, the mean levels of innovation produced by the two strategies are not significantly different. This demonstrates support for the paradox of institution: Devoting more resources to search in the context of routine organizational functioning does not increase the level of innovation by the unit compared to the baseline strategy. Second, Figure 2.5 depicts the total number of refinements. The institution condition produces a higher level of refinement than the baseline condition throughout the entire run of the simulation; in fact, the level of refinement produced by the insitution condition is significantly higher than that produced in the baseline condition ($p < 0.05$).

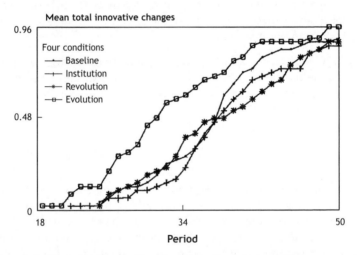

Figure 2.4   Mean total innovative changes in the four conditions

Support for the paradox of revolution is also indicated in Figures 2.4 and 2.5, by comparing the revolution and baseline conditions. The baseline condition produces innovations first, with the revolution condition producing its first innovations four periods after the baseline condition first yields innovations. However, from that point onward, the mean levels of innovation produced by the two strategies are not significantly different. Thus, as suggested by the paradox of revolution, the additional resources devoted to the search for innovations in the

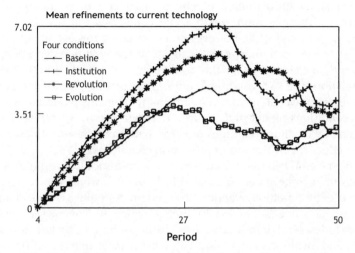

Figure 2.5   Mean refinements to current technology in the four conditions

revolution condition do not produce a significant increment to the level of innovation by the unit. Figure 2.5 demonstrates that the mean refinements produced by the revolution condition are at all times greater than the number of refinements produced by the baseline condition; this difference is statistically significant ($p < 0.05$). Thus, we found two types of support for the paradox of revolution: First, the additional resources spent on innovative search in the revolution condition do not yield significant increases in innovation relative to the baseline condition. Second, the additional resources spent on innovative search in the revolution condition actually result in significant increases in refinements relative to the baseline condition.

Finally, support for the proposition concerning the value of variance can be deduced from Figures 2.4 and 2.5. Figure 2.4 demonstrates the most substantive result: In terms of innovation, the evolution condition clearly dominates the baseline condition, producing a significantly higher ($p < 0.05$) level of mean total innovations. The evolution condition begins producing innovations in period 18 while the baseline condition does not produce an innovation until period 22. From that point forward, the evolution condition produces a higher level of innovation than the baseline condition in every period. Figure 2.5 demonstrates that the mean number of refinements to current technology produced by the evolution condition is somewhat less than that in the baseline condition. In the early part of the simulation, through about

period 20, the mean number of refinements to current technology produced by the evolution and baseline conditions is fairly identical.
Beginning in period 20, however, and continuing through about period 40, the mean number of refinements in the evolution condition is
lower than that in the baseline condition. In the final periods of the
simulation, the two conditions once again produce similar levels of
refinement. Overall, the mean number of refinements produced by the
two conditions are not statistically different; importantly, both the evolution and baseline conditions produce significantly fewer refinements
than either the institution or revolution conditions.

The trade-off between the costs and benefits associated with different
innovation strategies are illustrated in Figure 2.6, which depicts mean
resources by condition over time. The pattern of findings is evident and
consistent from about period 20 through period 50. The order of highest to lowest level of mean resources are the evolution, baseline, revolution, and institution conditions. This demonstrates that the costs associated with more resource intensive strategies for managing innovation,
i.e. the institutional and revolutional approaches, are not sufficiently
offset by the returns from the additional search that these resources buy.
The average level of total resources in both of these conditions is significantly less than the level of resources observed in the baseline condition. While the size and timing of the gap in Figure 2.6 depends on
parameter settings, several conclusions that arise from this line of rea-
soning do not.[7] First, the tenability of innovation strategies will be a
function of how their costs are distributed over time. Resource intensive
strategies to manage innovation will be sustainable only so long as the
increment to performance justifies the expense. Second, the tenability
of resource intensive strategies will probably be a function of competitive conditions. For the sake of simplicity, we have excluded competitive
effects from our model, but we believe they are of central importance for
future work. For example, we do not believe that is a coincidence that
Brown's (1991) pioneering strategy, which we categorize as a revolutional approach to innovation, was developed in the context of an
industry in which the basic production technology is changing rapidly.
In such contexts, the value of innovation will recover more quickly following the adoption of one innovation as the underlying technology
undergoes rapid transformation. Third, the long-run untenability of
resource intensive strategies might actually assist managers in deciding
when to devote more resources to the search for new technologies. For
purposes of illustration, we have adopted a model of these strategies as
binary, either off (baseline) or on (either the institution or revolution

conditions). More sophisticated switching rules based on performance and resources might do better than the simplistic strategies we have outlined here. As managers interpret ambiguous experience to adjust search routines, feedback about the apparent costs and benefits of search could be an important piece of information (Nelson and Winter, 1982).

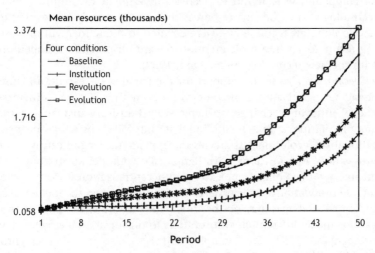

Figure 2.6 Mean resources in the four conditions

Conclusions and implications

We used a simulation methodology to explore the theoretical implications of following different innovation strategies in business units of large, bureaucratic organizations over time. Drawing from the organizational literature, we developed a framework of three key strategies used to encourage innovation in established firms: institutional, revolutional, and evolutional approaches. An organizational learning perspective was adopted to conceptualize the dynamics of the innovation process. This perspective suggested a focus on three key variables: search, performance, and change. We assessed the effects of the strategies on a business units' innovation record (i.e., refinement versus innovation) and resources. Overall, the findings support Damanpour's (1991) contention that different organizational types, particularly as they may be defined by their strategic orientation, can influence the degree of organizational innovativeness. Furthermore, the results are noteworthy in several respects.

First, we found that intentional strategies may have unintended consequences. We found support for the paradox of institution: Units
engaging in an institutional strategy did not tend to experience more
innovation, in spite of increased resources devoted to search. Our result
has a parallel in the real world of organizations: In a recent study, 32 of
34 companies were found to decrease investment in promising new
technologies. Instead, the resources that would have been devoted to
developing new technologies were devoted to the refinement of existing technologies in a futile attempt to ward off potential competitors
with the new technology (Blanchard, 1989).

Second, we also found support for the paradox of revolution: Units
engaging in a revolutional strategy, purportedly designed to increase
radical innovative change, garnered only transitory increases in the
amount of innovation. The finding that units following either the institutional or revolutional strategies did not produce significantly more
innovation is consistent with empirical work demonstrating that
greater organizational complexity and decentralization leads to incremental innovations (Ettlie et al. 1984). This finding on the incidence of
these two strategies may not be trivial, for the different types of innovations make differential contributions to organizational effectiveness
(Damanpour, 1991). For example, Hull, Hage and Azumi (1985) proposed that the success of Japanese manufacturing companies in the
1960s and 1970s might be attributed to their ability to make incremental innovations, while the success of American companies in this
sector and during the same time might be related to their introduction
of radical innovations.

Third, we found that a loosening of controls is beneficial when
tighter controls lower the variance of stochastic search. There was a
noticeable value of variance, in both discovering significantly more
innovations and making significantly fewer refinements to current
technology. Damanpour's (1991) meta-analysis of the innovation literature may offer a partial explanation for this result. His analysis of the
existing research indicated that an organization's technical knowledge
resources were more strongly related to radical innovation than incremental innovation. Perhaps organizations with more expansive knowledge bases are better able to take advantage of opportunistic search and
the serendipitous discoveries it may yield (Cohen and Levinthal, 1990).

The findings of our simulation point to interesting questions about
the role of management in the process of corporate renewal and
innovation. Tushman, Newman, and Romanelli (1986) emphasize
the importance of executive leadership, even attributing successful

organizational performance and adaptation to visionary leadership. In the simulation presented here, management was assumed to operate in the context of a rigid organizational structure, not unlike that found in large, bureaucratic firms. Once a strategic direction for innovation was set, choices about search rules, performance, and change followed a set of routines. Thus, our results adhere to the perspective articulated by Lant and Mezias (1992: 65): '...system dynamics limit the frontiers of individual efficacy and the possibilities for managerial leadership.' By demonstrating how these rules followed consistently and unswervingly over time, affected outcomes, we have suggested some of the ways in which routines provide important bounds on managerial discretion and control. Moreover, support found for the paradoxes of institution and revolution suggests that under such limitations, managerial interventions may have unintended results. What such paradoxes suggest is the need for managerial attention to structural routines in the process of strategic decision-making. In addition, the demonstrated value of loosening organizational controls and introducing variance into routine processes invites non-traditional definitions of the role of the executive and the management of organizational slack. Our results also speak to the centrality of attending to the costs and benefits of managing innovation while illustrating some of the complexities of attempting to do so. Strategies that attempted to induce a higher frequency of innovation by devoting more resources to search, i.e. both the institutional and revolutional approaches, resulted in markedly lower resources over time than the evolutional and baseline conditions.

Of course, the generalizability and external validity of the results are important concerns. The use of a simulation model was chosen to underscore our belief that the roles of chance and routine have been relatively underemphasized in the literature of innovation and corporate renewal. We attempted to make our simulation as descriptive as possible and included empirical measures of parameters whenever possible. In addition, in order to build on past literature using simulation methodology to study strategic management, many parts of our program were replications of code from Levinthal and March (1981). This strategy of replication facilitated the tasks of premise description and partial model tests (Morecroft, 1985), thus addressing the question of generalizability directly. We believe that a strategy of replication and extension in applying simulation methodology to questions of strategic management, as we have done here, has merit. Moreover, the simulation results do not simply reflect the suppositions built into the model, but yield knowledge that adds value beyond its explicit assumptions. The evidence for this is twofold:

First, we base our simulation on assumptions drawn from empirical and theoretical work elaborating a view of organizations as experiential learning systems; this represents a statement of premise description, which, by articulating how assumptions of a learning model of organizations lead to simulated behaviors of organizational units, should make the link between equations and results clearer (Morecroft, 1985). This descriptive architecture of complexity does not present ready opportunities to 'rig' the results. Second, the sensitivity analysis indicates that the findings are fairly robust, even when parameter values and structural equations are varied. In order to encourage further research in this area, we close our conclusions with a discussion of some straightforward extensions of the analysis presented here.

A first possibility for future research would be to place this model of innovation in an interorganizational context. Competitive conditions could be modeled explicitly by having organizations pay some penalty for spending resources innovating in the absence of a significant increase in returns. Industry dynamics in the pattern of innovation could be modeled and various ideas about them could be tested. For example, in industries characterized by rapid technological change, greater expenditures on innovation might be tolerated because all organizations would be forced to make them. Second, the whole question of imitability (Lippman and Rumelt, 1982) could be explored. Returns to innovation can be related directly to the ability of the organization making the innovation to reap its rewards. Various imitability conditions, spanning a continuum from more to less imitable, could be explored. In addition, stochastic errors in imitation could be modeled as a source of innovation in and of themselves (DiMaggio and Powell, 1983). Third, simulations of organizational innovation could be used to pursue a course proposed by Sterman (1989): using computer simulations as a tool to produce a controlled environment in which to run experiments. Simulations might be used to examine the effects of different specifications of mechanisms that relate individual units to their organization and the organizations to an interorganizational context. The implications of these findings might then be used to structure a set of experiments regarding how people interact with the proposed organizational mechanisms. It is our belief that the strength of these research projects would be their emphasis on a clear set of organizational routines as the source of corporate renewal and innovation. Such a clear set of routines in a setting of stochastic outcomes offers a real possibility for advancing our understanding of corporate renewal, change, and innovation.

Appendix: simulation particulars

Choice of parameter values

Two basic considerations were most fundamental in the choice of parameter values. First, for reasons of cumulative knowledge building, many of our assumptions about search processes and parameter values correspond to Levinthal and March (1981). This contributes to cumulative knowledge because our results can be seen as a direct extension of theirs. The cumulative relationship between Levinthal and March (1981) and this study is further reinforced because this is an entirely original program written in Turbo Pascal.[8] Since Levinthal and March (1981) used Basic, similarities in the conclusions demonstrate that they do not depend on choice of computer language. Second, in trying to set realistic parameter values, we relied on Tushman, Newman, and Romanelli's (1986: 34) characterization of incremental adjustment: 'A popular expression is that almost any organization can tolerate a "ten percent change." ... these changes are still compatible with the prevailing structures, systems, and processes.' Thus, parameters meant to capture routine adjustment were set at 10\% based on an empirical tendency for such adjustments to be near that level.

We also decided to initialize the simulation as if each unit had been founded in the period prior to the first. Thus, time since adoption of the current technology is set to zero. Thus, the search and change clocks of the unit are reset to zero. The unit is moved to the bottom of its learning curve on the current technology. Also, the unit incurs maximum search costs; since it has no prior experience with either innovative or refinement search, it does not have the requisite experience to begin lowering the costs of performing them.

Operationalization of search routines

The discussion of the operationalization of search routines will follow the flow chart for search given in Figure 2.1: The window of no search or change imposed by the search clock of the unit is set to two periods. An amount equal to the total resources devoted to search in the period of innovation is deducted in each of these periods but there is no search or change. Both innovative and refinement search are draws from uniform distributions. Innovative searches are draws from a uniform distribution with range as follows:

$$R_{it}^{\ i} = \pm \,(Ptl_{it} + \tau^2\,) \tag{1}$$

Ptl_{it} is defined to be the underlying potential of the technology used by unit i at time t; following Levinthal and March (1981), it is set to 50 in the first period. τ is defined to be the count of the number of periods since the adoption of the most recent innovation. Thus, the mean value of technologies discovered by innovative search is always zero, since the distribution is symmetric around zero, but the variance increases with the range.[9]

As a result, the probability that the best technology discovered by innovative search will be an improvement over current technology increases with time since adoption of the current technology.

Refinement searches are draws from a uniform distribution with a range as follows:

$$R_{it}^{\ r} = (1 \pm \delta_{it}) \times Ptl_{it} \tag{2}$$

Ptl_{it} is as defined above. δ_{it} is defined as follows: In the period immediately following an innovation, δ_{it} is set to ⅛ and remains at that value until three refinements have been adopted. From that point forward δ_{it} is set to $1/(TR_{it}^{\ 2})$, where TR_{it} is the total number of refinements made to current technology since adoption by the unit. Thus, the probability that current technology can be improved by further refinement decreases with the number of refinements already made.

The cost of search is proportional to the value of the underlying potential of the current technology. To initialize the simulation, the costs of both innovative and refinement search are set at the levels used by Levinthal and March (1981). Thus, the initial value of the minimum cost of innovative search is set to 0.0135 × 50, the initial value of the potential of technology, and the minimum cost of refinement search is 0.01 × 50. Units start out with a cost of search equal to the minimum cost of search raised to the power of 3/2.[10] With each search they perform, the exponent on the minimum cost of search decreases one half the remaining distance between its value and one. This results in the cost of search decreasing with the number of searches but at a decreasing rate. The exact functional form that results is depicted for the initial values of innovative search in Figure 2.7. When a unit does not search in a particular period, the cost of search increases at the same rate it decreases when the unit does search. Thus, the functional form of decay along the search cost curve is the obverse of the functional form of the decrease in search cost.

The assessment of past search proceeds as described in Table 2.1. The decisions involve three variables: Total Search Potential, TSP_{it}, Innovative Search Potential, ISP_{it}, and Refinement Search Potential, RSP_{it}. Following both Levinthal and March (1981) and the 10% rule, we operationalize increases and decreases to search resources as follows: If the assessment of total search is that it has been associated with failure, then TSP_{it} is reduced by 10%; if it has been associated with success, then TSP_{it} is increased by 10%. The assessments of innovative search and refinement search are operationalized identically. Actual resources available for search are defined by two equations. The first defines innovative search resources, ISR_{it}:

$$ISP_{it} = TSP_{it} \times ISP_{it} \times TP_{it} \qquad (3)$$

where TP_{it} is defined to be the actual performance the unit achieved with its technology in the most recent period. RSR_{it} is defined as in (3) with the substitution of RSR_{it} for ISP_{it}.

Actual resources devoted to search depend on the assessment of performance. If performance meets or exceeds aspiration level, then $RSR_{it} = RSR_{it}^{1/1.1}$ and ISR_{it} is left as is. Conversely, if performance is below aspiration level, then $ISR_{it} = ISR_{it}^{1/1.1}$ and RSR_{it} is left as is. The allowed number of searches is determined by taking the resources to be devoted to each type of search, dividing by the cost of that type of search, and rounding to the nearest integer. The unit takes a number of draws from the appropriate distribution equal to the number of searches. To operationalize myopia with respect to new technology, the value of innovative draws are deflated by raising them to the 0.75 power.

Operationalization of performance routines

The discussion of the operationalization of performance routines will follow the flow chart for performance given in Figure 2.2. As indicated in the figure, the value of technological potential drifts in each period, the draws from drift are uniform on the interval $(-0.1, 0.1)$, thus the value of technological potential in the current period is in between 90% and 110% of the value of the technological potential in the previous period. Movement on the learning curve is as follows: The technological performance of the unit, TP_{it}, is a function of the underlying value of the potential of the current technology. The form of this relation is as follows: $TP_{it} = Ptl_{it}^{\lambda}\tau$. The subscript τ on λ is meant to signify that it is a function of time since adoption of the current technology. In the period of adoption of the new technology, λ_0 is set to 0.75. In all subsequent periods until adoption of the next technology, the value of λ_τ is set by the following incremental formula:

$$\lambda_t = \lambda_\tau - 1\} + (1 - \lambda_\tau - 1)/2) \qquad (4)$$

In keeping with empirical data, the rate at which performance increases as a function of experience decreases as a function of time; the shape of this function is analogous to that presented in Figure 2.7. Refinements change the value of the underlying potential of the current technology but do not affect the learning curve. Adoption of a new technology automatically resets the exponent to 3/4, and movement on the learning curve begins anew. Performance, P_{it}, is defined as follows:

$$P_{it} = TP_{it} - ISR_{it} - RSR_{it} \qquad (5)$$

Thus, performance is determined by how well the unit does with its current technology minus the costs of all innovative and refinement search.

Aspiration levels, AL_{it} are set using the attainment discrepancy model (Lant and Mezias, 1990; 1992; Glynn et al. 1991; Lant, 1992):

$$AL_{it} = \beta_0 + \beta_1 AL_{i,t-1} + \beta_2 (AL_{i,t-1} - P_{i,t-1}) \qquad (6)$$

The parameter β_1 determines the level of incrementalism in aspiration level updating while the parameter β_2 determines the responsiveness of the process to performance feedback. The actual values of the β_s used are uniform on the range of the highest and lowest values of each parameter estimated by Lant (1992).

Operationalization of change routines

The discussion of the operationalization of change routines will follow the flow chart for change given in Figure 2.3. The change clock of the unit is set to two periods; for two periods following the adoption of an innovation the unit cannot change. Performance is assessed relative to target by comparing P_{it} and AL_{it}. If performance equals or exceeds the aspiration level, the probability of change depends on whether the best alternative technology found through search is an innovation or a refinement. For innovations, the probability of change equals the difference between the performance with current technology and the best technology found through innovative search divided by τ (cf. equation (1)). If performance equals or exceeds the aspiration level and the best alternative technology found through search is a refinement, then the probability of change equals the best refinement draw divided by δ_{it} (cf. equation (2)). If performance is less than aspiration level, then the actual amount by which performance falls below aspiration level is divided by $MinAL_{it} - P_{it}$ to obtain the probability of change.

To determine whether a unit changes in a given period, a draw is taken from a binomial distribution with the probability of success equal to the probability of change determined in the previous step. If that draw is a failure, then the unit exits the change routines. However, if the draw is a success then the unit proceeds to evaluate the available alternative technologies, both refinements and innovations, found through search. If no alternative superior to current technology is available, then the unit exits.

Operationalizing the four variants

Four conditions were used to operationalize the theoretical framework: In the baseline condition, all parameters are set exactly as described above. In the institution condition, TSP_{it} is multiplied by 1.25 to operationalize the 25% increase in resources devoted to search. In the revolution condition, ISP_{it} is multiplied by 1.25 to operationalize the 25% increase in resources devoted to innovative search. In the evolution condition, the range of innovative search is multiplied by 1.25 to operationalize a 25% increase in the variance of innovative search.

Operationalizing the sensitivity analysis

To assess the stability of our results, a sensitivity analysis was conducted; we varied both parameters and structural equations to test the sensitivity of our results to several features of the simulation program. We will first discuss how we varied parameters and then how we varied structural equations; both will be discussed in the order they were presented above. The first parameter varied was the length of the change and search clock. The value of 2 periods was the one used in the simulation presented in the body of the paper; the values of 0 and 10 were used as minimum and maximum to test the sensitivity of the results to this parameter. The second parameter varied was the level of technological drift. A value of 10% was used in the body of the paper; we chose the values of 20% and 33% to test the sensitivity of the results to this parameter. The first structural equation that we varied was the exponent of τ in equation (1). We ran three variations on this equation to test the robustness of the results under conditions of slow ($\tau = 1.5$), moderate ($\tau = 2$), and rapid ($\tau = 2.5$) technological change. The second structural equation variation involved substituting an additive relation for the multiplicative relation of search potentials in determining search expenditures. To do this we changed equation (3) as follows and made the same changes for the calculation of RST_{it}:

$$ISR_{it} = (TSP_{it} \times TP_{it})\,/4 + (ISP_{it} \times TP_{it})\,/4$$

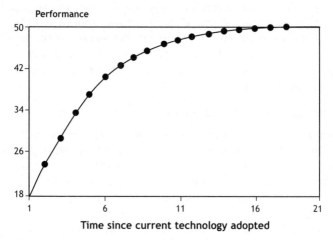

Figure 2.7   The learning curve assuming no innovation and a maximum of 50

3
Mimetic Learning and the Evolution of Organizational Populations

Stephen J. Mezias and Theresa K. Lant

The ecological (Hannan and Freeman, 1977) and institutional (Meyer and Rowan, 1977) perspectives have emerged as two dominant but distinct paradigms in organizational theory since their inceptions over a decade ago. Initially, one reason why these theories may have seemed irreconcilable, at least superficially, was the difference in the research questions that the original authors posed. Hannan and Freeman (1977) pointed to an apparent diversity of organizational forms and offered an ecological explanation for this multitude. Meyer and Rowan (1977) and especially DiMaggio and Powell (1983) stressed the lack of diversity of forms and proposed the mechanism of institutional isomorphism by which this diversity is eliminated. More recent work concerning populations of organizations has recognized the similarity of the inter organizational field (DiMaggio and Powell, 1983; Meyer and Scott, 1983) and the population (Hannan and Freeman, 1977; 1984; McKelvey and Aldrich, 1983) as units of analysis. For example, both institutional and ecological perspectives have been used in explaining the evolution of a population of Voluntary Social Service Organizations in the greater Toronto area (Singh, House, and Tucker, 1986; Singh, Tucker, and House, 1986; Singh, Tucker, and Meinhard, 1988; Tucker, Singh, and Meinhard, 1990). Singh and Lumsden (1990: 182) argue that this convergence of the ecological and institutional paradigms '... may be viewed as one of the more exciting research developments in organization theory.'

In this study, we will focus on the role of organization level change in the evolution of organizational populations. Ecological theory has been dominated by Hannan and Freeman's (1984: 150) argument that '(i)n a world of high uncertainty, adaptive efforts ... turn out to be essentially random with respect to future value.' Given the assumptions of costly change and negative selection, the random value of change assumption guarantees that organizations that change their structures will suffer higher mortality rates than organizations that do not change. This study relaxes the assumption of random change based on two developments in the ecological literature: The first is the increasing amount of empirical evidence to suggest that the relation between organization level change and the evolution of organizational populations may be more complicated than current conceptualizations, which are dominated almost exclusively by the argument that change increases mortality (Singh and Lumsden, 1990: 179–182). The second is the rapprochement of the institutional and selection perspectives, which suggest that organizational level change, can be linked to selection perspectives by positing a role for institutional theory in guiding organizational change (Singh and Lumsden, 1990: 182–184). As an alternative to the assumption of random change, we will describe organizational level change as the outcome of an experiential learning process guided by mimetic search.

We believe that this combination of the institutional and organizational learning perspectives offers three enhancements to current theory about the role of organization level change in the evolution of organizational populations: First, although we maintain the argument that successful adaptation is made more difficult and costly under conditions of uncertainty (Hannan and Freeman, 1984), we recognize explicitly that in the face of uncertainty, organizations may substitute institutional rules for technical rules (Meyer, Scott, and Deal, 1983). For example, if mimetic search can overcome the random value of change under conditions of high uncertainty, then such institutional rules may mitigate the liability of organizational level change. Second, an organization learning perspective is used to model the change processes of individual organizations that make up the population; the elaboration of organizational level processes allows for a more complete analysis of the role of organization level change in the evolution of organizational populations. Third, we model firms as engaging in a mimetic search process without assuming the existence of a highly developed institutional order. A finding that organizations using mimetic search can survive without extensive institutional support is a conservative test of the argument that the use of these rules mitigates the liability of organizational change. It also provides a theoretical basis for understanding the rise of institutional environments. Using this model, we conduct a simulation study to determine the conditions under which some significant proportion of a population consists of firms that change their core features according to a mimetic search process. These conditions establish a baseline for the study of institutionally guided change as an engine of change in the characteristics of the population. In the discussion and conclusions, implications for organizational theory and research are suggested; in particular, we speculate on the use of an institutionally informed ecology of learning as a tool to understand institutional effects on population dynamics.

An ecology of learning

This attempt to understand the role of organizational change in the evolution of organizational populations follows from a growing body of literature summarized by Fombrun (1988: 224): 'Indeed, the changing mix of characteristics in surviving organizations is increasingly regarded as a joint effect of both institutional and ecological influences.' This paper develops a model of an institutionally informed ecology of learning. Our use of ecology follows from the fact that the unit of our study is the population of organizations, and all of the results are reported at the population level. In addition, there is selection of organizational characteristics through different death rates for organizations with different characteristics. It is an ecology of learning because we argue that organization level change is guided by a process of experiential learning (Levitt and March, 1988); thus, organizational learning may have a significant impact on the evolution of organizational populations. The ecology is institutionally informed because the model focuses on particular patterns of organizational learning and change that are based on the mimetic processes discussed in the institutional literature. The following sections specify our model by describing the characteristics of the individual organizations and the environment in which they learn.

Characteristics of organizations

Organizations as Experiential Learning Systems. Organizations in this ecology learn from experience through a process that is '... routine-based, history-dependent, and target oriented' (Levitt and March, 1988: 319). The learning process has three basic components: First, unlike the typical actors of neoclassical economics that optimize in obtaining information (Varian, 1978: 231–248), a learning model suggests that the acquisition of information by organizations takes place in a routinized, heuristic process of search (Cyert and March, 1963; Nelson and Winter,

1982). Second, organizations have a target level of performance or aspiration level to which they compare their actual performance. In each period, they determine whether they have performed above or below this aspiration level (Cyert and March, 1963; Payne, Laughunn, and Crum, 1980). Third, performance above or below aspiration level affects the likelihood of organizational change. Change to core features of the organization is more likely when performance is below aspiration level (March and Simon, 1958; Cyert and March, 1963; Levitt and March, 1988). In sum, an organizational learning model suggests that the principal impetus for organizational change and adaptation is performance below aspiration level; the content of change depends on the outcomes of an organizational search process.

The growth of an experiential learning systems can be represented as follows:

$$R_{it} = R_{it-1} + P_{it} - c_1 n1_{it} - c_2 n2_{it} R_{it-1}. \tag{1}$$

We assume that there are I distinct firms observed over T time periods; thus, we have $i = 1,..., I$ and $t = 1,..., T$. R_{it} are the resources of firm i at time t. Pit is the realized performance of firm i at time t. c_1 is the cost of search, and $n1_{it}$ is the number of searches performed by firm i at time t. c_2 is the proportion of resources consumed in making one change to the core features of the organization, $n2_{it}$ is the number of changes to core features made by firm i at time t, and thus $c_2 n2_{it} R_{it-1}$ is the cost of change.

Organizations and search rules.   The organizational search process consists of routine activities directed toward examining alternative modes of organizing and assessing their effectiveness. Two types of search are possible: The first type of search takes place at the beginning of the organizational life cycle to determine the characteristics of the organization to be founded. Following Hannan and Freeman (1987: 911), this search is assumed to be directed in such a way that foundings have two main effects on the population of organizations: 'Some foundings initiate an entirely new form and thus contribute qualitatively to the diversity of organizational forms in society. Most foundings replicate an existing form and contribute quantitatively to diversity.' For this reason, founding search is modeled as an attempt to discover the relationship between firm type and performance rather than as an attempt to imitate. In this way, new firm types can be introduced to the population and existing types can be replicated.

The second type of search occurs subsequent to founding and follows rules derived from either the selection or the institutional perspectives. The first search rule is derived from the assumptions of the selection perspective; after an initial founding period, firms experience a variety of inertial forces that make them structurally inflexible. These firms follow a fixed strategy, and do not search or change at any time after founding. In terms of equation (1), this assumes that both $n1_{it}$ and $n2_{it}$ are zero for all fixed firms in all periods. The second search rule is derived from the institutional perspective. These firms follow a mimetic strategy; they search for information about what organizational characteristics are legitimated in their environmental niche. Fombrun (1988: 227) emphasizes the centrality of a mimetic search process in crafting an institutionally informed ecology of organizations: 'For organizations, this points to the importance of modeling the search processes through which managers acquire information about environments with which they then imitate competitors.' In our model, we assume that legitimated characteristics are those that have been adopted by key firms or industry leaders (DiMaggio and Powell, 1983), which we define as the largest firm in the population. In periods subsequent to founding, there is a non-zero probability that mimetic firms will change their core features so as to become more similar to this industry leader. In terms of equation (1), this implies that both $n1_{it}$ and $n2_{it}$ may be greater than zero for any mimetic firm in any period.

Mimetic firms continue to engage in stochastic search behavior throughout their existence; the distribution of these searches depends on total resources and performance relative to aspiration level (Cyert and March, 1963; Levinthal and March, 1981). Each search involves examining one other firm type to determine if it is the type of the largest firm in the population; for each such search conducted the firm incurs a cost equal to c_1 units of firm resources. Both problemistic and innovative search occur (Cyert and March, 1963; Levinthal and March, 1981; Mezias and Glynn, 1993); both types of search incur identical costs and are directed towards finding the type of the largest firm in the population. They differ, however, in two ways: First, problemistic search increases with the amount by which performance is below aspiration level. By contrast, innovative search increases as the focal firm becomes wealthy relative to other firms in the population. Second, they differ in terms of 'where' organizational attention is allocated relative to the current firm type. In problemistic search, firms consider those changes that alter the status quo only slightly. Innovative search may be focused more widely and can lead to fundamental change.

Aspiration levels and change.   Since fixed firms never change after founding, aspiration levels are irrelevant for this portion of the population. Among mimetic firms, however, performance relative to aspiration level is the principal determinant of whether observable organizational change will result from post-founding search. Mimetic organizations have a target level of performance or aspiration level that adapts over time according to a formula of the general form estimated in empirical studies of aspiration level adaptation (Lant and Montgomery, 1987; Glynn, Lant, and Mezias, 1990; Lant, 1992):

$$AL_{it} = A_0 + A_1 + AL_{it-1} + A_2 \times (P_{it} - AL_{it-1}) \tag{2}$$

where AL_{it} is the aspiration level of firm i at time t. A_0, A_1 and A_2 are parameters that govern the aspiration level updating process. In each period, firms determine whether they have performed above or below this aspiration level. The probability that a firm will change one or more characteristics depends on the difference between aspiration level and performance.[1] Consistent with research in this area, the distribution of the probability is discontinuous at the point where performance equals aspiration (Cyert and March, 1963; Mezias, 1988). For performance below aspiration level, the probability of change is an increasing function of the size of the discrepancy between actual performance and aspiration level. Although the probability of change is highest when performance is below aspiration level, there is a small probability that firms change even when performance is above aspiration level. Occasionally, as a direct result of search, firms discover good opportunities. In these situations, the probability of change depends on serendipity in the form of a conjunction between a good opportunity and a decision to act on it even in the absence of performance below aspiration level (Cyert and March, 1963; Levinthal and March, 1981). Each change to the core dimensions of the organization is assumed to be very costly (Hannan and Freeman, 1984); a proportion of the resources of the firm equal to c_2 in equation (1) is consumed by each change.

The characteristics of the environment

The environment in this ecology provides a mapping between organizational characteristics and performance. Both adaptive theories (Child, 1972; Galbraith, 1973; Tushman and Romanelli, 1985) and ecological theories (Carroll, 1984; Hannan and Freeman, 1977; 1984) argue that organizational performance is contingent on the fit between organizational characteristics and the environment. We assume that the relevant characteristics of organizations can be categorized into distinct firm types, designated $l = 1,...,L$. Each firm type, l, has a base performance, BP_{it}, which may vary by type l and over time t. This number, BP_{it}, is a measure of the fit between firm type l and the environment at time t.

Fixed characteristics of environments. The environment is characterized by a level of carrying capacity that is fixed. As the level of carrying capacity increases, the environment can sustain more firms and competition among firms is less intense.[2] The population size is constrained by the carrying capacity via negative selection. A firm goes bankrupt when its resources fall to zero; if the number of firms is above the carrying capacity of the niche, then that firm is not replaced. If the number of firms is at the carrying capacity of the niche, the bankrupt firm is replaced. The search rule of the replacement firm is determined by a random draw from the surviving firms that had positive performance in the current period. For the sake of simplicity, this simulation focuses on established populations where competition is high (population size is at or near carrying capacity). Empirical study of the evolution of organizational populations has demonstrated that population size tends to increase until it reaches a peak (Carroll and Hannan, 1989: 411): 'Once the peak is reached, there is usually a sharp decline and sometimes stabilization.' We simulate this period where the population moves back toward a size that the environment can sustain in the long term.

The second fixed characteristic of the environment is the level of ambiguity in the relationship between firm types and performance. In the real world of organizations, the true relationship between firm characteristics and performance is difficult to determine because of ambiguity (March and Olsen, 1976). The role of ambiguity is modeled here by assuming that firm performance consists of a systematic component based on firm type and a random component that differs for each firm in the population (March, 1988; Lant and Mezias, 1990, 1992). This relationship is summarized by the following equation:

$$P_{it} = BP_{it} + \mu_{it} \qquad (3)$$

μ_{it} is a random component that is added to the base performance of the firm's type in computing the actual performance of firm i at time t. These random components come from a distribution with a mean of zero; the level of ambiguity increases with the variance of the distribution of these random components. Defined in this way, ambiguity directly and differentially affects each firm in the population in determining actual performance in each period.

Ambiguity affects search at the time of founding as well. All firms in the population search at founding through the L firm types, and examine the following relation for each of the l types:

$$FP_{ilt} = BP_{lt} + \mu_{ilt} \qquad (4)$$

The decision rule is that firm i founded at time t becomes the type l that yielded the largest FP_{ilt} observation; more formally, organizations choose the firm type they will become, l, such that $\max l\ FP_{it}$ is satisfied.[3] Following initialization, all firms that replace bankrupt firms also engage in founding search to determine which firm type they will become. As discussed above, however, whether firms are fixed or mimetic is a property inherited from a firm randomly drawn from among all those with positive performance in the period of the replacement. Comparisons of different firm types to find a good type at the time of founding include both the actual base performance of type l and the random component mit that differs for each of L types. The distribution of μ_{it} is the same as the distribution of μ_{it}. Ambiguity in the founding search process creates a liability of founding search for both fixed and mimetic firms; the larger the level of ambiguity, the more likely it is that firms will experience an error during founding search. As a result, firms may adopt a type that does not have high performance.

Characteristics of environmental change. The frequency of change in the environment is captured by the probability that the relationship between firm type and base performance will change in any period of the simulation. The probability that this relationship will change in any of T periods is a Bernoulli random variable with a probability of 'success' or change given by $P(\Delta)$, $0 < P(\Delta) < 1$. The value of $P(\Delta)$ is a fixed characteristic of the environment.

The level of grain, or the magnitude of change, in the environment determines the size of the Bernoulli changes when they take place. Fine-grained environments involve changes of relatively small magnitude, while coarse-grained environments involve changes of relatively large magnitude (Hannan and Freeman, 1984; Hannan and Freeman,

1977). Given that a stochastic change in the environment has occurred, BP_{lt}, the base performance of type l at time t, will be a weighted combination of the previous base performance, BP_{lt-1}, and a new base performance, NBP_{lt}, drawn from the same distribution as the BP_{lt}. w_1 and $(1 - w_1)$, with $0 < w_1 < 1$, are the weights assigned to BP_{lt-1} and NBP_{lt}, respectively. Thus, the magnitude of an environmental change at time t is determined as follows:

$$BP_{lt} = w_1 \, BP_{lt-1} + (1 - w_1) \, NBP_{lt}. \tag{5}$$

A fine-grained environment will have a w_1 that is close to one, with a new base performance that is close to the old base performance.

Propositions

In order to derive the implications of organizational level change for the evolution of organizational populations, we examine the degree to which mimetic firms will survive in a population that consists of both fixed and mimetic firms. A finding that a significant proportion of firms in our simulated populations are mimetic would call into question the assumption that organizational level change does not impact population characteristics significantly. Our model of an institutionally informed ecology of learning suggests several theoretical propositions concerning the relative proportions of fixed and mimetic firms in the population. The propositions suggest several variables that might affect the proportion of mimetic firms in the population, denoted Y_{jt}, the proportion of mimetic firms in population j at time t. These variables, along with a description of the process by which parameter values were assigned, are discussed below.

Stable survival of mimetic firms

In order to conclude that mimetic firms might be important to population dynamics from the observation of a finite sample of time periods, the proportion of mimetic firms in the population must be moving toward a stable level greater than zero. We must demonstrate that the system is approaching an equilibrium at the point where we measure the proportion of surviving mimetic firms. System stability implies that the rate of change in the proportions of fixed and mimetic firms should decrease over time, approaching zero. If mimetic firms survive in substantial numbers, and the proportion of fixed and mimetic firms is stable, then we will have demonstrated that mimetic firms will be a fairly permanent component of the population. The stable survival of mimetic firms suggests that institutional processes may be important in the evolution of organizational populations. Thus, in order to adequately understand how populations of organizations come to have certain characteristics, it may be necessary to consider organizational level change explicitly in models of population dynamics.

Fixed characteristics of environments

As described in the preceding section, certain features of the environment in our model are fixed for each population at the beginning of each run of the simulation and do not change. The effect of carrying capacity is explored by randomly assigning the number of firms that the niche can support, designated K. The values of K are drawn from the uniform distribution of integers between 20 and 99. Since all populations are initialized with 100 firms, the value of K is a measure of the degree of downward pressure on the number of firms. This downward pressure on the size of the population constitutes the form of competition in this simulation and is operationalized via negative selection.[4] We do not include elements of mass or concentration in our operationalization of competition. Thus, in our model, competition increases when carrying capacity decreases. Hannan and Freeman (1984) argue that selection pressures favor firms that do not change their structure. In general, the smaller the carrying capacity of a niche, the greater are selection pressures. Thus, mimetic firms will be at a disadvantage compared to fixed firms due to negative selection in niches with limited carrying capacity.

> **Proposition 1**: A proportion of mimetic firms will increase as the carrying capacity of the niche increases.

The second fixed feature of the environment is the level of ambiguity in the relationship between firm characteristics and performance. The effect of ambiguity is explored by operationalizing μ_{it} in equation (3) and μ_{ilt} in equation (4) as random draws from the uniform distribution over the interval $-A$ to A. A is a random draw from the integers 0 to 25 that establishes the level of ambiguity at the start of each run of the simulation. In this ecology of learning ambiguity may impose two liabilities on firms: the liability of organizational change and the liability of founding search.

The liability of organizational change was presented quite effectively by Hannan and Freeman (1984); they argued that high levels of ambiguity render attempts at adaptive change essentially random with respect to future value. Since change is costly but of random value, there is a significant liability of organizational change. Thus, the proportion of mimetic firms should decrease with the level of ambiguity.

Proposition 2A: The proportion of mimetic firms in the population will decrease as the level of ambiguity increases.

The liability of founding search is derived from applying this argument to understanding how firms become a certain type in the founding search process. The greater is ambiguity, the less effective is the founding search process at discovering the relationship between firm type and performance, producing a liability of founding search. Although mimetic and fixed firms will make mistakes during ambiguous founding search at approximately the same rate, the ability of mimetic firms to make adaptive changes after founding may help them to overcome this liability. Thus, the proportion of mimetic firms should increase with the level of ambiguity.

Proposition 2B: The proportion of mimetic firms in the population will increase as the level of ambiguity increases.

Unsure as to how these two effects will balance out, we will predict that the proportion of mimetic firms will be affected by the level of ambiguity. A negative effect is consistent with a greater liability of change; a positive effect is consistent with a greater liability of founding search.

The final fixed parameters of the environment are the costs of search and the cost of change; these are invariant over time and identical for all search and change by all firms in the population for the entire length of the simulation. The cost of search, c_1 in equation (1), is expressed in the same units as organizational resources. This is the cost per search and determined by a random draw from the real numbers between 0 and 1. The cost of change to a core dimension of the firm, c_2 in equation (1), is expressed as a percentage of the total resources of the firm. Since change to core dimensions is very costly (Hannan and Freeman, 1984), the percentage of resources consumed by each change is determined by a random draw from the uniform distribution of real numbers between 0 and 0.5.[5] Thus, the type of change we are interested in modeling results in significant changes to the characteristics of an organization. Some institutional theorists (Meyer and Rowan, 1977) have suggested that organizations change peripheral features while buffering their core characteristics. Under the assumption that core changes are more costly than peripheral changes, the continuum from core to peripheral changes can be represented by the distribution of the cost of change across populations in the simulation. Thus, the implications of this simulation are not necessarily limited to a discussion of changes to core dimensions. Hannan and Freeman (1984) suggest that spending resources to change the core dimensions of organizations will have detrimental effects on organizational survival. The organizational learning perspective highlights the costs of search. Thus, we propose that there will be both a liability of organizational change and a liability of organizational search.

Proposition 3: The proportion of mimetic firms in the population will decrease as the cost of search and the cost of change increase.

Characteristics of environmental change

Our final arguments concern the mediating effects of environmental change on the different liabilities faced by firms in the population. Two components of environmental change are considered important: the probability of environmental change and the magnitude of environmental change. The parameter $P(\Delta)$ governs the probability that the environment will change in any period; when the environment changes, the fit of a firm type, as measured by its base performance, changes as well. The greater is $P(\Delta)$, the more likely it is that the environment will change in any period. The magnitude of environmental change (Hannan and Freeman, 1984) is operationalized as the weight used in determining the new relationship between firm characteristics and performance at the time of an environmental change. The magnitude of environmental change decreases with the value of w_1 in equation (5). Both the values of w_1 and $P(\Delta)$ are assigned randomly from the uniform distribution of real numbers between 0 and 1 at the start of each run of the simulation.

Analysis based on the institutionally informed ecology of learning suggests two effects of environmental change. The first is an effect on the liability of founding search. In stable environments, the information about the relationship between firm type and performance gathered during founding search is more likely to remain valid since the relationship is unlikely to change. Similarly, lower performing types adopted due to errors committed in founding search remain lower performing. As a result, the liability of founding search may be a more serious problem for firms under conditions of environmental stability than under conditions of environmental change. The second effect of environmental change may be to produce a liability for firms resulting directly from the fact that the environment does change. Under conditions of environmental stability, firms that do not incur the costs of search and change have an advantage over firms that do, *ceteris paribus*. These firms do not search when there is nothing to find and, better yet, do not change when there is no advantage to gain. Under conditions of environmental change, however, there will be a liability of environmental change for firms that cannot adapt their structures to new environmental configurations. Thus, the expected effects of environmental change are captured by two predictions. First, in highly stable environments, mimetic firms will be helped by their ability to overcome the liability of founding search. Second, in changing environments, mimetic firms will be helped by their ability to overcome the liability of environmental change. If these predictions are correct, then the proportion of mimetic firms should be higher in environments characterized by very low or high levels of change. Propositions 4 and 5 predict that the effects of both the probability and magnitude of environmental change on the proportion of mimetic firms are U-shaped:

Proposition 4: The proportion of mimetic firms will increase with very low or very high probabilities of environmental change.

Proposition 4 will be supported if the effect of the probability of environmental change is initially downward sloping from low rates of environmental change to intermediate rates of environmental change, and becomes upward sloping as the probability of environmental change reaches very high levels. To capture this U-shaped relation in a linear model, both the probability of environmental change, $P(\Delta)$, and its exponent are included in the analysis.

Proposition 5: The proportion of mimetic firms will increase with a very low or a very high magnitude of environmental change.

Proposition 5 will be supported if the effect of the magnitude of environmental change is initially downward sloping from a high magnitude of environmental change to an intermediate magnitude of environmental change, and becomes upward sloping as the magnitude of environmental change reaches very low levels. To capture this U-shaped relation in a linear model, both the magnitude of environmental change, w_1, and its exponent are included in the analysis.

The results of the simulation

Operationalizing the ecology

The model we develop assumes that organizations are distinguished by four core dimensions (Hannan and Freeman, 1984; Tushman and Romanelli, 1985); for the purposes of this simulation, the choice of labels for these dimensions is arbitrary. Distinct firm types are determined by different characteristics on these four core dimensions. For the sake of simplicity, we assume that firms have only two alternatives on each of these four dimensions; as a result, there are $2^4 = 16$ distinct firm types. Changes to core dimensions in this simulation involve movement from one of these sixteen firm types to another. At the start of the simulation, each of the sixteen firm types is assigned randomly a base performance level, BP_{l0}, $l = 1,..., 16$ at time $t = 0$. This base performance reflects the degree of fit of the lth firm type with the environment during the first time period. This base performance is stated as an integer that represents the increment to total resources that results from a given firm being a type l at this time. The range of possible values for performance has been restricted to the integers between -10 to 10. All sixteen types may be ranked from highest to lowest on this base performance.

A population is initialized with 100 firms, with 50 assigned to each of the mimetic and fixed search processes. The organization being founded becomes one of the sixteen firm types through the founding search process as per equation (4). The resources of all firms are set to an initial allocation of 30 units of resources at the time of founding. This level of resources imposes a significant liability of newness: firms of this initial small size are more likely to go bankrupt than larger firms because performance decrements in early periods can easily exhaust the initial allocation of resources. First, negative values of μ in equation (3) decrease performance, even leading to negative performance that can result in bankruptcy. Second, mistakes during founding search, affected by the size of μ in equation (4), may lead organizations to choose poor performing types as a result of founding search. Finally, the mimetic firms must bear the costs of search and change that can consume a considerable proportion of resources and can lead to bankruptcy; thus, mimetic firms face a greater liability of newness than fixed firms, *ceteris paribus*. In each period the performance of the firm, as defined in equation (3), is added to its resources. Subsequent to founding, fixed organizations get performance draws in each period, but never search or change. By contrast, mimetic organizations get performance draws in each period, make search and change decisions, and update their aspiration levels.

To evaluate the propositions, a linear regression of the following form is estimated:

$$Y_j^{500} = \beta_0 + \beta_1 K + \beta_2 A + \beta_3 C_1 + \beta_4 C_2 + \beta_5 P(\Delta) + \beta_6 \, exp(P(\Delta) + \beta_7 w_1 + \beta_8 \, exp(w_1) + e_{jt} \qquad (6)$$

where K is carrying capacity, A is ambiguity, c_1 is the cost of search, c_2 is the cost of change, $P(\Delta)$ is likelihood of environmental change, $exp[P(\Delta)]$ is the exponent of the likelihood of environmental change, w_1 is the magnitude of environmental change, and $exp(w_1)$ is the exponent of the magnitude of environmental change. We estimate this equation for 500 populations after 500 periods have elapsed; thus, $j = 1, ..., 500$. The results are used to obtain an estimate of the effect of each of the independent variables once the system has reached an equilibrium. Table 3.1 provides a summary of the variables and related research propositions.

Table 3.1   The effects of organizational and environmental characteristics on the proportion of mimetic firms in a population

	See equation (6)	
Variable name	Proposition	Predicted effect
K (carrying capacity)	1	$\beta_1 > 0$
A (ambiguity)	2	$\beta_2 < 0, \beta_2 > 0$
c_1 (cost of search)	3	$\beta_3 < 0$
c_2 (cost of change)	3	$\beta_4 < 0$
$P(\Delta)$ (environmental stability)	4	$\beta_5 < 0$
$exp(P(\Delta)$	4	$\beta_6 > 0$
w_1 (magnitude of change)	5	$\beta_7 < 0$
$exp(w_1)$	5	$\beta_8 > 0$

Findings and discussion

Proposition 1 predicted that some proportion of mimetic firms would survive in the long run. Figure 3.1 demonstrates that by period 500,

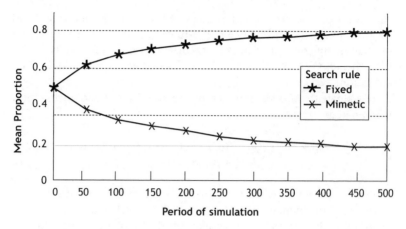

Figure 3.1   Mean proportion of surviving firms of each type as a function of
time

approximately 20% of the firms are mimetic, compared with 80% that
are fixed firms. Further, Figure 3.1 also indicates that the rate of change
in the proportion of firms of both types decreases over time. In particular, the slope of the lines tracking the proportion of fixed and mimetic firms in the population appears to be zero by period 500. We take this
as evidence that the proportion of fixed and mimetic firms in the population in period 500 is similar to what we would observe over an
extended period of time; that is, approximately 20% of the population
will consist of mimetic firms over the long run. Thus, Figure 3.1 illustrates strong support for the proposition that some proportion of
mimetic firms will survive in the population even after an arbitrarily
long period of time. The results of testing propositions 2 through 6 are
presented in Table 3.2, which reports the significance of estimated coefficients from an ordinary least squares regression of the effects of carrying capacity, ambiguity, costs of search and change, and the rate and
magnitude of environmental change on the proportion of mimetic
firms in the population in period 500.

The effect of carrying capacity on the proportion of mimetic firms is
significant and positive as predicted by Proposition 2. Thus, as carrying
capacity increased, the proportion of mimetic firms that survived in the
population also increased. This result supports the argument that
decreased selection pressures help mimetic firms. Contrary to
Proposition 3, the level of ambiguity in the environment did not have a
significant effect on the proportion of mimetic firms in the population.

Table 3.2   The effects of organizational and environmental characteristics on the proportion of mimetic firms in a population

	See equation (6)	
Variable name	**Coefficient**	**T-statistics**
Intercept	−.5994	−4.3930**
K (carrying capacity)	.0007	2.2333*
A (ambiguity)	.0005	.4190
c_1 (cost of search)	−.1848	−6.9569**
c_2 (cost of change)	−.2540	−5.4825**
$P(\Delta)$ (environmental stability)	−.5785	−3.1076**
$\exp(P(\Delta)$	.4466	3.9939**
w_1 (magnitude of change)	_.7224	−3.6594**
$\exp(w_1)$	.4640	−4.0064**

Note: T-statistics are presented for interested readers, They do not imply that these are empirical results. Futhermore, T-statistics depend on sample size and sample size could be increased by conducting more simulation runs; thus, such statistics should be interpreted with these caveats in mind.

The effects of the cost of search and the cost of change are negative and significant, as predicted by Proposition 4. These results point to the significant liabilities of search and change: mimetic firms are at an increasing disadvantage compared to fixed firms as the cost of learning increases.

Proposition 4 predicted that the proportion of mimetic firms would increase in environments with either very low or very high probabilities of change. The results offer evidence of the predicted U-shaped relationship. The measure of the probability of environmental change, $P(\Delta)$, is negative and significant. This result indicates that the proportion of mimetic firms decreases as the probability of environmental change rises from a low to an intermediate level. The exponent of $P(\Delta)$ is significant and positive, indicating that the proportion of mimetic firms increases again as the probability of environmental change rises to a very high level. Figure 3.2 illustrates this curvilinear relationship.

Proposition 5 predicted that the proportion of mimetic firms would increase in environments with either a very low or a very high magnitude of change. The results offer evidence of the predicted U-shaped relationship. The measure of environmental grain, w_1, is significant and negative. This result indicates that the proportion of mimetic firms decreases as the magnitude of environmental change falls from a high

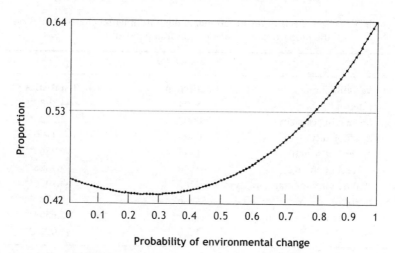

Figure 3.2   Effect of the probability of environmental change on the mean proportion of mimetic firms

level to an intermediate level. The exponent of w_1 is significant and positive, suggesting that the proportion of mimetic firms increases again as the magnitude of environmental change reaches a very small level. Figure 3.3 illustrates this curvilinear relationship.

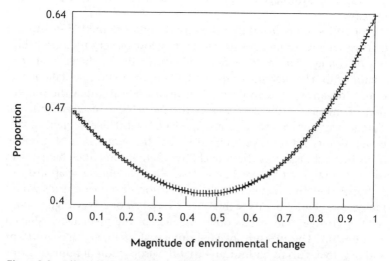

Figure 3.3   Effect of the magnitude of environmental change on the mean proportion of mimetic firms

Limitations and suggestions for future research

The generality of the results from the simulation may be limited by the particular choices we made in operationalizing this ecology of organizational learning. In this section, we suggest several dimensions on which the simulation could be expanded, and we discuss the possible implications of such changes. One possible limitation is that organizations in our ecology do not increase their competency at search and change activities as their age and experience increased. Allowing firms to increase their competence at search and change could give mimetic firms a better chance of survival if the cost of search and change decreased as competence increased. With respect to search, firms in our simulation do not improve on their ability to search by searching, and all firms in the population have identical costs of search (cf. Levinthal and March, 1981). Further, problemistic and innovative search (Cyert and March, 1963) have the same cost. These are simplifying assumptions to facilitate understanding the direct effect of the cost of search on the probability of survival of firms that search. With respect to change, we do not include an explicit term to measure the probability of successful change; for purposes of this simulation, a lower probability of successful change increases the expected number of change attempts required to achieve a successful completion of change. This increases the cost of a successful change: More difficult change is regarded as more costly change.

In addition, it might be useful to take into account the suggestion of Hannan and Freeman (1984) that organizations will be less likely to change as they grow larger. Such a pattern of change might result in older, successful mimetic firms behaving more and more like fixed firms over time. Presuming that mimetic firms had achieved a good fit with the environment, reducing the amount of resources devoted to search and change would be an advantage in stable environments. However, it would result in mimetic firms experiencing the liability of environmental change typically experienced by fixed firms. These implications lead us to ask: What if firms could change from one search process to another? In stable environments, we might see an increasing number of mimetic firms adopting a fixed search process, whereas in changing environments, we might see a large number of fixed firms adopting a mimetic search process. In ambiguous environments, we might see the majority of firms in an emerging population choosing a mimetic search process, since they will be able to correct mistakes made in an ambiguous founding search process. In unambiguous environments, however, we might see the majority of firms in an emerging population choosing a fixed search process, since there will be no benefit to searching or changing after the initial founding search. These speculations suggest what might happen if we simulated organizational populations while they were emerging and growing as well as during the periods of peak and decline. In order to simulate this emergent period, we would also need to include an ongoing birth process, rather than just the replacement birth process operationalized in this model. We might also examine the effect of population density on the rate at which firms go bankrupt. That is, as competition increases (as the population gets closer to its carrying capacity), some firms will be forced out of the population before their resources fall to zero. We expect that the effect of such competition on mimetic firms would depend on the variables we examined in this simulation, such as the cost of search and change, and the frequency and magnitude of environmental changes. All of these changes represent extensions to the institutionally informed ecology of learning that would further demonstrate its utility.

The role of mimetic learning

The results of this simulation offer an interesting illustration of how different assumptions lead to different conclusions about the importance of organization level change in understanding population dynamics. Hannan and Freeman's (1984) contention that change is random with respect to future value implies that the study of inert firms replacing each other is all that is necessary in order to understand the evolution of organizational populations. This implies that organization level change is not an important focus for the study of the evolution of organizational populations. In this paper, the assumption of random change has been relaxed based on two developments in the ecological literature: The first is the increasing amount of empirical evidence suggesting that organization level change may play an important role in the evolution of organizational populations (Singh and Lumsden, 1990: 179–182). The second is the rapprochement of the institutional and selection perspectives, which guided the choice of the type of organizational level change addressed explicitly in this study (Singh and Lumsden, 1990: 182–184). We replaced the assumption of random change with the assumption that firms engage in institutionally guided mimetic search and change. Using this alternative assumption, we highlighted the liabilities of founding search and environmental change in addition to the liabilities of organizational change usually considered in ecological models (Hannan and Freeman, 1984; Carroll, 1984). A simulation methodology was used to assess the minimum conditions under which a significant proportion of mimetic firms would persist in the population. The survival of mimetic firms in our simulation did not depend on the existence of an elaborate institutional environment. Thus, we suggest that the operationalizations in our model provide the baseline conditions under which organizational level change guided by a mimetic process may be an important element in models of the evolution of organizational populations.

Our results suggest that understanding mimetic learning and organization level change will be more important in understanding the evolution of organizational populations under the following conditions: (1) Low levels of competition, as measured by higher carrying capacity, increase the proportion of mimetic firms. (2) Low costs of search and change increase the proportion of mimetic firms. Thus, mimetic firms do experience a liability of both search and change. (3) A relatively low or a relatively high magnitude of environmental change increases the proportion of mimetic firms relative to an intermediate magnitude of change. (4) A relatively low or a relatively high probability of environmental change increases the proportion of mimetic firms relative to an intermediate probability of change. The third and fourth points suggest that mimetic firms are helped not only by their ability to overcome the liability of environmental change, but also by their ability to overcome the liability of founding search under conditions of environmental stability.

Evolution and organization level change

In general, the results of the simulation suggest that a significant proportion of mimetic firms can survive under a wide range of conditions. Our choice of ranges used in operationalizing the simulation are based on empirical measures or are consonant with theoretical treatments of the underlying concepts. These assumptions define some boundary conditions under which organizations that are capable of mimetic learning will survive over relatively long periods of time. These results are obtained by making relatively few assumptions about the institutional environment. The only institutional process operationalized in the simulation is mimetic: Mimetic firms in the population engaged in search that enabled them to imitate the largest firm in the population. There is no cooperation among the mimetic firms to pool or otherwise lower the costs of search and change. There is no transfer of resources from a centralized authority to those firms that follow the mimetic search process. There is no central coordination at the level of the institutional environment or diffusion of professionalized personnel to increase normative or coercive pressures to adopt certain characteristics (DiMaggio and Powell, 1983; Meyer and Scott, 1983). The ability of a significant proportion of mimetic firms to survive for long periods of time absent such additional support suggests how mimetic organization level change might evolve even in the absence of a well-developed institutional environment.

Imitation of the largest firm in the population, a search process based on institutional theory and the literature on organizational learning, is a robust strategy over time, even under conditions of competition, ambiguity, costly search and change, and environmental variability. This is illustrated by the fact that the average proportion of mimetic firms in the population is still above 20% even after 500 periods (Figure 3.1). This result suggests that under a fairly general set of conditions, a significant proportion of organizations in a population that have the ability to change core features of their structure may survive. Based on this conclusion, we believe that models of the evolution of organizational populations have an obligation to take into account the potential effects of change at the level of individual organizations. We do not believe that dismissal of the possibility of organization level change is acceptable as a principle for the study of the evolution of populations of organizations. In addition, we believe that our results suggest an intriguing possibility: What if mimetic firms, recognizing their common interest, form a coalition to influence, strengthen, or even create the institutional environment?

Pursuing the implications of the formation of an institutional environment by a coalition or coalitions among firms that have the ability to change core features also may be an important area for future research. The institutional literature has suggested two phenomena that might be the result, and both may form interesting areas for future research. First, the institutional literature has suggested that there will be increases in the legitimate and coercive power of the nation-state. The findings of Barnett and Carroll (1992) regarding the effect of governmental action, The Kingsbury Commitment, on the evolution of populations of telephone companies provides evidence of how state action might affect the evolution of organizational populations. Second, the institutional literature has predicted the rise of professionalized sectors (Meyer and Rowan, 1977; Meyer and Scott, 1983; DiMaggio and Powell, 1983). The recent consolidation of the formerly

Big Eight firms into the Big Six represents an obvious example of how these sectors change over time. The interrelationship of the evolution of populations of professional organizations and the evolution of the populations of organizations that they serve may be one way to link the rise of professional sectors explicitly with the evolution of populations of organizations. We believe the exploration of both of these phenomena form an important and interesting agenda for future evolutionary research.

Appendix

The values of the parameters of the aspiration level formula, A_0, A_1, and A_2 in equation (2), were assigned randomly from the values of these parameters estimated by Lant (1992) in a study of aspiration level adaptation. The results reported here are not changed by effects from any combination of these values. When mimetic firms search, they attempt to discover the type of the largest firm in the population and adopt its characteristics; this is true for both problemistic and innovative search. Problemistic search occurs if and only if firm performance is below aspiration level and involves searching any of the four types that would require only one change to firms structure. For example, a firm type 1111 engaging in problemistic search might search types 1110, 1101, 1011, or 0111. Thus, no more than four problemistic searches will be conducted; the actual number conducted is binomial with n=4 and pi given as follows:

$$\pi = \frac{P_{it} - AL_{it-1}}{min_i \, (P_{it} - AL_{it-1})} \tag{7}$$

Thus, the probability of one problemistic search is the ratio of the amount by which the focal firm fell below its aspiration level and the largest amount by which any firm in the population performed below its aspiration level. Innovative searches can be performed by any mimetic firm in any period; these can involve examination of any of the 15 firm types other than the current type of the focal firm. Thus, the number of innovative searches will be binomial with n=15 and π given as follows:

$$\pi = \frac{R_{it}}{max_i(R_{it})} \tag{8}$$

Thus, the probability of one innovative search is the ratio of the focal firm's resources to the resources of the largest firm in the population at time t. Problemistic searches are conducted first, and those firm types searched in the problemistic process are not considered in the innovative search process. Thus, no firm type will be searched twice in the same period.

For firms performing below aspiration level in a given period, the probability of change is binomial with n=4 and Π as given in equation (7) for problemistic search. For firms performing above aspiration level the probability of change is binomial with n=4 and $\Pi = 0.05$.

This study attempts a simultaneous development of both the ecological and institutional perspectives by focusing on the role of change at the level of the individual organization in understanding the dynamics of populations of organizations.

Several theoretical propositions are derived and examined using data obtained by observing 500 simulated populations at 50 period intervals for 500 periods. Separate cross population regression equations are estimated for the 500 observations obtained at each of the 50 period intervals; the time subscript on the variables is t=50, 100,..., 500. The dependent variable, Y_{jt}, is the proportion of mimetic firms in population j, j=1,...,500 , at time t. Each of the independent variables suggested by the propositions are discussed below along with a description of the process by which parameter values were assigned in each run of the simulation.

Periodicity

The finding of movement toward stability is complemented by the periodicity suggested in the results. The effects of the independent variables occur in different periods and some variables have different effects at different points in time. The variables tracking system stability illustrate the most general form of periodicity. The coefficient on the previous proportion of mimetic firms is not significantly different from zero in period 100, and it is significantly less than one in periods 150, 200, and 300 through 450. The coefficient on the exponent of previous percent is significantly greater than zero in periods 100 through 200 and 300 through 450. This suggests that the movement toward stability was non-linear. The constant is significant and positive in period 50, and significant and negative in periods 100, 150, 200, 300, and 450. This suggests that on average the movement towards stability, after controlling for the effects of the independent variables, involved decreases in the proportion of mimetic firms.

The significant effects of variables in periods later than 350 also suggest some continuing periodicity in the stabilizing system. The pattern of effects for several variables suggests that there may continue to be some small but systematic changes to the proportion of mimetic firms even after 500 periods. The effect of carrying capacity seems to have a pattern of oscillation between a positive effect and no effect; the pattern seems to be dampening after period 350, but there is a small, positive, significant effect on the proportion of mimetic firms as late as period 450. The small but significant negative effect of ambiguity in period 350, which contradicts Proposition 3, is followed by a smaller, but significant, positive effect in period 450. There is an apparent oscillation of the effect of cost of change between a negative effect and no effect over time. However, the pattern of oscillation seems to dampen after period 250. Nonetheless, the cost of change has small but significant negative effects as late as periods 400 and 500. Finally, the effect of stability seems to enter a period of oscillation in period 400, having a small, but significant, effect in period 450. Interestingly, the effect has an inverse U-shaped relation with the proportion of mimetic firms in period 450, contradicting Proposition 5. This offers an intriguing anomaly both in terms of system stability and the inversion of the expected effect.

Some of the mechanisms by which this process would proceed have been suggested in previous literature. The potential ways in which the evolution of legitimacy might influence selection pressures can be illustrated within an institutionally informed ecology of learning.

The institutional environment can control resources that directly affect the survival of individual firms (Scott, 1987); such transfers of resources might mitigate the effects of lower carrying capacities, costly search, and costly change on mimetic firms.

Institutional environments might bring down the costs of search and change by centralizing these functions and pooling the resources of many organizations interested in discovering the same information; in our simple example, the information of interest was the type of the largest firm in the population. Such pooling of knowledge and resources might alter significantly the cost of change or the probability of success once a change has been undertaken. The institutional environment may function to substitute institutional rules for technical rules as a guide to the structuring of organizations (Meyer, Scott, and Deal, 1983). As Scott (1981: 274) points out: 'Ritually defined categories can provide order and meaning, and rational myths can supply rationales for choice and action.' Following from this, it is quite easy to imagine scenarios under conditions of ambiguity where the substitution of institutional for technical rules might reduce the costs of search and change. The institutionalization and professionalization of the management of organizations might alter what March (1981) calls the level of altruism in the population. Imagine a world where the amount of organization level change that maximizes the survival of individual organizations is different from the amount of change that maximizes the wealth of the population. The institutional environment offers a mechanism for balancing what is sensible at these different levels of analysis. Hannan and Freeman (1984) argue that selection pressures favor firms that are inert with respect to core features. At the level of the institutional environment the propensity for organizations to change core features could be altered by the creation of an ideology of management. In this way, the propensity to change core features of organizations produced by selection pressures could be changed by the operations of the institutional environment. Differences in the rates at which the environment and definitions of legitimacy change can serve as a buffer between the firm and the direct effects of the rate and magnitude of environmental change, at least in the short run. This opens up many interesting possibilities for modeling how institutional environments mediate the perception and effects of shifts in underlying relations between firm types and performance. For example, certain combinations of the rates of environmental variability and rates of change in centralized definitions of legitimacy could increase movement towards the turbulent environments described by Emery and Trist (1965).

In conclusion, future research on population dynamics should consider the reciprocal relationships between legitimacy and competition on the one hand, and organizational learning, change, births, and deaths on the other. We hope that this paper has demonstrated the potential usefulness of an institutionally informed ecology of learning in performing such analyses.

Part II
The Evolutionary Dynamics of New Industry Creation

In this section we assemble evidence of the strong influence evolutionary population dynamics and the social context of organizations play in the occurrence of entrepreneurship and in new industry creation. In Chapter 4: Resource Partitioning, the founding of specialist firms, and innovation: The American feature film industry, 1912–1929, provides additional support for our claim in section one that incumbent firm change can play a significant role in new industry emergence. Incumbent firms in the early American film industry affected the founding of specialist organizations and genre innovation directly and indirectly. Because the industry became highly concentrated very quickly, specialist firm foundings were fostered as is predicted by resource partitioning theory. In turn, specialist firms are shown to be more innovative in the area of introducing new genres, such as the Western, to film audiences. By successfully applying the resource-partitioning model to an industry that is still in its infancy, this chapter provides further support for our contention that the ecological level of analysis.

In Chapter 5: The Community Dynamics Of Entrepreneurship: The Birth of The American Film Industry 1895–1929, the concepts of second and related sourcing from the technological literature are used to shed light on the founding dynamics of the American film industry. This chapter shows how firms in each part of the value chain are dependent upon entrepreneurship in other parts of the value chain in order to thrive. For example, rapid growth in film production only occurred after entrepreneurs in the exhibition part of the value chain introduced the nickelodeon. The nickelodeon was an inexpensive but stable venue in which movies could be seen. Reliable exhibition space simultaneously increased demand for films and film production. The interdependence of producers and exhibitors provides further support for our belief that in order to fully understand the phenomenon of entrepreneurship we must broaden our focus beyond single founders or single firms.

4
Resource Partitioning, the Founding of Specialist Firms and Innovation: the American Feature Film Industry, 1912–1929

John M. Mezias and Stephen J. Mezias

The so-called independent film production companies dominated the 1996 Academy Awards. Of the five nominees for best picture, a Hollywood studio produced only one. Van Gelder (1996: 9) described the phenomena of the rise of the much smaller and more specialized independents, asserting that the films produced and distributed by these firms demonstrated '... their dominance over the products of the Big Hollywood studios.' Despite somewhat greater success of studio films in the Academy awards during the subsequent two years, independent films continue to command attention. This continuing trend was epitomized by the surprise win for best picture of 1998 by *Shakespeare in Love*.

One of the more interesting aspects of the recent attention given to independent producers, especially during the period since the 1996 awards, was the linking of these firms with innovative products and artistic freedom. Weinraub (1997: 11) quoted the prominent actress, Jodie Foster, as follows: 'Independents are not so much a financial state of mind but a creative state of mind. Studios ... want the most risk averse films. Quality films that studios used to make aren't on their agenda. That's where the independents come in.'

These recent developments in the film industry are consistent with differences among organizations, particularly with regards to the degree of product innovation. Summarizing the literature on innovation, Mezias and Glynn (1993: 77) stated the following: 'Traditionally, organizational size, formalization, and complexity have been viewed as obstacles to innovation.' Thus, the presence and vitality of smaller less structured and relatively specialized may be crucial to the ability of an industry to generate needed innovations. The failure to do so may be especially damaging in cultural industries, reducing both artistic quality and product diversity; this failure to serve audiences can be made even more acute where a few large firms exercise market control (Perrow, 1986: 184).

The increased visibility of high quality films from smaller, more specialized producers and distributors seem to suggest that there is something new or different. In fact, such smaller specialized firms have existed along with a few dominant firms in the U.S. feature film industry since its emergence in the early years of this century (Mezias and Kuperman, 2000). In this study, we begin with the development of an ecological perspective on such a bifurcation of the population firms within the film industry. Specifically, we use the resource-partitioning model to predict that the presence of large, generalist firms in a highly concentrated feature film industry will increase the foundings of strategically specialized firms.

The basic resource-partitioning argument is straightforward: Within a population, large generalist organizations compete with each other to occupy the center of the market. This competition for similar resources frees up peripheral resources that are often exploited by strategically specialized organizations within the population (Carroll, 1985). So as concentration among generalists' increases, the environment becomes more munificent for specialist organizations that utilize different resources. Consequently, increasing concentration among generalists, which decreases the vital rates of generalist organizations, actually increases the vital rates of specialist organizations.

To support this claim in the context of the beginnings of the American feature film industry, we will discuss the emergence of the large firms that eventually came to be known as the Hollywood studios. As these firms grew, high levels of concentration in the industry were the result, with a few highly similar, vertically integrated firms dominating the production and distribution of films. As the dominance of these firms increased, the resource-partitioning model predicts that foundings of specialist firms will increase. Our first objective will be to provide evidence that this happened during the emergence of the American feature film industry.

Our next objective will be to assess the relative innovativeness of these specialist firms during the early years of the American feature film industry. In a study of the microprocessor market, Wade (1996: 1241) found that innovations were more likely to come from small firms entering after a dominant technology had emerged. However, as he noted, '... the number of entries and analyzable events was relatively small'. As a result, he suggested that this finding '... should be taken as suggestive rather than definitive.' By examining more systematic evidence concerning the relative innovativeness of specialists, we increase the power of the test by providing a larger sample. The sharp historical, industry, and technological differences in the settings of the two studies augment the robustness of any confirmation of Wade's (1996) result.

We proceed as follows: The next section provides a brief outline the early history of the feature film industry in the United States. The subsequent section will discuss the resource-partitioning model and detail the research hypotheses suggested by this model. We proceed by discussing a measure of innovativeness among specialist and generalist firms. Following that, the data, method, and results will be reported. We will conclude with a discussion of the implications of our findings for the study of cultural industries, the ecological and resource-partitioning models, and the relative innovativeness of specialists.

Evolution of the early feature film industry

Examining the American feature film industry beginning with its birth in 1912 and ending with 1929 provides an opportunity to track a cultural industry from its inception to the first stages of its development into a major industry. We chose the demarcation of 1912 as the beginning of the early feature film industry because the first companies to produce or distribute feature length films emerged in this year (Mezias and Kuperman, 2000). While 1913 marked the first emergence of a generalist firm, the population began a year earlier with the founding of specialist producers and distributors. We believe that 1929 is the appropriate end of the early feature length film industry because it demarcates the period immediately before two dramatic changes altered the industry. The first was widespread introduction of talkies. Cook (1981: 243) argued that 1929 ended an era in film because of the: 'near total conversion to sound by the end of 1929 which radically changed the structure of the film industry and revolutionized the practice of cinema all over the world.' The second was widespread integration by generalists into film exhibition (Mezias and Kuperman, 2000).

These eighteen years cover a period in which this industry underwent phenomenal growth, with the number of annual releases jumping from a handful of films to almost a thousand films (Mezias, Eisner, Mezias and Kuperman, 1996). Attendance at movies also tripled during this period. One of the major challenges facing the entrepreneurs who spearheaded the emergence of the feature film industry was the development of organizational infrastructure capable of handling the demands of feature film production (Mezias and Kuperman, 2000).

By comparison with the production of short films, the production of feature-length films required the development of new organizational and creative skills. In terms of film production, longer narratives had to be sustained, requiring longer production times and bigger budgets. The organizational solution, first developed by Thomas Ince, was the central producer system, which was widely adopted by almost all major producers in very short order. This system gave primary responsibility for each film to a single person, allowing it to be treated as a unique product while monitoring costs and maintaining quality (Koszarski, 1990: 108).

A second major challenge faced by those who developed the new industry of feature film production concerned the distribution of films. During the era of short films, turnover of product had been very rapid as the films themselves were of such a short duration that the potential audience could be exhausted fairly quickly. Distribution was handled by relatively informal exchanges that were in close geographic proximity to the theaters that showed the films and were more like spot markets than well-defined organizations. These independent exchanges were organized somewhat toward the end of the era of short films into umbrella organizations such as the Motion Picture Distributing and Sales Company and General Film Company. However, once feature-length films became dominant, with longer exhibition times and less rapid turnover of films, a new form of distribution emerged. This involved formal organizations that oversaw the distribution and promotion of films (Mezias and Kuperman, 2000).

Meeting these challenges, especially the rapidly growing centralization of distribution, resulted in the creation of increasingly larger organizations. On the production side, the demands for greater coordination and materials costs resulting from the switch from short to feature-length films threatened the volume of films. One solution to this problem was the creation of ties between the increasingly powerful distribution organizations and the production firms. Eventually, some of these alliances resulted in vertical integration, combining both production and distribution. The first of these integrated firms appeared in 1913 after Universal absorbed affiliated producers. Pathe and Fox Film Corporation quickly followed suit. World Film Corporation took a different route by being founded as a generalist firm in 1914 with substantial Wall Street financing and story material provided by

Broadway's Shuberts (Mezias and Kuperman, 2000). The rise of the vertically integrated firms that would come to dominate film production and distribution in the next few years had begun. The eventual result was the founding of the Hollywood studio system that persists in a somewhat altered form to this day.

Even in the early years of its development, the feature film industry was beginning to show the emergence of two different organizational forms. On the one hand, there was the rise of generalist firms, committed to a strategy of vertical integration and engaged in both the production and distribution of films. On the other hand, there was the growth of specialist firms, which had not vertically integrated because of their commitment to a more focused strategy of either production or distribution of films. Figure 4.1 illustrates the percentage of films produced and distributed by generalists between 1912 and 1929. The importance of ties among firms is illustrated by the fact that the market share of generalists for production and distribution differ. In addition to distributing films they produced, generalists also distributed films produced by specialists. As a result, the number of films produced and distributed by generalists are not always equal. Further inspection of Figure 4.1 also reveals that the vertically integrated firms came to dominate both the production and distribution of films quite rapidly. Indeed, the generalists' share of both the production and distribution of films exceeded half the market by 1917. The rise of vertically integrated generalist firms that controlled the vast majority of both production and distribution is one of the major developments that occurred during the early years of the film industry. It is worth noting a key fact relevant to the resource-partitioning argument: This rise in dominance came at a time of increasing generalist concentration. By 1929 the number of generalist firms had decreased by approximately 50% from its high point in 1925, even as their share of both production and distribution continued to increase.

Despite the overwhelming domination of the industry by generalists, both in terms of production and distribution, specialist firms did not disappear. In 1929, there were twice as many specialist producers as generalists and an approximately equal number of specialist distributors. In fact, this is the crux of the resource-partitioning argument: A high concentration among large generalist firms drawing on the same environmental resources leaves open the possibility that firms will arise to occupy specialized niches not served by large generalists. Our analysis of the population dynamics of generalists and specialists is focused on providing evidence to support this resource-partitioning claim.

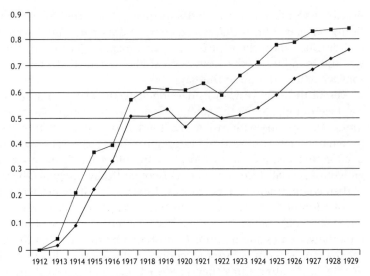

Figure 4.1 Proportion of films produced and distributed by generalist firms

Furthermore, the meaning of these ecological arguments may be especially important in the context of a cultural industry. As the observers of the 1996 surge of independent films noted, the modern independent film companies are making films and serving audiences that the large studios had neglected. It is possible that the vibrancy, creativity, and innovation that may renew interest in cultural products and even culture itself depend vitally on the presence of firms that occupy these specialized niches. This is the crux of our interest in the relative innovativeness of specialist firms: Were specialist firms more innovative than generalist firms during the early years of the American film industry?

Research hypotheses

The population dynamics of generalists and specialists

Empirical studies reporting systematic differences in organizational vital rates based on organizational strategies span a wide range of organizational populations. The range of these populations is impressive; they include newspapers (Carroll 1985; Dobrev 2001), early telephone companies (Barnett and Carroll, 1987), the deregulated telephone industry (Barnett, 1991), breweries (Swaminathan and Wiedenmayer, 1991; Wade, 1991; Carroll and Swaminathan, 1992; 1993), banking cooperatives (Freeman and Lomi, 1994), manufacturers of medical diagnostic: imaging equipment (Mitchell, 1994), wineries (Swaminathan, 1995; 1998), manufacturers (Torres, 1995), microprocessor manufacturers (Wade, 1996), airline passenger services (Seidel, 1997), savings and loan institutions (Haveman and Nonnemaker, 1998), and auditing firms (Boone, Brocheler, and Carroll, 1998).

Following the lead of these authors, we investigate the early years of American feature film industry beginning with its birth in 1912 and ending in 1929. We use a resource-partitioning model to study the foundings of specialist firms during these early years of the American feature-film industry. The basic argument is as follows: Organizations pursuing different strategies within the same population should experience varied effects from competition with larger firms dominating the market (Carroll, 1985; Barnett, 1991; Carroll and Wade, 1991; Swaminathan and Wiedenmayer, 1991; Hannan and Freeman, 1989). Carroll (1985) labeled this process resource partitioning; one of its key predictions is that concentration among large, generalist firms will increase the founding rate of firms pursuing a specialist strategy within the same population. For example, generalist firms likely compete for resources in the center of an industry. Concentration among generalists and their competition for 'central resources' creates an opportunity for firms that can utilize the resources on the fringes. Testing this model, Carroll (1985) found that concentration among generalist newspaper firms increased the founding rate of specialist newspaper firms.

As Wade (1996: 1234) noted, '... models using concentration to investigate resource partitioning should be tested only after scale economies become significant.' Despite the fact that our study examines the emergence of a new industry, we believe that significant scale economies existed from the outset of feature film production. In part, this is due to the fact that short films had been in existence for nearly two decades prior to the release of the first feature film in 1912. Significant scale economies for film production, such as spreading out the costs of equipment, stages, and studios, had developed during the era of the production of shorts. Similarly, the development of an infrastructure for the distribution of short films had created scale economies. For example, by 1912, firms enjoyed scale economies from spreading the cost of expensive film duplication equipment needed for distribution to multiple places over many different films. These scale economies only increased in the wake of more capital-intensive feature films and the emergence of national distribution and advertising (Mezias and Kuperman, 2000).

Based on this, we study resource partitioning during the emergence of the American feature film industry. To do this, we partition firms in the early film industry into generalists and specialist. The mutualist argument of the resource-partitioning model, first put forth by Carroll (1985), is that concentration levels among the generalist firms will enhance the vital rates of specialist firms. Our specific interest is in the relationship between concentration among generalist firms and the founding of specialist firms. We state this argument formally as follows:

Hypothesis 1: Greater concentration levels among generalists will have a positive effect on founding events of specialists.

Innovativeness among generalists and specialists

There is a large literature suggesting that a disproportionate amount of innovation in organizational populations may be done by small firms (Kanter, 1983). In fact, our summary of the discussion that followed the 1996 Academy Awards focused on the more innovative films of the companies characterized as independent of the studios. Wade (1996) found suggestive evidence that innovations were more likely to come from small firms entering the microprocessor market after a dominant technology had emerged. We were interested in investigating whether there was evidence that specialist firms were more innovative during the early years of the American feature film industry.

Interestingly, some measures of innovativeness that might have appropriateness in the context of the modern feature film industry, such as garnering awards, critical acclaim, or a massive box office opening, either cannot be measured, are not relevant for this period, or both. The Academy Awards and other well-known indicators of critical acclaim were not established until the late 1920s. The concept of the massive opening also was alien in this era, with films opening only in a few select cities before slowly moving out into the rest of the country. Also, for much of the period of our study, box office figures are extremely unreliable (Mezias and Kuperman, 2000).

At the same time, it is clearly true that important innovations characterized the emergence of feature length films. This new product allowed for innovations in story line and character development that were not afforded by short films. What ensued was a golden era of theme development that witnessed the emergence of many of the film-making genres that still exist in the industry today, such as science fiction, western, horror and mystery. As Bowser (1990: 167) noted: 'Genre films certainly existed before this period, but with the organization of the industry they were incorporated in the system of production, distribution, and exhibition.' Continuing the discussion of the importance of genre creation and transformation during this period, Bowser (1990: 169) interpreted film industry coverage in the popular press of the day as signaling '... some of the changes in film genres and subjects that were taking place in the midst of the shift from short film production to the feature.' One hypothesis consistent with the claim that specialist firms are more innovative than generalist firms is that specialist firms would be more likely to participate in the creation of genres and subjects that accompanied the emergence of feature-length films.

Hypothesis 2: Specialist firms will be more likely to participate in the creation of film genres.

Data and methods

The sample

The two volumes of the American Film Institute (AFI) Catalog of Motion Pictures: 1911–1920 (American Film Institute, 1988) and 1921–1930 (American Film Institute, 1971) served as the primary sources of data on companies and their strategies. The AFI Catalog comprehensively lists all feature-length films released during the sample period. Since we focus on the commercial population, all films handled by government agencies (i.e., War Department, Department of Health, etc.) have been removed from the database. Films were documented by their initial release date, including month, day, and year. Reported release dates are very accurate estimates for distribution, but in establishing the presence of producers we also use release dates to approximate production dates. Although information is sketchy, it is quite clear that the time between production and distribution during this era was much shorter than it is today. For example, Musser (1990: p. 469) indicates that for Famous Players, the first company to regularly release full-length feature films, the time from production to release was one month. Consequently, we believe that film release dates are a good approximation for production dates as well.

Our data, which is organized by month, consist of all commercial firms listed in the AFI Catalog. To construct a database that includes all firms that produced, distributed, or produced and distributed films in the United States between 1912 and 1929, we had to make certain extrapolations from the available data. The following text discusses these extrapolations, the rationale behind them, and the procedures utilized to implement them:

(1) The 1911–1920 volume details production and distribution credits for every film and provides explanations when credit information cannot be found; however, the 1921–1930 volume was edited differently: The name of the distributing company is sometimes omitted without explanation. AFI informed us that in these cases, the producer almost always handled distribution, but gave us a heuristic for checking individual firms: When plot information was given, AFI informed us that the producers handled distribution. In the few cases where plot information was not provided, and the distributor was unknown, the following rules were sufficient: (a) Distribution credit went to the producers that had three or more such occurrences in any year. (b) Any company producing a film without plot information was given distribution credit if they were documented as generalists in the same year.

(2) The AFI Catalog does not provide background information on company histories. Documenting mergers and acquisitions required an extensive review of film history. We used the following additional sources to construct this history: Balio (1976), Berg (1989), Bowser (1990), Eyman (1990), Hampton (1931), Highan (1973), Jewell and Harbin (1982), Kozarski (1990), Lahue (1971), Slide (1986), and Slide and Gevinson (1987). We discovered that 15 firms in our sample began as subsidiaries of already existing firms. These subsidiaries were removed and their film counts were added to their parent company's totals.

(3) When researching the formative years of any developing industry, some record-keeping and documentation problems emerge. The American Film Institute (1988: 225) noted, 'The determination of exact names was as difficult for corporate as personal names, and, in some cases, nearly impossible. Research among reviews, advertisements, and news items often resulted in conflicting information. For these cases, we gave the most credence to the name as it appeared in company records, followed by advertisements, copyright records and studio directories.' All corporate or personal credits listed by AFI as a unique entity were included in our database. However, given the uncertainty of those early, turbulent years, some unique names may be the result of inadequate or inconsistent documentation and may not represent unique corporations. Entities with personal names cause most of the problem. For these cases, we

created a rule-based heuristic to identify questionable cases and merge records when appropriate. (a) In the same or consecutive years, company names that were identical except the ending of Co., Inc., or Corp. were combined into a single record. (b) In the same year, company names that were proper names or proper names followed by anything, e.g. Thomas H. Ince, were combined with any entities that were called by that same proper name followed by anything. (c) In consecutive years, company names that were proper names were combined with any entities that were called by that same proper name regardless of what other words were included in the title of the company.

Resource partitioning and the founding of specialist firms

In order to use these data to study the population dynamics of generalists and specialists, we had to categorize organizations based on their strategies. Our population was categorized into three mutually exclusive and exhaustive categories based on the activities of the firms. The first category included *generalist producer-distributors*, any firms that were involved in both production and distribution activities in a given year were placed in this category. The second category included all *specialist producers*; any firms that only engaged in activities resulting in the creation of feature films in a given year were placed in this category. The third and final category included all *specialist distributors*; any firms that only engaged in activities to ensure that the films were available to potential exhibitors in a given year were placed in this category.

Dependent variables. To test the resource-partitioning model, the foundings of specialist firms were tabulated for each month starting in January of 1914 to December of 1929. We did these tabulations separately for the two kinds of specialist firms, resulting in two dependent variables defined and named as follows: (1) **Producer Foundings** is defined as the number of new firms founded as specialist producers in the population during a given month. (2) **Distributor Foundings** is defined as the number of new firms founded as specialist distributors in the population during a given month.

Independent variables. To test the resource-partitioning model, we calculate the concentration level of generalist producer-distributors with respect to both production and distribution. This allows us to run separate models to capture the effects on specialist foundings events stemming from the level of concentration among large generalists. To do this, we created two independent concentration variables. Carroll (1985: 1275) used GINI coefficients to measure '... resource concentration in the general mass market.' In his study, the concentration of the generalist mass market corresponded to the concentration of generalist newspapers. Following his lead, our generalist concentration variables are GINI measures of concentration levels only among generalists. The GINI measures concentration by assessing the variability in the distribution of firms with respect to either film production or film distribution in a given year. The formula is:

$$\frac{1 - G / 2}{\mu}$$

G is defined to be the absolute mean difference in film production or distribution for all pairs of generalists in a given year. μ is defined to be the mean of the variable of interest, either film production or film distribution, in that same year (Dorfman, 1980).

For each year, generalist film production and distribution were determined separately. This enabled annual calculation of GINI concentration coefficients for both production and distribution. These concentration variables focus on the effects of competition as predicted by the resource-partitioning argument. These variables help assess how generalists concentration for production affects the foundings of specialist producers and how generalists concentration for distribution affects the foundings of specialist distributors.

- **Production GINI** is defined as the GINI estimate of film production concentration among generalists during a given year.

- **Distribution GINI** is defined as the GINI estimate of film distribution concentration among generalists during a given year.

Control variables.   We included three variables to control for the effects of various measures of competition that past research would suggest may impact founding rates. First, we use the most frequent ecological measure of competition within a population: the count of organizations – density, in the context of the density dependence model. Baum (1994) articulated the density dependence argument of competition: Initial increases in density increase the legitimacy of the population (mutualism), while subsequent increases in density induce competitive effects. Since the density dependence argument suggests a curvilinear relationship, we control for effects of both density and density squared on foundings. These two control variables focus on the effects of competition and mutualism as predicted by the density dependence argument and are measured as follows:

- **Density** is defined as the number of firms in the population, measured by counting the number of firms during a given year. Past research would suggest density to have a positive effect on foundings.

- **Density Squared** is defined as the square of density divided by 1000. Past research would suggest density squared to have a negative effect on foundings.

Mass dependent competition suggests that increases in total population size will have a competitive effect on organizations. To do this, we must account for organizational size as well as the count of organizations. Although 'traditional' measures of size, such as number of employees, budgets, or revenues, are not available for the early feature-film industry, Winter (1990) argued that researchers should use capacity-based measures of size. Following his suggestion, we develop a metric for assessing organizational size based on the number of films handled by an organization, which we believe is a good approximation for capacity. Specialist producer size is measured by counting the number of films produced. Specialist distributor size is measured by counting the number of films distributed. Generalist size is measured by counting the total number of films handled: the sum of all films produced and distributed. For each year, population mass was determined by summing the size for all organizations in the population. The mass variable focuses on competitive effects as predicted by the mass argument and was measured as follows:

- **Mass** is defined as the annual sum of the size of all firms in the population divided by 1000. It is predicted to have a negative effect on foundings.

As other authors, e.g., Dacin (1997), have noted, economic forces may well effect ecological outcomes – organizational foundings likely increase during periods of economic expansion. To control for this plausible explanation of organizational foundings, we incorporate the annual gross national product growth rate as a control variable. Economic conditions fluctuate and, following Baum and Mezias (1992), we controlled for the domestic business cycle by including a variable measuring annual changes in the Gross National Product

(GNP) growth rate (U.S. Department of Commerce, Bureau of the Census, 1975).

- **GNP Growth** is defined as the rate of annual growth in the Gross National Product.

Previous studies of organizational foundings have found positive contagion or a significant relationship between organizational foundings in one period and foundings in subsequent periods (Delacroix and Carroll, 1983; Delacroix and Solt, 1988; Ranger-Moore, Banaszak-Holl and Hannan, 1991). The relationship was curvilinear: prior foundings had a positive effect on subsequent foundings and prior foundings squared had a negative effect on subsequent foundings. To control for positive contagion in our study we incorporate the number of the prior months' foundings and its square as control variables. We calculate these variables for both types of specialist organizations: specialist producers and specialist distributors.

- **Producer Foundings Lag** is defined as the number of specialist producers that were founded in the previous year.
- **Producer Foundings Lag Squared** is defined as the number of specialist producers that were founded in the previous year squared.
- **Distributor Foundings Lag** is defined as the number of specialist distributors that were founded in the previous year.
- **Distributor Foundings Lag Squared** is defined as the number of specialist distributors that were founded in the previous year squared.

Estimation methods.   Both dependent variables are counts of events; consequently, we use a Poisson process as the baseline model (Maddala, 1984). The basic Poisson model for event count data is the following:

$$\Pr(Y_t = y) = e^{\lambda(X_t)} \, [\lambda(X_t)^y / y!]$$

λ is the rate at which events occur, which is a function of a set of independent variables X_t. This model assumes that both the expected number of events and the variance of the expected number of events equal the rate, $\lambda(X_t)$, which is estimated by using the values of X_t. The estimation equation for λ_t is the following: $l_t = exp(X_t)\varepsilon_t$. Ranger-Moore, Banaszak-Holl, and Hannan (1991) suggest that for certain types of count data, e.g., annual counts of organizational foundings, the assumption of equal mean and variance may be violated. They suggest using the negative binomial regression model to correct for possible violation of this assumption. For estimation of both resource-partitioning our models, we use the *LIMDEP* program (Greene, 1989), which allows for estimation of both the negative binomial and Poisson models.

The innovativeness of specialist firms

The distinction between generalist and specialist firms is also central to our test of our hypothesis that specialists will be more likely to participate in the creation and transformation of film genres. We will test this by comparing the participation of specialists in the population as a whole with their participation in the production and distribution of films within a genre in the first year that genre appeared. Bowser (1990: 167–169) argued that the emergence of feature-length films resulted in the creation and transformation of film genres. To track this innovation of genres we relied once again on the AFI catalog, which used 27 genres to categorize films during the years from 1912 to 1920. The AFI catalog provides information regarding the year in which the first feature-length films that they categorized in each genre appeared. For purposes of our analysis, we consider all firms that produced or distributed films in any of these 27 genres during the first year that it appeared as having innovated. We interpret the claim that specialist participation in new genre creation will be disproportionately large to suggest predictions about both specialist producers and specialist distributors. First, the proportion of films produced within an emerging genre attributable to specialists will be more than the proportion of films in the population produced by specialists during the same year. Second, the proportion of films distributed within an emerging genre attributable to specialists will be more than the proportion of films in the population distributed by specialists during the same year.

For each year that a new genre emerged, we computed these proportions by creating variables equal to the counts of films produced or distributed by specialist firms both within the genre and in the population as a whole. The null hypothesis is that there should be no difference between the proportion of specialists within the genre and proportion of specialists in the population as a whole. The alternative hypothesis is that the difference between proportion of specialists within the genre and in the population as a whole should be positive. Thus, the representation of specialists within the genre exceeds their representation in the population as a whole, which we interpret as indicative of a higher level of innovativeness among these firms. To assess these null and alternative hypotheses, we use non-parametric tests. McClave and Benson (1988: 944) summarized the benefits of these tests as follows: 'These techniques...require fewer or less stringent assumptions concerning the nature of the probability distributions of the populations....' The first is the sign test and the other is the Mann-Whitney-Wilcoxon test.

Results

With respect to the tests of the first hypothesis, descriptive statistics for all variables are reported in Table 4.1, and a correlation matrix for all variables is provided in Table 4.2. Results for estimation of specialist producer foundings and specialist distributor foundings models are reported in Table 4.3. For both models, we ran the Poisson and negative binomial regressions and indicated which regression was used in the table under the sample size. This choice of which regression to use is based on the alpha variable: A significant alpha indicates overdispersion or unexplained heterogeneity in the data. When this is indicated, as it is for our specialist producer model, then negative binomial regression should be used because it has an additional scaling parameter that controls for heterogeneity. When alpha is not significant at the 0.05 level, as is the case for our specialist distributor data, then the Poisson model can be used.

Table 4.1   Descriptive statistics

Variable	Mean	Standard Deviation	Minimum	Maximum
1. Producer Foundings	6.583	3.738	0.000	19.000
2. Distributor Foundings	1.896	1.712	0.000	8.000
3. Production GINI	0.630	0.065	0.455	0.725
4. Distribution GINI	0.642	0.055	0.540	0.717
5. Density	198.500	65.345	48.000	306.000
6. Density Squared/1000	43.650	25.719	2.300	93.640
7. Mass/1000	1.301	0.428	0.080	1.897
8. GNP Growth	3.644	6.454	−8.700	15.800
9. Producer Foundings Lag	6.557	3.766	0.000	19.000
10. Distributor Foundings Lag	1.896	1.712	0.000	8.000
11. Producer Foundings Lag Squared	57.109	60.429	0.000	361.000
12. Distributor Foundings Lag Squared	6.510	10.690	0.000	64.000

n = 192 for all descriptive statistics

Table 4.2 Correlation matrix

Variable	1	2	3	4	5	6	7	8	9	10	11
1. Producer Foundings	1										
2. Distributor Foundings	.427**	1									
3. Production GINI	.263**	.180*	1								
4. Distribution GINI	.443**	.302**	.476**	1							
5. Density	.336**	.023	.647**	.087	1						
6. Density Squared/1000	.434**	.025	.563**	.158*	.974**	1					
7. Mass	.086	.095	.585**	-.169*	.529**	.380**	1				
8. GNP Growth	-.206**	.000	-.221**	-.417**	-.266**	-.338**	-.046	1			
9. Producer Foundings Lag	.509**	.283**	.271**	.418**	.397**	.458**	.114	-.219**	1		
10. Distributor Foundings Lag	.243**	.102	.186**	.302**	.024	.027	.097	.004	.413**	1	
11. Producer Foundings Lag Squared	.433**	.252**	.288**	.402**	.352**	.412**	.111	-.199**	.947**	.405**	1
12. Distributor Foundings Lag Squared	.217**	.113	.170*	.255**	.002	-.003	.105	.045	.379**	.918**	.362**

* Significant at the 0.05 level; ** Significant at the 0.01 level; n = 192

Table 4.3   Regression results for specialist foundings

Variable	Producer Foundings	Distributor Foundings
Constant	1.141***	–3.374***
Production GINI	1.791**	
Distribution GINI		6.734***
Density	–0.017***	–0.012**
Density Squared/1000	0.049***	0.026*
Mass/1000	0.261**	0.736***
GNP Growth	0.011*	0.023**
Producer Foundings Lag	0.143***	
Producer Foundings Lag Squared	–0.006***	
Distributor Foundings Lag		–0.084
Distributor Foundings Lag Squared		0.008
ALPHA	0.048**	
Chi-square	7.283	45.159
p-value	0.007	0.000
N	192	192
Model	Negative Binomial	Poisson

*p < .1, **P< .05, ***p <.01

An alternative method for determining which model to use, based on a comparison of the log likelihood of different estimation models, yielded the same choice between Poisson and Negative Binomial estimation for our two sets of data on specialist foundings. The number of observations was 192 for both models, and each model included a constant, which controls for the base rate of foundings. Positive coefficients indicate that the variable is associated with increases in the number of foundings for the specialist organization. Conversely, when coefficients are negative, the variable is associated with reductions in the number of foundings for the specialist organization.

Effects of these variables on organizational foundings of specialist producers and specialist distributors can be determined by inspection of Table 4.3. For both models, hypothesis 1 received strong support: Production GINI and distribution GINI were both significant in the predicted positive direction. This result emerges even after controlling for the effects of density, density squared, mass, GNP growth, prior foundings, and prior foundings squared. This demonstrates that increasing concentration among generalists had a positive effect on specialist foundings for both film production and film distribution.

For both models, density and density squared were significant, but opposite the directions typical in other research. These findings suggest that low levels of density had a negative effect on foundings of specialist organizations and density squared had a positive effect. Mass was also significant, but opposite the expected direction based on a mass-dependence argument. This indicates that increasing size of organizations had a positive effect on the foundings of both specialist producers and distributors. It is plausible that production mass might be very different than distribution mass. We therefore ran tests to see if calculating production and distribution mass separately would affect our findings. The results indicate that using separate mass measures does not affect our findings. They are either not significant or significant in a direction opposite that expected. GNP growth was significant and positive for the foundings of specialist producers and specialist distributors. This suggests that economic growth also had a positive effect on the foundings of both specialist producers and specialist distributors. The constant was significant and positive for the specialist producer model, but was significant and negative for the specialist distributor model.

Consistent with results from other studies investigating the effects of prior foundings on subsequent foundings (Delacroix and Carroll, 1983; Delacroix and Solt, 1988; Ranger-Moore, Banaszak-Holl and Hannan, 1991) we found some evidence of positive contagion: a significant relationship between organizational foundings in one year and foundings in subsequent years. Significant curvilinear effects were found in the specialist producer, but not in the specialist distributor models. Producer Foundings Lag had a positive effect on subsequent producer foundings and Producer Foundings Lag Squared had a negative effect on subsequent producer foundings. However, neither Distributor Foundings Lag nor Distributor Foundings Lag Squared was significant.

In Table 4.4, we list each of the 27 genres followed by the year that feature-length films in that genre first appeared. This table also provides the counts of films produced and distributed by specialists and generalists in that genre during this first year. While this table gives an idea of the differences among genres and the participation of generalist and specialists in each, we did not believe it was appropriate to base our analysis of participation on counts. We felt it was important to control for overall representation of firms with different strategies in both

Table 4.4   New genre production and distribution by generalists and specialists

Film Genre	First Year	Specialist Producer	Generalist Producer	Specialist Distributor	Generalist Distributor
Adventure	1913	3	0	3	0
Comedy-Drama	1913	2	0	2	0
Crime	1913	4	0	4	0
Detective	1913	4	0	4	0
Documentary	1913	3	0	3	0
Drama*	1913	38	3	37	3
Fantasy	1913	1	0	1	0
Historical*	1913	7	2	8	2
Social*	1913	6	1	4	1
War Drama	1913	3	0	3	0
Western*	1913	3	0	2	0
Allegory	1914	4	0	3	1
Biographical*	1914	3	0	5	0
Comedy	1914	19	0	19	0
Melodrama	1914	11	0	11	0
Mystery*	1914	6	1	3	1
Northwest drama	1914	4	1	4	1
Wild animals	1914	1	0	1	0
World War I*	1914	2	1	2	2
Espionage	1915	3	0	2	1
Horror	1915	2	0	2	0
Instructional	1915	1	0	0	1
Rural*	1915	19	1	16	3
Society	1915	17	5	14	8
War Preparedness	1915	2	1	2	1
Compilation	1917	N/A (+)	N/A (+)	1	0
Science Fiction	1919	0	1	0	1

* Some films were produced or distributed by more than one firm; thus, production and distribution counts do not match.

+ The only film in this genre this year was produced by an industry group, not a specific firm.

the population and the genre. Support for the hypothesis that specialists will be more likely to engage in early genre production requires that the proportion of specialists in the genre exceed the proportion of specialist in the population. Data appropriate to test support for this hypothesis are given in Table 4.5, which like Table 4.4 lists each film genre and the year it first emerged in feature film in the first two columns.

Table 4.5   Specialist proportions in genre and population

Film Genre	First Year	Specialist Proportion of Genre Production	Specialist Proportion of Population Production	Specialist Proportion of Genre Distribution	Specialist Proportion of Population Distribution
Adventure	1913	1.0000	0.9825	1.0000	0.9565
Comedy-Drama	1913	1.0000	0.9825	1.0000	0.9565
Crime	1913	1.0000	0.9825	1.0000	0.9565
Detective*	1913	1.0000	0.9825	1.0000	0.9565
Documentary*	1913	1.0000	0.9825	1.0000	0.9565
Drama*	1913	0.9268	0.9825	0.9250	0.9565
Fantasy	1913	1.0000	0.9825	1.0000	0.9565
Historical*	1913	0.7778	0.9825	0.8000	0.9565
Social	1913	0.8571	0.9825	0.8000	0.9565
War Drama	1913	1.0000	0.9825	1.0000	0.9565
Western	1913	1.0000	0.9825	1.0000	0.9565
Allegory	1914	1.0000	0.9070	0.7500	0.7831
Biographical	1914	1.0000	0.9070	1.0000	0.7831
Comedy*	1914	1.0000	0.9070	1.0000	0.7831
Melodrama	1914	1.0000	0.9070	1.0000	0.7831
Mystery	1914	0.8571	0.9070	0.7500	0.7831
Northwest drama	1914	0.8000	0.9070	0.8000	0.7831
Wild animals	1914	1.0000	0.9070	1.0000	0.7831
World War I	1914	0.6667	0.9070	0.5000	0.7831
Espionage	1915	1.0000	0.7699	0.6667	0.6296
Horror	1915	1.0000	0.7699	1.0000	0.6296
Instructional	1915	1.0000	0.7699	0.0000	0.6296
Rural*	1915	0.9500	0.7699	0.8421	0.6296
Society	1915	0.7727	0.7699	0.6364	0.6296
War Preparedness	1915	0.6667	0.7699	0.6667	0.6296
Compilation	1917	N/A (+)	N/A (+)	1.0000	0.4290
Science Fiction	1919	0.0000	0.4645	0.0000	0.3902

* These genres began in 1912. Since generalists first appeared in 1913, we begin analysis in the second year for these genres.

+ The only film in this genre this year was produced by an industry group, not a specific firm.

Five genres actually began in 1912; these are noted in Table 4.5. Since generalists did not appear in the population until 1913, we could not examine the hypothesis that specialists were more likely to innovate in this year. Consequently, we used the second year of their existence to examine the relative innovativeness of specialists and generalists for these genres. Given the small number of feature-length films that were produced and distributed in 1912, we believe that excluding these genres for 1912 is not of great consequence. Further, if specialists are more likely to enter a genre early in its existence, then excluding the first year of a genre's emergence mitigates against finding that specialists are more innovative.

The data in the third through sixth columns all pertain to proportions of films produced or distributed by specialists in the year of the emergence of the indicated genre. Column 3 gives the proportion of films produced by specialists within the genre. Column 4 gives the proportion of all films produced by specialists in the population. Column 5 gives the proportion of films distributed by specialists within the genre; column 6 gives the proportion of films distributed by specialists in the population. These proportions are used to test two different null hypotheses implied by Hypothesis 2. The first null hypothesis is that there is no difference between the participation of specialists in the population and in the genre in the indicated year. Thus, taking the difference of proportion within the genre and in the population yields numbers that are no more likely to be positive than negative. Our alternative hypothesis is that the differences between the proportions will be positive, indicating that specialists were more active in creating or transforming genres. We test the null hypothesis against this one-sided alternative hypothesis separately for production and distribution using a sign test. For production, we reject the null hypotheses in favor of the alternative hypotheses, $p = 0.0377$. For distribution, we reject the null hypotheses in favor of the alternative hypotheses, $p = 0.0261$.

We augmented our findings from the sign test by using a more powerful, but somewhat more restrictive test: the Mann-Whitney-Wilcoxon test. This is a two-sample test that uses ranks to test the null hypothesis that the difference between two sets of numbers has a median of zero. For our data, the two sets of numbers are the proportion of specialists in the genre and the proportion of specialists in the population. Given our hypothesis that specialists are more likely to engage in early genre production, we test the null that the median difference is zero against the one-sided alternative hypothesis that median is greater than zero. This will be supported if the proportion of specialists in the genre is greater than the proportion of specialists in the population. The alternative hypothesis is that the proportion of specialists in the genre is greater than the proportion in the population, indicating that specialists were more active in creating or transforming genres. We tested this separately for production and distribution. For production, we reject the null hypothesis in favor of the alternative hypothesis based on a Mann-Whitney-Wilcoxon statistic of 834.0, p = 0.008. The estimated median difference between the proportions for production is 0.0175. For distribution, we reject the null hypothesis in favor of the alternative hypothesis based on a Mann-Whitney-Wilcoxon statistic of 878.0, p = 0.0195. The estimated median difference between the proportions for distribution is 0.0435.

All four tests provide uniform support of Hypothesis 2. First, we reject the null hypothesis that the difference between the proportion of specialists producing films in the population and the proportion of specialists producing films in the genre is zero. This suggests that we accept the alternative hypothesis that the difference between these proportions is positive. Second, we reject the null hypothesis that the difference between the proportion of specialists distributing films in the population and the proportion of specialists distributing films is zero. Once again, we accept the alternative hypothesis that the difference between these proportions is positive. Third, we reject the null hypothesis that the median proportion of film production by specialists in the population is equal to the median proportion of film production by specialists within the genre. We reject the null hypothesis in favor of the alternative that the median proportion within the genre is more than that in the population. Fourth and finally, we reject the alternative hypothesis that the median proportion of films distributed by specialists in the population is equal to the median proportion of films distributed by specialists within the genre. Once again we accept the alternative hypothesis that the median proportion of specialist distributors in the genre is greater than that in the population. All of these tests indicate that specialists are significantly more likely to participate in the production and distribution of films that mark the creation or transformation of a genre. We interpret this to suggest that specialists are more likely to engage in the production and distribution of innovative films than the generalists are.

Discussion

The pattern of results across the two models of foundings, those of specialist producers and those of specialist distributors, is remarkably consistent. Higher levels of generalist concentration, as measured by the GINI coefficient, were associated with a greater likelihood of foundings of both types of specialist firms. These findings emerged in a model that included a constant, which controls for the base rate of foundings; ecological variables; which control for other competitive effects, GNP growth, which controls for economic conditions; and prior foundings variables, which control for positive contagion. We interpret these findings as strong support for the resource-partitioning model of the founding of specialist firms. In addition, the results of all four tests of Hypothesis 2 indicate that specialists were more involved in the creation and transformation of new film genres.

Although previous studies have shown that concentration among generalists enhances the vital rates of specialists, few studies included population density variables. Of those that included density variables, only Swaminathan (1995) included a measure of population mass. Our study includes these previous variables as well as a control measure of economic conditions, such as GNP growth, which was significant in both foundings models. We also control for prior foundings, which significantly affected specialist producer foundings. Including these variables helps to extend the theory by controlling for possible alternative explanations of the results.

However, our contribution to the empirical study of resource partitioning goes beyond mere replication or extension to a new context. We have also provided a large sample study of the relative innovativeness of generalists and specialists in the same context where we have documented the effects of resource partitioning. Many have argued that smaller firms are more innovative (Kanter, 1983). Going a step further, Wade (1996) has provided suggestive evidence that the emergence of dominant designs is accompanied by increased market entry of new technology sponsors. We have systematized these general notions in the context of the innovativeness of generalists and specialists in an environment characterized by significant effects of resource partitioning on the foundings of specialists. We have provided systematic evidence that specialists are more innovative.

Three limitations to our results are worth noting. The first limitation relates to our resource-partitioning study: The dependent variable is calculated on a monthly basis while many of our independent variables are calculated annually. Unfortunately it is not possible to obtain monthly data for many of the independent variables, which would have been preferable. However, we do have some reasons to believe that the effects of this may not be so serious as to undermine the credibility of the study. First, the variables that are calculated monthly, including the foundings lag variable, are significant in the predicted direction. Second, some of the variables calculated annually are highly significant, notably our GINI coefficient. Third, there are plausible alternative explanations for the failure to demonstrate the significance of other annual variables. For example, density, density squared, and mass may all fail to achieve their levels of significance in the expected direction due to the rapid growth in the industry.

A second limitation is related to our study of the innovativeness of specialists: The time period for our study of resource partitioning was from 1912 to 1929, while the time period for our study of new genre creation and transformation was from 1913 to 1919. From the point of view of establishing evidence concerning the innovativeness of specialists in the context of resource partitioning, it would have been preferable if the time periods of the two studies had been identical. This leads directly to the third limitation. The level of generalist market share that characterized the time period of our study of innovation is considerably lower than during subsequent years included in our study of resource partitioning. In fact, generalist market share was greater than specialist market share for only three of the seven years included in the time period of our study of genres. By contrast, during the eighteen year time period of our resource-partitioning study, generalist market share was greater than specialist market share in eleven years for production and in twelve years for distribution. The reason for this is that new genre creation and transformation were completed by 1919, while generalists did not dominate both production and distribution until 1917. Obviously, the selection of films for Academy awards and nominations in recent years has been interpreted to suggest that specialists continue to be more innovative. However, the evidence concerning any potential relationship between resource partitioning and innovation should be viewed with caution; subsequent work to replicate this finding is necessary.

Implications and conclusions

A key implication of this research for ecological models concerns the merging of models of competitive dynamics and resource partitioning. We have shown that both variables associated with models of competition and variables associated with resource partitioning have significant effects on the foundings of specialist firms. Future studies can focus on the interaction of these factors interact and investigate their effect on organizational mortality and change. One key question would be whether the mortality of specialists is reduced by concentration among generalists. Another would concern whether transitions between generalist and specialist strategies are affected by concentration among generalists.

In doing this, we also believe that future work should consider possible implications of our findings that are contrary to previous ecological findings regarding the density dependence models and the competitive effects of mass. We found that density has a curvilinear effect, with low levels of density being associated with a decreased probability of foundings and higher levels being associated with an enhanced likelihood of founding. We also found that population mass had a positive effect on the founding of specialist organizations. A possible explanation for this lack of competitive effects from density and population mass may be that we are investigating effects only on the foundings of specialists. As Figure 4.1 illustrates, the large generalists quickly came to dominate this industry. Their output accounts for most of the population mass, so a competitive effect from mass may affect generalists, but would be less likely to affect specialists.

An alternative possible explanation for the lack of competitive effects from density and mass might focus on the role of competition in a rapidly growing new industry, such as feature film production and distribution between 1912 and 1929. The results for the density dependence model in this population are reversed: Low levels of density are associated with a lower probability and high levels of density are associated with a higher probability of founding of specialist firms. This is consistent with the conjecture that over the short run in a rapidly growing industry, only the legitimacy enhancing effect of numbers might be observed. The negative coefficient of density indicates that legitimacy was still low in this industry when numbers were low. As numbers rose, however, the legitimacy of the feature film industry was enhanced, and foundings of specialist firms became more likely.

This finding also suggest that resource partitioning, the concentration of large generalist firms, may occur before the competitive effects of density and mass dependence take hold. However, our study alone is far from conclusive in this regard. We have shown that the foundings of specialist firms during the rapid growth of the early film industry do not conform to the predictions of density dependence. This finding will need to be extended to include other key population vital rates, e.g., the foundings of all firms and their mortality across a wider range of industries, before any conclusions can be drawn. It is our hope that this interesting and anomalous finding will trigger research designed to examine our conjecture.

We want to close the paper by returning to how we opened, addressing what we view as a key issue in cultural production – innovation in products and serving diverse audiences. Clearly, one strategy, and apparently one pursued by the studios according to observers of the 1996 phenomenon of the independent film, is massification (Perrow, 1986: 188). The argument is that the large firms want only to produce blockbusters, films that will be seen by large numbers of people around the world. Beck and Smith (1996: 1) quote Barry Reardon, then president of Warner Brothers Distribution, making exactly this argument with respect to the success of the independents in 1996: 'We'd be out of business if we had to depend on the pull of most of the films that have been nominated this year – *Shine* has only brought in $30 million, *Sling Blade* about $8.5 million, *Fargo* ... $24 million ... Warner has always leaned towards more commercial product.' These observations suggest two avenues for future research.

Clearly, a massification strategy is consistent with the finding in the innovation literature that large, complex, bureaucratic firms are less likely to innovate (Kanter, 1983). This points to the issue of the relationship between size and innovativeness. It is important to note that our results do control for average size by comparing proportions of specialists in the population with the proportion in the genre. Thus, even though specialists were most frequently smaller than generalists were, and size and strategic specialization are likely to be highly correlated, we believe we have evidence that strategy might matter in determining the level of innovativeness of a firm even after controlling for size. Careful investigation is required to determine the relative importance of size and strategic specialization in promoting innovative firm activity. Future work could determine the extent to which both size and strategic specialization are associated with innovation.

A second avenue for future research is related to a question that was implicit in the discussion of the 1996 Academy Awards that opened our paper: What are the sources of innovation in the context of a cultural industry dominated by an oligopoly of large firms pursuing a massification strategy? Our paper has provided part of the answer to this question. We have shown that the presence of highly concentrated generalists in the early feature film industry was associated with the foundings of specialist firms, as would be predicted by a resource-partitioning model. Furthermore, we have shown that specialists are systematically more likely to participate in the creation and transformation of film genres. This higher level of innovation among specialist may be particularly vital in cultural industries. However, it is not necessarily true that increases in the foundings of more innovative specialists as concentration increases can insure the vitality of cultural products. Of particular relevance to the level of innovativeness of cultural products is one question that our research cannot answer: Under what conditions are specialists successful in getting their products to audiences when the market is dominated by highly concentrated generalists?

Perrow (1986: 181) argued that highly concentrated industries will be those with the lowest levels of innovation: 'The charges of bias, favoritism, suppression of innovation, and so on often occur in the cultural industry for the simple reason that potential suppliers and supplies exist in vast numbers, but very few of them are selected.' This observation suggests that where the few media potentates (Barnouw, 1978) can choose among vast numbers of smaller producers and distributors, the results in terms of innovative cultural product may be very negative indeed. While it is plausible, perhaps likely, that the presence of smaller firms willing to take risks is a necessary condition for the presence of innovative cultural products, this alone is not necessarily sufficient. Future work needs to address the question of when specialist firms are successful in producing or distributing innovative cultural products (Glynn, 1996), including films. Given the dependence between generalists and specialists, it would be interesting to investigate when alliances between a specialist and a generalist will successfully transfer skills and tacit knowledge that will improve their joint product (Levitas, Hitt, and Dacin, 1997).

In fact our results combined with the arguments of Perrow (1986), Peterson and Berger (1971; 1975), and Hirsch (1969; 1972) suggest the possibility of a paradox. The high levels of concentration that we found to be associated with enhanced chances of foundings of specialist firms may in fact represent a market structure in which innovative cultural products are least likely to flourish. A more complete understanding of market structure and resource partitioning and how these are linked with the content of films and other cultural products might go a long way toward improving our understanding of how and when innovative cultural products are successfully delivered to a sizable audience. We believe this is an important question for cultural industries and hope that our results can trigger future research that will give us a more complete understanding of the dynamics of cultural industries.

5

The Community Dynamics of Entrepreneurship: the Birth of the American Film Industry, 1895–1929

Stephen J. Mezias and Jerome C. Kuperman

Introduction

The study of entrepreneurship has traditionally focused on the founders of new organizations, especially those that emerge as leaders in the creation of new industries. Much of this work follows what Gartner (1989) called the 'traits' approach. Studies of this type posit a causal link between the founding and success of new organizations and the personal attributes of the entrepreneurs. However, more recent research has documented the many ways in which successful entrepreneurship requires more than just the 'right' person; a multitude of factors, operating at both the organizational and evironmental levels of analysis, also affect the success of entrepreneurial efforts. Examples include technological change (Shane, 1996), changes in sources of firm capital (Cable and Shane, 1997), changes in strategic alliances (Eisenhardt and Schoonhoven, 1996), personal networks (Ostgaard and Birley, 1996), national environments (Shane and Kolvereid, 1995), location choice (Stearns, Carter, Reynolds, and Williams, 1995), and national culture (Shane, 1992).

As Stearns and Hills (1996) observed, the study of entrepreneurship is increasingly moving away from the focus on the individual entrepreneur by emphasizing process models that include the consideration of other factors. Such models explicitly recognize that entrepreneurs do not exist independent of organizational and societal contexts (Granovetter, 1985; Van de Ven, 1993a; 1993b); thus, their actions cannot be completely understood without attention to those contexts. We agree with Van de Ven (1993b) and Romanelli (1989) that while the individual entrepreneur is important, the study of entrepreneurship is incomplete if it ignores the collective process of entrepreneurship in the context of the organizational community (Astley, 1985). In parallel with the more recent emphasis in entrepreneurship research on the role of social contexts, a literature addressing the organizational (Lawless and Price, 1992), social network (Abrahamson and Rosenkopf, 1997), product family (Meyer and Utterback, 1993) and cultural (Rao, 1994) contexts of technology competition and innovation has also developed. We believe that both these literatures converge on a key theoretical point: the importance of community context and dynamics. By emphasizing the role of community dynamics (Wade, 1995; 1996) in entrepreneurship and the emergence of new industries, the theory developed in this paper helps contribute to some integration of this literature on technological change and the emergence of dominant designs with the social systems model of entrepreneurship.

In particular, we believe that a study of the emerging film industry points to the importance of two concepts from this literature on technological change. A first is what Wade (1995) called second sourcing; we interpret our case study to suggest that second sourcing is an important concept even outside of the high technology context. Further, we believe that the importance of second sourcing in the emergence of new industries highlights the potential importance of imitation to successful entrepreneurship. A second important concept is that of related sourcing, also suggested by Wade (1995) in the context of a technological community. As was the case with second sourcing, we interpret our case study of the early film industry to suggest the generalizability of the phenomenon of related sourcing. While Wade (1995) was careful to suggest the high technology context of his study as a potential limitation to his findings regarding second sourcing and related sourcing, we believe that its importance to the emergence of the early film industry suggests that the concepts may have wider applicability. We use a review of the history of the early film industry to discuss some observations about how both second sourcing and related sourcing can provide benefits to particular entrepreneurial initiatives, especially in the context of an emerging industry. Further, our proposed definition of entrepreneurial behavior and our propositions formalize these observations, suggesting the importance of these concepts in the context of new industry emergence, not just in the context of technological communities.

Our focus on community dynamics reflects an underlying assumption that communities are comprised of unique populations of firms. We believe that focusing on events at both the population and community levels enhances our understanding of the role of entrepreneurship in the emergence of new industries. A number of researchers have noted the benefits gained in using an ecological perspective to study the entrepreneurial environment (Shane and Kolvereid, 1995; Baum and Singh, 1994a; 1994b; Aldrich, 1990; Reynolds, 1991; Romanelli, 1989), but there are also those who are critical of using an ecological perspective. For example, Bygrave and Hofer (1991) questioned the value of ecology to the study of entrepreneurship, pointing out that ecological findings cannot deterministically predict the future and are uninformative regarding crucial aspects of process. We do not dispute that there are limitations in using an ecological approach for the study of entrepreneurship. However, these limitations do not necessarily mean that the ecological approach is not useful for understanding entrepreneurial activity. We believe this is especially true when drawing from an evolutionary perspective (Baum and Singh, 1994a), which admits organization level change as an important mechanism in population dynamics (Mezias and Lant, 1994).

We develop two applications of an evolutionary perspective to the field of entrepreneurship in this study. First, we argue that many of the findings of population ecology research, especially those related to the population dynamics of foundings, can augment our understanding of entrepreneurship (Romanelli, 1989). This focus fits with other work that has examined both foundings (Aldrich, 1990) and survival as variables in understanding entrepreneurship (Bruno, McQuarrie, and Torgrimson, 1992; Carter, Williams, and Reynolds, 1997; Stearns, et al., 1995; Harmon, Ardishvili, Cardozo, Elder, et al., 1997). Second, we argue that both the population and community levels of analysis are useful in the study of entrepreneurship; specifically, we argue that our understanding can be augmented by locating entrepreneurial activity in the larger setting of a community of organizational populations. Entrepreneurial behaviors in a focal population can have effects on evolutionary processes not only within their own populations, but in other populations within the community as well.

The remainder of this paper illustrates the importance of community dynamics in the emergence of the American feature film industry during the period from 1895 to 1929. We develop a community dynamics model and use this specific application to provide some illustrative discussion of the kinds of assumptions, mechanisms, and propositions that are suggested. To do this, we organize the subsequent sections as follows. The next section introduces the social systems framework (Van de Ven, 1993b; Van de Ven and Garud, 1989) and establishes the relevance of this framework in the context of the early

American film industry. The third section discusses the evolution of the early American film industry as necessary background leading to theory development. The fourth section emphasizes the social systems framework and the role of community dynamics in new industry creation and the study of entrepreneurship. In this section, we use examples from the history of the early American film industry to suggest the need for a broad definition of entrepreneurship, which would include second sourcing. We also derive two propositions concerning related sourcing and the community dynamics of entrepreneurship in the context of new industry creation. We close with a discussion of some of the implications of our study for both the practice and theory of entrepreneurship.

The emergence of new industries: a community dynamics model

It is our contention that a better understanding of the roles of entrepreneurship in the emergence of new industries can be developed by applying a social system framework (Van de Ven, 1993a; 1993b). This theoretical framework, drawn from earlier work by Van de Ven and Garud (1989), depicted the industrial infrastructure supporting entrepreneurship in terms of three primary components – institutional arrangements, resource endowments and proprietary functions. We focus on one component of the industrial infrastructure of entrepreneurship, proprietary functions, which Van de Ven (1993b: 214–215) considered to include technological development functions, the commercialization of innovation and the creation of markets and consumer demand. There are at least two justifications for this focus. First, as evidenced in the early American film industry, these functions are especially important in the creation of new industries. Second, we believe that we can augment Van De Ven's (1993a; 1993b) earlier work by incorporating related literatures to form a community dynamics model of proprietary functions in new industry creation. Thus, the primary focus of this paper is to broaden the social systems framework by developing a model of the community dynamics of proprietary functions and examining the implications of this model for the study of entrepreneurship.

Proprietary functions including technological development functions, the commercialization of innovations, and the creation of consumer demand and markets have been studied in a variety of different industry settings (e.g., Abrahamson and Rosenkopf, 1997; Anderson and Tushman, 1990; Dosi, 1984; Utterback and Abernathy, 1975; Utterback and Suárez, 1993; Wade, 1995). Nonetheless, we believe that the early American film industry is particularly interesting in that it is both 'low tech' and also first appeared a full century ago. Compared to the emerging industries of the late 20th Century, e.g., microcomputers, technological change in the early film industry was relatively slow. In terms of the social systems framework, it is interesting that social setting appears to be important in the early American film industry despite the fact that the institutional environment at the turn of the century was fairly simple by today's standards. We believe that this suggests the importance of social systems in the entrepreneurial process even in the absence of powerful governmental regulatory bodies, industry associations, or other institutional actors. In fact, the early film industry may be a particularly revealing setting for understanding the community dynamics of entrepreneurship precisely because it was relatively 'low tech' and occurred when the institutional environment was still fairly weak in comparison with later years. This observation is not meant to imply that we disagree with authors who have argued that social setting becomes more important as the rate of technological change increases and as entities in the environment become more organized and powerful. Rather, we believe that a closer study of the early film industry may allow insights into basic processes that are still operative even in the presence of rapid technological change and high levels of institutionalization.

According to Van de Ven (1993b: 219) the social infrastructure of entrepreneurship emerges '... through the accretion of numerous institutional, resource, and proprietary events involving many entrepreneurs located in the public and private sectors over an extended period.' The weak institutional environment during the early years of the American film industry allows us to de-emphasize institutional events and focus on how resources were acquired as a result of proprietary events largely in the private sector. Following Van deVen (1993: 214), our focus '... is on the actions of individual entrepreneurs and firms who typically appropriate basic knowledge from the public domain and transform it into proprietary knowledge.' By developing a community dynamics model of these proprietary functions, we attempt to both augment the social systems framework and demonstrate its applicability to the creation of the American film industry.

In delineating a community to study the dynamics of proprietary events, we followed Van de Ven (1993b: 214), who characterized proprietary events as incorporating '... the traditional industrial economic definition of an industry.' In industrial economics literature, a simple but typical industry value chain would include three fundamental functions – production, distribution, and retailing. In the early American film industry, researchers (e.g., Allen and Gomery, 1985) have typically identified three analogous functional tasks – production of films, distribution of films, and the exhibition of the films. Not surprising given the emerging nature of the industry, these functions tended to be entirely separate in the initial years of the industry. Thus, it is reasonable to model the early film industry as consisting of three populations of different kinds of firms that formed the larger film industry community:

1. Production – This function involves the production of films that will be shown to the general public.

2. Distribution – This function involves activities that included the storage, promotion, and physical distribution of films.

3. Exhibition – This function involves the showing of films to paying audiences.

For purposes of the remainder of this paper, the community where we will study the dynamics of new industry emergence consists of these three populations, which pursued the three proprietary functions in the industry value chain. We will emphasize their roles in the development of an infrastructure for entrepreneurship in the early American film industry. We delineate the period encompassing the emergence of the film industry in the U.S. as the years during which the populations of firms pursuing each of these functions grew into the giant studios that we now collectively know as 'Hollywood.'

The early American film industry

The struggle to develop a first commercially feasible technology in film industry began shortly after basic moving picture technology was first invented. As suggested by Aldrich and Fiol (1994), entrepreneurs who participated in the birth of the industry faced considerable difficulty in creating the cognitive and sociopolitical legitimacy that would allow success. Indeed, in many industries the development of a first commercially feasible technology might be considered at least as great a struggle as the subsequent competition among technologies for the establishment of a dominant design (Anderson and Tushman, 1990; Dosi, 1984; Utterback and Abernathy, 1975).

It is our contention that the period prior to the emergence of a dominant design is, to use the words of Utterback and Suárez (1993: 17), '... predominantly entrepreneurial.' Two implications of this contention are central to this study. First, this predominantly entrepreneurial activity is worthy of closer study because it helps us to understand what Utterback and Suárez (1993: 2) characterized as '... the creative synthesis of a new product innovation.' Second, both generally and in the specific case of the early American film industry, a social systems framework is useful for understanding this activity.

In the early American film industry, this entrepreneurial period begins in 1894 with Edison's commercialization of the peephole kinescope and ends sometime in the 1920s with the creation of the studios, which incorporated all three of the industry value chain activities within a single corporate entity. It is likely not possible to pick a precise date for the end of this period, and, in fact, some consolidation, particularly of theater chains, continued into the 1930s. However, by the end of the 1920s it is clear that the industry had matured beyond its initial entrepreneurial period: All of the primary organizational forms that we are familiar with in the modern era of filmmaking had been established. The remainder of this section discusses the history of the early American film industry, providing the raw material for later theoretical discussion. Key innovations in each of the populations that make up the community are listed in Table 5.1 along with the approximate year in which they were introduced.

Edison Manufacturing Company was the first commercial film company, inventing the peephole kinetoscope in 1892 and commercializing it for operation in 1894. As the name implies, patrons viewed movies individually through a peephole, a technology that was more of a novelty than a commercial success. At the same time, Louis Lumière was working in France on an alternative technology, film projection, and was documented to have made a workable projector as early as 1895 (Rhode, 1976). By 1897, both Edison and an American competitor, Biograph Co., had developed projectors as well. In these early years, film exhibition took place many different locations, including church socials, fairs, music halls, penny arcades, and travelling road shows. Although the superiority of projection over a peephole machine in terms of audience size for a single run of the film was immediately obvious, during the first several years of the industry, both peephole machines and projectors were in use. The problem for film projection was simple: There were few reliable venues for projecting a film to a large audience, perhaps because the itinerant exhibitor population was

Table 5.1   Key innovations in the emergence of the film industry

Year	Production Function	Distribution Function	Exhibition Function
1894	1) Peephole kinetoscope introduced		1) Films exhibited in a variety of outlets
1897	2) Projectors appear		
1899			2) Films begin to appear in vaudeville programs
1905			3) Nickelodeons begin to appear as dedicated exhibition outlets for films
1906		1) Local exchanges appear	
1909	3) Motion Picture Patents Corporation is created 4) Multi-reel films appear	2) Travelling road shows and the states rights system appear as distribution alternatives for multi-reel films	
1910		3) Distribution companies appear following earlier cartel activity	
1912	5) The first feature film is released	4) Independent distribution companies with more proactive roles begin to appear	4) Movie theaters begin to displace nickelodeons
1914	6) Producers and distributors begin to vertically integrate	5) Producers and distributors begin to vertically integrate	5) Movie palaces begin to appear
1916	7) The central producer system is introduced		
1920s			6) Studios begin buying theaters

largely unwilling to make the site-specific investments that creating such venues required.

Realizing the potential for greater audiences with projection, producers searched in these early years for a more stable exhibition outlet, and, in 1899, Biograph pioneered a critical change in industry dynamics.

The company solved their demand problem by marketing their revolutionary entertainment product to vaudeville theaters. This linkage of film production companies with vaudeville theaters allowed for negotiated long-term agreements that both increased the demand for films and stabilized that demand for producers. By 1899, the linkage between moving pictures and vaudeville was well established (Musser, 1990: 273); films could now be viewed regularly by mass audiences as part of existing vaudeville theater presentations.

At this point, projected films became enormously popular, and the kinetoscope rapidly faded from importance. Albert E. Smith (1952: 254), the founder of Vitagraph, one of the largest producers of films during this period, wrote in his autobiography, 'The first ten years of this century were the heyday of the one-reeler.' During these years, virtually all firms that produced films concentrated their energies on making single reel, short subject films (henceforth shorts). Each of these shorts tended to have it own story line and ran for approximately twenty minutes; even those shorts produced by the same company had no connection in story or content to other shorts.

As the popularity of shorts in the vaudeville venue became established, it was not long before the development of film exhibition as a separate and distinct business from vaudeville occurred. Most film historians (Musser, 1990; Rhode, 1976) credit Harry Davis, a leading vaudeville magnate, with opening the first dedicated film exhibition hall in 1905. To enter his theater and be entertained by shorts, patrons were charged a nickel; thus, the theaters that he and legions of imitators founded were called nickelodeons. A *Saturday Evening Post* article in 1907 offered the following description of these early film exhibition outlets:

'The nickelodeon is usually a tiny theater containing 199 seats, giving from twelve to eighteen performances a day, seven days a week. Its walls are painted red. The seats are ordinary kitchen chairs which are fastened to the floor ... Nickelodeons which seat 199 people have only to take out amusement licenses whereas theaters which seat two hundred or more people must take out theatrical licenses costing $500 a year (Writers' Program – NY, 1985: 305).'

Following their introduction in 1905, the population of nickelodeons quickly grew at an amazing rate. In 1907, *Moving Picture World* estimated that 2500 to 3000 nickelodeons were in existence (Writers' Program – NY, 1985: 303); by 1910, the total was approximately 10 000 (Bowser,

1990: 81). With all the new exhibition outlets, film production grew as well. New subject footage released by all production companies combined increased from approximately 7000 feet per month in January 1906 to 30000 feet per month just 20 months later in August 1907 (Musser, 1990: 449). This rapid increase in both film production and the number of exhibition outlets created an obvious opportunity for entrepreneurs to become more active in the distribution function and provide some necessary organization. Both producers and exhibitors had an interest in creating more structure within the community. Producers wanted to increase their market reach by selling to as many nickelodeons as possible. Nickelodeons had an even more pressing need; in order to thrive, they had to be able to turn product over relatively quickly because the potential audience for a given single reel film shown repeatedly throughout the day was exhausted in fairly short order. Rapid turnover of films was the only way to continue to attract audiences, and this could be facilitated by more formal organization of the distribution function.

The first formal distribution organizations developed when entrepreneurs, some of them nickelodeon owners, organized exchanges to serve as intermediaries between producers and nickelodeons. Exchanges were libraries where nickelodeon managers would go to rent new product. They simply served a warehousing function and had no influence over either production or promotion. These early exchanges were essentially localized spot markets and did not provide a vehicle for the coordination of distribution across larger regions or nationally. Bowser (1990: 103) described how the system was organized. A producing firm:

> '...advertised and distributed its product by the brand. Under the system of the release day and the standing order, exhibitors, exchanges, and the public were expected to request films by company names, not by specific titles or stars. The price to the exchange was the same for any brand and any film. Competition among producers consisted of selling a greater number of prints to the exchanges ... Such a system depended upon the uniformity of the product manufactured.'

Several factors came together in this period of rapid growth between 1905 and 1909 that directly hurt the profits of producers. First, as a direct result of organizing within the community in the manner described above, the films themselves became commodity products. Second, demand growth was also slowing as the novelty of short films was fading quickly by the end of the decade. A third problem for American producers was the influx of imported films; in 1909, approximately half of the total industry production was by foreign companies (Bowser, 1990: 23). In sum, producers faced the challenge that their product had become a commodity at the same time that the growth in demand was slowing and new entrants were plentiful. The net effect of these factors was that those operating in the distribution and exhibition functions were making the greatest profits (Bowser, 1990); in essence, producers were being squeezed.

The major production companies, led by Edison and Biograph, responded to the situation by forming a cooperative cartel called The Motion Picture Patents Corporation (MPPC). The cartel was intended to reduce competition among producers and increase their power relative to producers outside the cartel as well as both distributors and exhibitors (Burt, 1980; Pfeffer and Salancik, 1978). After over a year of bargaining and negotiating, eleven producers, including the two largest foreign producers, came together in January 1909 to form the MPPC. This production cartel was organized as a holding company with shares equally owned by Edison and Biograph, the two companies that controlled all the major patents. They agreed to license the use of their patented equipment exclusively to the nine other producers who joined the cartel.

The MPPC created production quotas and scheduled release dates for each member company. The organization also instituted a policy requiring the exclusive licensing of all exchanges receiving product from any of the eleven firms affiliated with the MPPC. The object was to force exchanges and nickelodeons to book product from only member companies at a price determined by the cartel. This policy was based on the belief that neither exchanges nor nickelodeons could find sufficient film product from any other source except the MPPC. In addition, member companies also challenged non-member producers in other ways, especially in terms of litigation alleging patent violations.

To avoid being effectively frozen out, producers that were not affiliated with the MPPC had to demonstrate to the exchanges still independent of MPPC control that they were capable of supplying sufficient product. The response of non-MPPC producers was not to organize as a production cartel, but to create a central distribution organization in April 1910 called the Motion Picture Distributing and Sales Company. This entity was essentially the first distribution company, and it engaged in many functions that had not been performed by exchanges. It took shorts from independent producers and, in essence, marketed them to the exchanges. This distribution company provided independent producers with market reach for their product and, even more importantly, gave exchanges independent confidence that there was a sufficient volume of films from producers outside of the MPPC to satisfy their needs.

Later that year, the MPPC, both in recognition of the new competition and also to manage the licensed exchanges more effectively, organized their own distribution cartel, The General Film Company. Similar to the distribution company founded by the independent producers, General Film exerted central control over the distribution of shorts produced by MPPC members. In addition, it also functioned as an umbrella organization for the acquisition of all exchanges that purchased MPPC films. Eventually, the organization also attempted to extend its control over exhibitors by setting guidelines for pricing and film changeovers. Clearly, these organizations represented a significant transformation of the distribution function, rendering it more proactive and moving it beyond the simple role of a film library. Because of this transformation, coordinated national distribution, not just regional distribution, became a reality. At least initially, the formation of production and distribution cartels was a successful response to the decline in the popularity of shorts

Ultimately, however, a different response to the declining popularity of short films, pioneered by the Vitagraph Company, proved more enduring. Albert Smith (1952: 254), Vitagraph's founder, made the following observation about the decline of the popularity of shorts in his autobiography: 'Public apathy toward "galloping tintypes" daily became more marked; some sort of move had to be made. A new era was in the offing, held back by the old order.' The 'old order' can only be referring to his MPPC associates who were rigidly trying to maintain order against all threats of change. Vitagraph broke rank with other MPPC members and began releasing short films with related story lines. Their first multi-reel production, released in 1909, was called *The Life of Moses*. Soon other producing organizations also began releasing multi-reel films. These products were still in the short film format, but attempted to maintain audience interest by building bridges across the narratives of a series of short films, maintaining characters and allowing for more complex story lines, e.g. *The Perils of Pauline*. Multi-reel stories were initially shown according to MPPC rules in installments one reel at a time, but eventually their very existence had a ripple effect leading to other changes throughout the community.

Most producers were initially unwilling to make serials or multi-reel films; only Vitagraph and some foreign companies such as the world's largest producer, Pathés Frères, were producing multi-reel films (2–3 reels) in 1909. Certainly, some producers simply lacked the capabilities to think and operate at the level of complexity and sophistication need-ed to produce serial shorts or multi-reel films as opposed to shorts. However, there was another, and we believe more important, problem for producers of these films: Even though these films were popular with the consumer, they were not popular with the distribution cartels. This is perhaps not surprising given the mindset of industry control that was the basis of the two cartels that dominated the distribution function during this period. Their refusal to distribute multi-reels or feature length films created opportunities in the distribution function, allow-ing road show operators and states rights distributors to become central players in promoting multi-reels. Bowser (1990: 192) described how this occurred:

'Feature films [term is used in this context to indicate any multi-reel production] could be road-shown, as plays were, with stock compa-nies playing the provinces. Features were shown as special attrac-tions in the local opera houses and town halls and legitimate the-aters at advanced prices and stayed for as long as there was enough business to support them . If the film was not being road-shown, or if that tour was completed, it could be sold by states rights ... The "states rights" system meant that individuals or small companies could buy the rights for a specific territory and then charge what-ever the market would bear.'

The proliferation of states rights distributors and road shows between 1909 and 1912 helped to ensure that serials and multi-reels were avail-able to audiences, preventing the cartels from blocking the emergence of longer films and serials. During these years, it became increasingly obvious that multi-reel films were much more popular with audiences than shorts. Longer films soon followed, culminating with the release of films that set the industry standard for a feature-length film (henceforth features), now recognized as a minimum of four reels or approximately 4000 feet (American Film Institute, 1988). By this definition, the first features did not appear until 1912, but the product was received enthu-siastically in the marketplace and adopted quickly by producers. From this point, the popularity of features grew extraordinarily quickly, evi-denced by a rapid increase in the number of firms making features. In

1912, only one firm released a feature; by 1914, there were 114 firms producing features (American Film Institute; 1988).

The emergence of features reflected a pronounced shift in consumer attitudes toward an increased recognition of stars and directors. Benjamin Hampton, a noted producer and director for the period, estimated that by 1917 only five percent of American features were without the protection of a star name (Koszarski, 1990: 260). The unique production qualities and star appeal that separated features from earlier multi-reels and shorts forced producers to develop many new organizational and creative skills. This included learning new approaches to functional tasks such as writing and directing, learning how to acquire and develop talent, and learning how to promote their films. Dependent on stars and substance, features could not be scheduled as shorts had been, using quotas like a commodity on an assembly line. Thomas H. Ince is credited with developing the 'central producer system', an administrative innovation that nearly every major producer soon adopted (Koszarski, 1990: 108). This system treated each film as a unique product, allowing for enhanced creative quality, but also monitored costs, controlling the financial threat posed by the greater capital expenditures required in the production of features.

Even before features had become readily available, some nickelodeon owners had begun a transformation process that would result in the displacement of nickelodeons by movie theaters. Following the introduction into the marketplace of multi-reel films and serials, some nickelodeon owners had begun to experiment with programming. Innovative operators were quick to substitute multi-reel films and serials, as these products became available, for a string of unrelated shorts. Because customers stayed for longer periods of time, the comfort of the exhibition hall became increasingly important. This resulted in the development of movie theaters with enhanced comfort (e.g., restrooms, carpeting, better seating, etc.). These establishments began to raise prices to a dime in order to recover capital improvement costs and, even more importantly, to compensate for revenues lost due to the reduced audience turnover that resulted from expanded programs (Bowser, 1990: 199). Given the popularity of extended multi-reel programs, almost all exhibitors were soon forced by competition to either close or renovate their nickelodeons into theaters. Thus, as multi-reels and eventually features replaced shorts, nickelodeons were replaced by movie theaters.

The final major innovation in exhibition venues occurred in 1914 with the opening of the Strand Theater in New York City. The Strand

Theater marked a dramatic variation in theater design resulting in the emergence of what came to be known as the movie palace or show palace. These show palaces, patterned after large Broadway playhouses, were the most opulent of theaters with seating capacities in the thousands. Bowser (1990: 126) described them as follows:

'All kind of amenities were brought in to make the new theaters comfortable, elegant, and refined ... Marble, beveled glass, polished oak and walnut, dazzling electric lights, lavish carpeting, and huge mirrors began to appear in newly redecorated theaters. Rest rooms became a necessity rather than a luxury with longer programs, and these were finer facilities than many customers had at home.'

The popularity of these opulent movie theaters proved undeniable, and they diffused quite rapidly (Kosarski, 1990).

The appearance of multi-reels and features also was creating opportunities for change in the distribution function. The distribution cartel formed by independent producers in 1910 was an uneasy amalgamation formed only as a response to actions by the MPPC. By 1912, the threat of the MPPC to independent producers had diminished; in fact, independent film production was nearly equivalent to the total MPPC production by that time (Bowser, 1990: 85). Also during that same year, the first suit under the Sherman Anti-Trust Act was brought against the MPPC. In addition to the diminished threat of the MPPC, the appearance of multi-reels had increased the ability of producers to differentiate their products. All of these factors provided an incentive for some larger independent producers to leave the distribution cartel and look for their own distribution arrangements. The independent distribution companies that resulted were very different entities than the cartels that preceded them. Distributors worked for their producer clients by actively engaging in new functions such as marketing, promotion, and product placement (e.g., first run vs. second run theaters). In particular, the longer showing time of features meant that larger audiences needed to be attracted; this led to an explosion of advertising expenditures. In 1913, the industry was spending five million dollars on advertising; a figure that increased to sixty-seven million dollars by 1925 (*Wid's Film Daily*, 1926:3). In some cases, these new distribution companies even helped arrange financing to help producers meet the increased costs incurred in the production and promotion of features.

The increasingly strong relationship between production and distribution companies culminated in 1914 with the appearance of the first vertically integrated companies. Universal, a large independent producer, began to distribute on its own in 1914. In addition, World Film Corporation entered the industry backed by extensive Wall Street financing with both production and distribution operations. The next several years saw the proliferation of the vertically integrated producer-distributor. In 1915, Pathé became the first MPPC producer to leave General Film and vertically integrate into distribution. That same year Fox Film Corp. (the predecessor to Twentieth Century Fox) also vertically integrated into distribution. In 1916, several production companies led by Famous Players (founded by Adolph Zukor) merged with their distributor, Paramount, to form the dominant company in the industry. As the industry entered the 1920s, the integrated production and distribution organizations had come to dominate both the production and distribution of feature length films in the US market. It is estimated that six integrated producer-distributors, the studios as they came to be called, accounted for 80% of total film production in 1923 (*Wid's Film Daily*, 1924: 7).

Having consolidated their hold over both production and distribution, some of these studios turned their attention to exhibition. By the mid-1920s the final trend to complete the creation of the studio system that still dominates the American film industry today began with forward integration of the studios to acquire theaters. Within the decade, a few studios came to control the production, distribution, and exhibition of feature length films in the United States. This development, which marks the end of our discussion of the emergence of the industry, created an oligopolistic system that remained in place until a 1948 anti-trust decision forced the studios to divest of their theater chains.

The community dynamics of new industry creation

This section relates key activities in the emergence of the early American film industry to the social systems model of entrepreneurship (Van de Ven, 1993b), ultimately suggesting a community dynamics model of proprietary functions. We begin by showing how the development of the industry seems to follow and support many of the propositions put forward by Van de Ven (1993b) as well as offering an opportunity for demonstrating the relevance of some related literature. We then go on to suggest how a community dynamics model of the development of proprietary functions augments our theoretical understanding of entrepreneurship in a social systems framework.

The early film industry and the social systems framework

The theoretical framework proposed in this paper begins with the social systems perspective of community-wide entrepreneurship discussed by Van de Ven (1993a; 1993b). The relevant aspects of this infrastructure for entrepreneurship emerge '... through the accretion of numerous institutional, resource, and proprietary events involving many entrepreneurs located in the public and private sectors over an extended period." In the years following the introduction of film projection technology, we find that the infrastructure discussed by Van de Ven (1993b) was central to the process of entrepreneurship that created the American film industry. Indeed, many of the important activities that led to the development of the American film industry can be understood in terms of many of the propositions of the social systems framework

Van de Ven (1993b: 221) predicted that the success of entrepreneurs would in part be determined by their progress in building institutional arrangements and resource endowments for a new technology. This point is well illustrated by the process that led to the emergence of shorts, the first commercial film product to become widespread. With short films, which began commercial production in 1895, there was initial widespread confusion about how to present a novel product to the public. Very early on, film exhibition took place in locations such as church socials, fairs, music halls, penny arcades and traveling roadshows. The linking of films with vaudeville theaters represented an important institutional arrangement that guaranteed film production companies greater demand stability, resulting in greater and more reliable resource endowments. This was followed by the development of exhibition outlets devoted exclusively to the viewing of short films. However, these outlets, called nickelodeons, did not become widespread until after 1905; more than ten years after the initial commercialization of short films. Thus, the success of short films was not assured until institutional arrangements had been developed and resource endowments stabilized.

Van de Ven (1993b: 222) also argued that a novel product like short films would face greater problems in developing a social infrastructure for entrepreneurship than an incremental development like moving from shorts to features. Indeed, the fact that it took so much longer for shorts to integrate fully into the consumer marketplace versus the time it took for features to become fully accepted lends support to this proposition. By contrast, the entrepreneurs who promoted serial shorts, multi-reel films, and ultimately features were able to capitalize on the institutional arrangements created during many years of short film production. The early producers and distributors of features immediately understood the importance of dedicated exhibition outlets. Further, they quickly realized the shortcomings of nickelodeons as outlets for longer films, which demanded a different philosophy on the part of exhibitors. Reduced turnover of film product meant that exhibitors needed to charge customers more for each showing; customers in turn required more comfortable surroundings than nickelodeons allowed. Ultimately, the revenue potential of longer films justified the greater capital expenses associated with larger and plusher exhibition halls. As a result, entrepreneurs found resource endowments that supported the creation of theaters and even the much more expensive movie palaces.

In addition, it is interesting to note that as Van de Ven (1993b: 223) predicted, the social infrastructure that promoted one technology, short films, became an inertial force during the technological transition (Cooper and Smith, 1992) from short films to more elaborate multi-reel productions and eventually to feature length films. This is apparent in the activities of the MPPC and the two distribution cartel companies. Leading producers, through their distribution cartels, imposed policies that delayed the diffusion of multi-reel films. They actively resisted the transition from shorts to features, even after the preference of the market for the latter became apparent. Ultimately, only one MPPC producer from the shorts era, Vitagraph Co., went on to become a major producer of features. The entrepreneurial activities of those who distributed feature films in new ways including the states rights system and road shows were critical in overcoming these inertial forces.

In discussing the role of individual entrepreneurial firms in the development of a social infrastructure, Van de Ven (1993b: 223–225) emphasized the notion of running in packs. In fact, going it alone was a rare event during the early years of the American film industry. Entrepreneurs located their production organizations in concentrated areas, principally New York City and Los Angeles. Actors, technicians, and directors moved between production companies frequently. Cooperative and competitive ties between firms (Van de Ven, 1993b: 224) were rife, with producers frequently making films of similar content, selling that product to the same exchange markets, and having their products exhibited in the same nickelodeons. Entrepreneurs in this industry did not simply settle for this informal level of cooperative ties; they went further with the formation of cartels. The MPPC was the first cartel, instituting standardized policies for all eleven members and marshaling resources to litigate alleged patent violations by non-members. In response, producers 'frozen out' by the MPPC formed their own cartel, resulting in the creation of a distribution cartel; the response of the MPPC was to create a rival distribution cartel. For approximately two years, virtually all films in the United States were distributed through these two cartels. Both the formation of the MPPC and the quick response of non-MPPC members epitomize the strategy of running in packs.

Finally, and again as Van de Ven (1993b: 226) predicted, the dominant technological design that prevailed early on did not go on to become the dominant design that ultimately was most profitable. The kinetoscope was the first film technology; it is clear that its commercial variant, the peephole kinetoscope, did not fare well in competition with the subsequent technology that allowed films to be projected. A similar squeezing out of an older technology by a new technology is illustrated by the emergence of features. By the time shorts had become widespread, producers had become stagnant and ceased to make either technological or aesthetic advances. In 1909, Vitagraph introduced multi-reel films, and within three years, the first feature was released. In a remarkably short time, shorts were nearly completely displaced by features; parallel changes occurred in distribution (remaining exchanges and distribution cartels becoming distribution companies) and exhibition (nickelodeons being displaced by theaters and movie palaces). The whole form of the movie industry community changed immensely as the underlying product shifted from shorts to features.

Our claim is that the patterns of entrepreneurship in the film industry, from the initial development of shorts to subsequent transitions associated with the rise of features, can be most comprehensively understood using a community dynamics perspective. The subsequent two sections develop aspects of how our understanding can be augmented. In the first, we argue for a broad definition of entrepreneurship based on events that occurred in the community dynamics of the emerging film industry. In particular, we believe that the importance of second sourcing (Wade, 1995) to any emerging industry suggests that even purely imitative activities must be considered for a fuller understanding of successful entrepreneurship. In the second, we focus on how the success of entrepreneurial behaviors in one population of a community may depend on entrepreneurial behaviors in another population in the community. We believe that this process of cross-population entrepreneurship is analogous to the related sourcing activities discussed by Wade (1995) in the context of technological communities.

Community dynamics and a broad definition of entrepreneurial behavior

Many researchers have noted the confusion that exists over the definition of entrepreneurship (Bygrave and Hofer, 1991; Gartner, 1990; Hornaday, 1992; Lant and Mezias, 1990). However, there is a common element to most existing definitions of entrepreneurship: Entrepreneurial activity in the literature is often conceptualized as the search for and discovery of alternative possibilities; the discovery of opportunities that have not yet been noticed (Kirzner, 1979) or fully exploited (Lant and Mezias, 1990). This broad definition is also consistent with Schumpeter's (1950: 72) conceptualization of entrepreneurship. He argued that the key requirement for an activity to be entrepreneurial was that it results in new combinations of productive activity: '...the function of entrepreneurship is to reform or revolutionize the pattern of production...' In this conceptualization of entrepreneurship, change is the key variable and not the specific activities that lead to change. In this paper, we emphasize the role of entrepreneurship in creating change at a community level and recognize that many activities contribute to change.

Based on a review of the historical literature, Hornaday (1992) identified three dimensions that he felt consistently were used in the literature to characterize the entrepreneurship process – economic innovation, organization creation, and profit-seeking in the market sector. Only profit-seeking firms are included in this study, so that dimension will not be discussed further. We agree that both economic innovation and organization creation are consistent with entrepreneurial activity, but believe that a fuller appreciation of their role can result by treating them as dichotomous variables. Table 5.2 uses these two variables in defining four types of entrepreneurial behaviors.

Table 5.2 Four categories of entrepreneurial behavior

	Economic innovation	No Economic Innovation
New Firm	Innovative Founding: Most entrepreneurial	Imitative Founding: Moderately entrepreneurial
No New Firm	Product or Service Innovation: Moderately entrepreneurial	Product or Service Imitation: Least entrepreneurial

Economic innovation is the first of the dimensions, presented across the top of the table. Based on the discussion of the history of the early film industry, we conclude that the concept of innovation necessary to understand the emergence of a new industry must be inclusive, referring to a broad range of activities that produce change. In particular, we agree with Williamson's (1983) assertion that change in the characteristics of existing organizations is as crucial to our understanding of economic change as technical and product innovation. This is especially well illustrated in the film industry with the transformation of producing organizations following the displacement of shorts with features (e.g., story development, the creation of star power, and the central producer system). It is further illustrated by the transformations of nickelodeons into theaters and theaters into movie palaces. This emphasis on organizational as well as technical and product innovations is echoed by Arrow (1969) and Chandler (1977), and expressed succinctly by Cole (1968: 61–62) who stated the argument as follows: '[I]f changes in business procedures and practices were patentable, the contributions of business change to the economic growth of the nation would be as widely recognized as the influence of mechanical innovations or the inflow of capital from abroad.' This broad definition of economic innovation implies that it can be conceived of not only as product or technological innovation; it also includes innovation in organizational structure and process (Mezias and Glynn, 1993).

Having defined economic innovation, there is still the question of whether economic innovation is necessary for a behavior to be considered entrepreneurial. We suggest that economic innovation is not necessary when entrepreneurship is considered not as an individual act but as a community-wide innovation process. Imitative activities also contribute to the innovation process; for example, Swann (1987) and Wade (1995: 112) have provided evidence that imitation enhances the probability of success of a technological standard. Wade (1995: 112) noted that the literature of technological competition suggests that foundings of microprocessors using a particular standard '... serves as an information externality indicating the status of the product.' We believe that a similar process occurs during the development of new industries, rendering imitation a crucial activity even in the absence of an analogous battle over technological standards.

Repeatedly, rapid contagion, involving extensive imitation, was central to the success of entrepreneurial innovation in the early film industry. The quick spread of links between early producers of shorts and vaudeville theaters is one example. The incredibly quick diffusion of nickelodeons and the rapid development of exchanges is another. Projected films as a product would likely have been no more successful than films for the peephole kinetoscope if there had not been rapid imitation of vaudeville contracts, the nickelodeon, and the development of local exchanges. Similarly, the ability of features to prevail as the dominant product despite the obstructionist efforts of the dominant distribution cartels depended heavily on imitative behaviors. Innovative entrepreneurs in the distribution function created mechanisms such as travelling road shows and 'states rights' systems to promote multi-reel films. However, without imitative follow-up activities by others, the form may never have reached the audience necessary to make it a viable alternative to shorts. Similarly, the transformation of nickelodeons into theaters and theaters into show palaces, driven in large part by imitation, were important to the success of features. We believe that a community dynamics model of the emergence of new industries suggests that imitation is an important aspect of entrepreneurship. Thus, we include activities that are both high and low on the dimension of economic innovation in our typology of entrepreneurial behaviors.

Hornaday's (1992) second dimension of entrepreneurial activity, depicted along the vertical axis of Table 5.2, is organization creation. As with economic innovation, we are interested in the question of whether firm founding is necessary for an action to be considered entrepreneurial. It is quite clear that many crucial administrative innovations have occurred in existing organizations. As an example, corporate venturing research (e.g., MacMillan, 1986; Burgelman, 1983) has demonstrated the critical role of such innovation in the success of new product ventures. Areas of organizational innovation that have been studied include organizational culture (Kanter, 1983; MacMillan, Block, and Narasimha, 1986), top management commitment (Fast and Pratt, 1981), strategic planning and strategy (Cooper, 1979; Biggadike, 1979), and the structure and design of the new venture effort (Burgelman, 1983; 1985). Such innovation represents a case of organization re-creation rather than organization creation. Thus, we emphasize that entrepreneurial activity in existing organizations may also be an important source of innovative activity (Covin and Slevin, 1994; Dougherty, 1995; Dougherty and Hardy, 1996; Hardy and Dougherty, 1997; Shane and Venkataraman, 1996; Tushman and O'Reilly, 1996; Tushman and Rosenkopf, 1996; Vandermerwe and Birley, 1997).

We believe that this emphasis is justified by the fact that the transformation of existing organizations was also important in the emergence of the feature film industry in the U.S. It was a vaudeville theater owner who is credited with founding the first nickelodeon; subsequently, many vaudeville organizations branched out into nickelodeons. The first few organizations to make multi-reel and features were producers of shorts attempting to increase audience interest in their films. A rapid transformation of nickelodeons into theaters was included in the next wave of transformations, even as some traveling shows and state rights organizations were transformed into film distribution organizations. The remaining developments that culminated in the rise of the Hollywood studios were all heavily influenced by the transformation of existing organizations; these included the rise of the central producer system, the integration of production and distribution firms, and, ultimately, forward integration to acquire theater chains. We believe that entrepreneurial activity is possible even in the absence of the creation of a new organization.

Ultimately, models that emphasize the collective nature of entrepreneurship (e.g. Romanelli, 1989; Tjosvold and Weicker, 1993; Van de Ven, 1993a; 1993b), view all of the activities accompanying the emergence of an industry as, to use the words of Utterback and Suárez (1993: 17) '... predominantly entrepreneurial.' Our analysis of the early film industry's emergence is supportive of this view that a broad range of behaviors collectively contribute to entrepreneurship at the community level. However, while we view all these behaviors to be necessary for entrepreneurial innovation at the community level, we do not consider them as being equally entrepreneurial. In fact, the dimensions of economic innovation and organizational founding provide a legitimate means of comparing the four categories of behavior depicted in Table 5.2 in terms of their level of entrepreneurship. Two of the behaviors lead to the creation of a new organization; that is, they relate to foundings, which are part of the traditional definition of entrepreneurship. Another type of behavior is entrepreneurial in terms of the traditional focus on economic innovation, even though it does not actually result in the creation of an organization. The problematic quadrant in terms of past research is the one labeled-product or service imitation. These firm behaviors have not traditionally been considered entrepreneurial, because they neither result in the founding of a new firm nor do they involve the discovery of new opportunities. However, from the Schumpeterian (1950) perspective, imitation can contribute to revolutionary changes in patterns of production. Further, imitation is critical in a community dynamics model of the emergence of new industries because it can have dramatic effects on the success of the new industry.

A first contribution of a community dynamics model of proprietary functions is that it provides a framework for distinguishing four types of entrepreneurial behaviors and comparing them in terms of their level of entrepreneurship. These four types of behavior are defined as follows:

Innovative Founding: This type of behavior results in both economic innovation and organizational creation. In the film industry, examples would include the creation of the first producers, first nickelodeons and the establishment of the first exchanges to distribute short films.

Imitative Founding: This type of behavior results in the creation of a new organization that is not innovative. It instead attempts to duplicate the processes of an existing organization and be its direct competitor in supplying a given good or service. In the film industry, three examples include production company foundings that followed the early producers (i.e., Edison, Biograph and Lumière), nickelodeon foundings that occurred in the years following the first establishments and the development of competing exchanges after an area was already being served by one.

Product or Service Innovation: This type of behavior results in innovation, the introduction of a new product or service within an existing organization, but does not include organizational creation. An example of product innovation is Vitagraph in 1909, which began producing multi-reel films in addition to the single-reel films that had been their main product. By so doing, Vitagraph became the first company to be a producer of multi-reel films. An example of service innovation is the introduction within established nickelodeon operators of more advanced design concepts leading to theaters and movie palaces.

Product or Service Imitation: This type of behavior results in neither economic innovation nor organizational creation. It involves the decision by an existing organization to change its existing products or services through imitation. This behavior has an impact on entrepreneurship at the community level by supporting previously introduced innovation. As an example of product imitation, the rapid diffusion of feature films following Vitagraph's lead required that many existing firms be willing to adopt the new product form represented by features. As an example of service imitation, the rapid diffusion of theaters could not have occurred without the acceptance by existing nickelodeon operators of the new form.

While it is clearly possible to compare these activities in terms of the level of entrepreneurship from high to moderate to low, as indicated in Table 5.2, we believe that all are essential. A community dynamics model of the role of entrepreneurship in the emergence of new industries highlights the crucial role of second sourcing, whether it is the result of a product or service imitation within a new or existing organization. Thus, while economic innovation clearly makes an activity more entrepreneurial, we do not believe it is required for an activity to be considered entrepreneurial. Similarly, it is evident from the early film industry that important entrepreneurial events often occurred at existing firms; thus, while organizational founding may render a particular behavior more entrepreneurial, we do not believe that founding is required for an activity to be considered entrepreneurial. To summarize, the community dynamics model of the role of proprietary functions in the emergence of new industries was interpreted to suggest four important categories of entrepreneurial behaviors. The occurrence of these behaviors across populations of firms in the community is the subject of the next section.

The community dynamics of cross population entrepreneurship

As we noted at the start of the paper, the film industry's value chain represents distinct populations of firms, especially in the early years of the industry when entrepreneurial activity is most intense. As an industry matures, firms frequently integrate, bringing other functions within the boundaries of the organization. However, when studying the emergence of an industry, we believe that it is appropriate to think of value chain activities in terms of ecologically distinct populations within the emerging community. It is from this premise that we begin our discussion of the community dynamics of cross-population entrepreneurship. Van de Ven (1993b: 219) asserted that the paths of independent entrepreneurs – acting out their own diverse intentions and ideas – intersect. We agree, arguing that entrepreneurial behaviors can impact entrepreneurship not only in the population where the entrepreneurial behavior originated but also in other populations within the community. Our study of the film industry shows that these spillover effects cross populations. Activities by firms in one part of the value chain can have significant effects on both the occurrences of entrepreneurial activities in other parts of the value chain as well as on the ultimate success of those activities. Following Wade (1995), we will refer to these spillover effects as related sourcing.

As examples from the film industry illustrate, the open resource space (Astley, 1985; Romanelli, 1989) that facilitates entrepreneurial behavior often depends on earlier entrepreneurial behavior elsewhere in the community. As we have discussed, the first commercialized technology was Edison's peephole kinetoscope. Within a few years, projectors were being sold as well by three main players – Edison, Biograph and Lumière. Following the introduction of projectors, the Biograph Co. was able to find a new and more dependable set of customers in vaudeville establishments. Thus, innovation in the production function, the introduction of projection technology, made possible innovation in the exhibition function, showing films as part of the vaudeville program. In the case of nickelodeons and exchanges, the innovation of nickelodeons in the exhibition function created an open area of resource space in the distribution function that allowed the introduction of exchanges. Exchanges served a warehousing function, facilitating exchanges between producers and exhibitors. Without the existence of strong and dedicated exhibition outlets, the creation of exchanges in the distribution function would have been unnecessary. Thus, innovation in the exhibition function, the introduction of nickelodeons, made possible innovation in the distribution function, the introduction of exchanges. The variation of multi-reel films, directly resulting from Vitagraph's independent activities in experimenting with serials, fostered opportunities for innovation in exhibition, leading to the creation of movie theaters and movie palaces to replace nickelodeons.

Wade (1995) has provided evidence for one example of this spillover phenomenon, which he called related sourcing, in technological communities defined both by design and architecture. His evidence suggested that foundings in one population within a technological community could have a mutualistic effect on foundings in another population of the same technological community. We believe this is also true in the emergence of new industries. Entrepreneurial behaviors in one population of a community can create opportunities for additional entrepreneurial behaviors elsewhere in the community. In general, we believe that the following will be true:

Proposition 1: During the emergence of a new industry, entrepreneurial behaviors in one population of the community may create opportunities for entrepreneurial behaviors elsewhere in the community.

Thus, it is our contention that innovative foundings in one population can have a positive effect on innovative foundings in another population, e.g., the foundings of firms producing features positively impacting the foundings of theaters. Similarly, innovative foundings in one population can also have a positive effect on other entrepreneurial behaviors in other populations, e.g., the foundings of traveling road shows positively impacting the transformation of firms producing to include multi-reel and feature-length film production as well. We would make analogous arguments concerning the potential impact of all four categories of entrepreneurial behaviors in one population on the potential for all categories in other populations. Our fundamental point is that an understanding of how this related sourcing contributes to a contagion of entrepreneurial behaviors across populations is important to the understanding of the emergence of new industries.

Entrepreneurial behaviors in one population not only have an impact on the occurrences of entrepreneurial behaviors elsewhere in the community but also impact on the success of those entrepreneurial initiatives. For example, imitative foundings of exchanges in the distribution function helped enable nickelodeons in the exhibition function to flourish. Nickelodeons changed their films often, and many of the first nickelodeon owners faced substantial uncertainty regarding the supply of film product. The founding of exchanges reduced this uncertainty, providing nickelodeon owners with a place where they could find the variety and quantity of product needed on a regular basis. The existence of exchanges made the external environment faced by prospective nickelodeon owners more supportive. This allowed even more imitative foundings of nickelodeons and helped in ensuring the success of the nascent film industry.

Similarly, innovative foundings of states rights distributors and road show organizers in the distribution function helped in the success of multi-reel films in the production function. Following the introduction of multi-reels in 1909, distribution cartels and exhibitors were reluctant to deal with the new film product, instead preferring shorts. The appearance of states rights distributors and road shows between 1909 and 1912 helped in the success of multi-reels by providing producers with a known outlet and ultimately an early market for their new form of film product. Thus, innovative foundings of states rights distributors and road show operators were important variations in the distribution function that helped ensure the success of multi-reel films in the production function.

As a final example, theaters in the exhibition function and multi-reel film producers in the production function were each important to the success of the other. Producers such as Vitagraph had started to experiment with multi-reel programs prior to the introduction of theaters. However, theaters still helped in supporting the proliferation of multi-reel film product by increasing the number of exhibition outlets available to such films. Multi-reel films were similarly important to the proliferation of theaters and show palaces. Although it quickly became obvious that audiences preferred multi-reel films to shorts, nickelodeons were reluctant to show them. This was because they only profitable when there was a quick turnover of audiences throughout the day, and multi-reel films slowed audience turnover. Thus, the existence of multi-reel films supports the movement away from nickelodeons and into theaters and movie palaces.

As these examples show, the ultimate success of entrepreneurial behaviors in one population within a community is often affected by behaviors of entrepreneurs in other parts of the community. Entrepreneurial behaviors in populations external to the focal population can render the environment of the focal population more munificent, affecting the success of entrepreneurial behaviors in the focal population. It is our contention that the survival of film production companies was dependent on the service innovation of vaudeville theaters showing shorts. Further, the imitative service changes of other vaudeville theaters following the lead of pioneers in the showing of films also aided the survival of firms producing shorts. Subsequently, both the innovative foundings of the first nickelodeons and the massive imitative second sourcing that followed were crucial to the survival of film production companies. In the same manner, the founding of exchanges was crucial for the survival and spread of nickelodeons. Thus, there is a reciprocal effect in addition to the effect of entrepreneurial behaviors in one population creating opportunities for entrepreneurial behaviors in other populations as suggested by Proposition 1. The opportunities exploited in a second population in response to entrepreneurial behaviors in a first population may also be important in ensuring the success of the entrepreneurial behaviors in the first population. Both the opportunities for and success of entrepreneurial behaviors in one population may be affected by entrepreneurial behaviors in another population; it is this latter effect that is summarized in the following proposition:

Proposition 2: During the emergence of a new industry, the success of entrepreneurial behaviors in one population may be supported by entrepreneurial behaviors in other populations.

Conclusions

Traditionally, entrepreneurship has often been thought of and even studied as an isolated event, focused on the actions of individuals without paying sufficient attention to the context nurturing the event and the person. The primary goal of this study has been to augment models of entrepreneurship and the emergence of new industries that take a more social perspective. Towards this end, we focused heavily on the social systems framework (Van de Ven 1993a; 1993b) and developed a community dynamics model of proprietary functions. The history of events in the film industry's emergence strongly reinforces the value of a social systems approach and lends support to many of the propositions forwarded by Van de Ven (1993b). In particular, it points to the need to continue working on a theory of entrepreneurship that considers it as both an evolutionary and a collective process taking place within a larger community context. We believe that this paper contributes to this research stream with its community dynamics model of the role of proprietary functions in the emergence of new industries, especially in terms of highlighting conceptual issues about the definition of entrepreneurship and cross-population effects in a community of organizations.

During the course of this research, it became clear that there are many meanings to the term entrepreneurship (Amit, Glosten, and Muller, 1993, Bygrave, 1993; Gartner, and Shane, 1995; Hofer and Bygrave, 1992; MacMillan and Katz, 1992; Sandberg, 1992; Stearns and Hills, 1996; Woo, Daellenbach, and Nicholls-Nixon, 1994). Some consider it the act of organizational creation; others consider it an innovative activity. Still others would say that an entrepreneur necessarily engages in both economic innovation and organization creation (Hornaday, 1992). In attempting to understand the role of entrepreneurship in the emergence of new industries, however, we believe that a broader definition is justified. Thus, we developed a four-quadrant typology of entrepreneurial behaviors where innovative behaviors are considered as not only being associated with new organizations, but as also occurring in the context of an existing organization. Further, the typology included imitative behaviors both in the context of new foundings and within existing organizations. It is often necessary that all these behaviors occur in order for entrepreneurship in a community setting to succeed. Van de Ven (1993b: 224) described it quite well: Running in packs means that entrepreneurs coordinate with others as they develop and commercialize their innovation.

Just as populations within communities are interdependent, so too are entrepreneurs within them. Van de Ven and Garud (1989) noted the importance of emerging social systems in their study of the cochlear implant industry. Stinchecombe (1965: 146) wrote that entrepreneurs find or learn about alternative, better ways of doing things that are not easily done within existing social arrangements. They thrive where variation around them is at a maximum, because this allows them to arrange a new social order that leads to new innovative opportunities. These social structures are constantly evolving as variations continue to occur throughout the various populations comprising the community. We found much evidence for these phenomena in the early film industry in the United States.

Specifically, we analyzed how entrepreneurial behaviors interacted in different parts of a community defined by the value chain. Different types of entrepreneurial behaviors, constrained by the path dependent nature of change in this empirical setting, impacted one another at every stage in the emergence of this new industry. More entrepreneurial behaviors, as we have conceptualized them, resulted in innovation, the creation of new organizations, or both. Minimally entrepreneurial activities, product and service imitations by existing firms, while involving neither innovation nor the creation of new organizations, were still crucial to the development and success of the emerging film industry. We are still left with the remnants of the exchange system, national and states rights distribution, four-reel features, and other more subtle influences that all have their roots in these community dynamics of the emergence of new industries.

In this paper, we focused narrowly on a single set of empirical developments in the hopes of developing an understanding of theoretical mechanisms that would apply more broadly (MacMillan and Katz, 1992). The community that formed the early American film industry consisted solely of populations engaged in performing proprietary functions within the industrial infrastructure of the film industry. Based on our analysis of this community, two propositions were derived that we believe are generalizable beyond this specific case and can be extended to other industries. However, the implications of this research are not limited to the study of entrepreneurship; there are at least two other literatures for which our study has clear implications. First, the literatures of population ecology and evolutionary perspectives must be brought to bear on the emergence of new industries (Mezias and Mezias, 1999). The population and community dynamics of the four types of entrepreneurial behaviors, innovative foundings, innovative organizational level change, imitative foundings, and imitative product and service changes, are one area to begin this work. Second, the literature on competition for technological standards might look to broaden the range of applicability of the mechanisms and theoretical constructs that it has emphasized. In this paper, both second and related sourcing were shown to be important concepts in the emergence of the early film industry. We have suggested that many of the same processes that characterize competition among standards after an industry has emerged may also characterize the search for a first feasible technology that accompanies the birth of any industry.

Beyond these two literatures, we also believe that there may be general lessons regarding the role of entrepreneurial behaviors in producing innovation, the creation of new organizations, and the ultimate successful emergence of a new industry. Our propositions provide a summary description outlining how entrepreneurial behaviors in one population in a community can affect the possibilities for and success of entrepreneurial behaviors in another population in the community. We feel confident that the community dynamics processes we have described are crucial to the creation of new industries and economic change. We look forward to working with others in pursuing the empirical and theoretical work that will deepen our understanding of these processes.

Part III
The Role of Institutions in New Industry Emergence

In this section we draw attention to the insights institutional theory brings to our understanding of new industry emergence. The primary question asked in the following chapters is: Does success in dealing with legitimacy problems enhance the foundings of new firms in an emerging industry? Aldrich and Fiol (1994) developed theory regarding how firms and networks of firms in a new industry attain legitimacy. They describe the creation of technological standards shared by all firms as fundamental to the attainment of both cognitive and socio-political legitimacy. They reasoned that if an industry does not share technological standards key stakeholder trust in the industry would be delayed or withheld entirely.

In Chapter 6: Legal Environments and the Population Dynamics of Entrepreneurship: Litigation and Foundings in the Early American Film Industry, 1897–1918, we focus on how the legal contests surrounding film making patents and copyrights frustrated efforts to establish a technological standard and as a result slowed the industries cognitive legitimation. Consistent with the theory proposed by Aldrich & Fiol (1994) we find that the lack of a technological standard created high levels of uncertainty for both incumbent firms and potential entrants. Further we hypothesize that high levels of uncertainty will suppress foundings during the periods when litigation is at its peak. Contrary to early institutional work that viewed organizations as passive recipients of state mandates, forced to conform to the inexorable tide of coercive isomorphism (DiMaggio and Powell, 1983) we find that the firms comprising the early American film industry were very active in shaping through litigation their legal institutional environment.

In Chapter 7: Industry Creation, Legitimacy, and Foundings: The Case of the American Film Industry, 1896–1928, we focus on the cognitive and sociopolitical legitimacy challenges an emerging industry faces. Rather than discussing legitimacy as an abstract construct we investigate three legitimacy challenges actually faced by the industry. We formulate these three challenges as questions: Is film a viable business?, Are motion pictures an unsavory, marginal business? and What is this product, and how do I consume it? In order to attain sociopolitical legitimacy firms in the film industry had to prove that they were operating mainstream viable businesses that produced and delivered product that consumers understood how to use and for which there was substantial demand. In this chapter we analyze a sample of headlines appearing in the main mass communication vehicle of the time, *The New York Times*, between 1897 and 1928, to test whether the success of the film industry is reflected in the number and mix of articles that undermine and enhance cognitive and sociopolitical legitimacy. Building on these findings we develop four propositions concerning the effects that the appearance of articles undermining or enhancing cognitive and/or sociopolitical legitimacy will have on organizational foundings.

We believe that by combining the ecological focus on the population as the unit of analysis, specifically the rate of foundings, and research on the creation of legitimacy for a new industry we can significantly improve our understanding of the dynamics of new industry emergence. We hope these chapters will persuade more researchers to join us in investigating these questions.

6

Legal Environments and the Population Dynamics of Entrepreneurship: Litigation and Foundings in the Early American Film Industry, 1897–1918

Elizabeth Boyle and Stephen J. Mezias

America is known as the litigious society (Lieberman, 1981), and American organizations have become increasingly legalistic (Sitkin and Bies, 1993; Sutton, Dobbin, Meyer, and Scott, 1994). Of current organizational theory perspectives, neo-institutional theory (DiMaggio and Powell, 1991) has had the clearest focus on how the state and the legal environment (Edelman, 1990) have impacted organizations. Early institutional work on the role of the state tended to view organizations as passive recipients of state mandates, forced to conform to the inexorable tide of coercive isomorphism (DiMaggio and Powell, 1983). Of course, one reason for this deemphasis of active agency was because the dominant theories at the time tended to be managerialist. Early institutional theorists took as part of their mission the creation of an alternative to positing causality at the organizational level of analysis and linking outcomes with the rational actions of managers. Empirical studies of isomorphic processes at the interorganizational field level soon revealed, however, that managers as well as professional and state actors were active participants in shaping normative environments (Baron, Dobbin, and Jennings, 1986; Edelman, 1990; 1992; Mezias, 1990). Without changing the emphasis on cultural sources of organizational structure, these theorists began to examine how these environments were shaped, not just how they shaped organizations.

One of the most active areas of research examining the interplay of organizations and cultural environments has been study of the legal environment (Edelman, 1990; 1992; Edelman and Suchman, 1997).

This work has documented how the legal environment has been linked with changes in organizational practices, including the diffusion of bureaucratic personnel procedures (Baron, Dobbin, and Jennings, 1986), the diffusion of grievance procedures (Edelman, 1990; 1992; Edelman, Uggen, and Erlanger, 1999; Sutton and Dobbin, 1996), employment-at-will clauses (Sutton and Dobbin, 1996), maternity leave policies (Kelly and Dobbin, 1999), the elaboration and diffusion of internal labor markets (Dobbin, Sutton, Meyer, and Scott, 1993), and the rise of human resource management divisions (Dobbin and Sutton, 1998). This work has documented how the courts, professionals such as human resource professionals and lawyers, and organizations shape the way organizations conform to normative expectations in the legal environment.

In order to apply some of the ideas from this literature to entrepreneurship, we will focus on the legal environment as a source of uncertainty that impacts organizations (Edelman, 1990; 1992). In this chapter we de-emphasize normative expectations of society as an aspect of legal environments because our goal is to link studies of the legal environment with studies of population ecology. We deemphasize normative expectation here, not because we would deny that normative expectations are important. In fact, we agree that explaining the role these expectations play during new industry and new firm founding is a critical key to increasing our understanding of this phenomenon. (Aldrich and Fiol, 1994; Lounsbury and Glynn, 2001); This is the principal reason why we focus on issues of legitimacy in Chapter 7. Here we have a different goal: It is our intent to link studies of the legal environment with studies of population ecology by proposing relationships between litigation and the foundings of firms during the early years of the American film industry. The integration we propose is very much in the spirit of the study of the effect of regulation on breweries by Wade, Swaminathan, and Saxon (1998). However, rather than study direct attempts at control by government actors, we will propose effects of litigation on entrepreneurship in a newly emerging industry.

We proceed as follows. In the next section we provide a brief review of the various kinds of litigation that characterized the early years of the American film industry. We conclude that both patent infringement and copyright litigation may have an effect on a key entrepreneurial activity: the founding of new firms. We also conclude that the extended fight over patent infringement, which became known as the patent wars, consisted of several periods that are likely to have different effects on founding rates. Finally, we discuss some implications of our framework for future research and some preliminary conclusions for work on legal environments, the population dynamics of new industry formation, and entrepreneurship.

Litigation in the early days of film

The early days of filmmaking and exhibition in the US were a time of severe legal disputes, particularly over two issues: patent infringement and copyright protection. We will begin by discussing the first of these because it lasted longer and had a more profound effect. Beginning with the kinetoscope, film production was inseparable from the production of technology to view it. Even after the Lumière Brothers had liberated film viewing from the peephole, film stock and the technology for projecting were not standardized. Each firm that produced a film also had to ensure the equipment to project it was produced and distributed along with it; thus, at this time, each film production company was also a manufacturer of film, projection, and related equipment. All of these technologies were proprietary, and each firm attempted to patent its specific system; thus, it is not surprising that disputes arose. Also, given Thomas Edison's central role in the development of motion pictures, it is not surprising that litigation came to be important. He was a veteran of patent wars in multiple industries, having been forced to sue to protect his inventions on numerous occasions before the beginnings of cinema (Shapiro and Varian, 1999); he had also learned important lessons in market control from his previous experiences with litigation (Bowser, 1990). Thus, Edison launched the first salvo of what came to be known as the 'patent wars' in 1897 in his ongoing effort to gain sole control of the industry, but this was not the only purpose of patent infringement litigation. It is also clear, at least in Edison's case that he used the patent wars as a signal of the quality of his system to consumers, at a time when the equipment was still intermittently unreliable and the quality of the projected images was widely varied. Short film clips of the Spanish-American War had become immensely popular; competition among the nascent film companies to quench the popular thirst for coverage was intense. Castonguay (1999) included an advertisement published in *The New York Clipper* in 1898 by F. Z. Maguire, the authorized selling agent for Edison's news shorts about Spanish-American war made in collaboration with *The New York Journal*. The ad is quite explicit: It tells the reader to remember the patent wars, declaring that the films exhibited using Edison's technology are '... producing the greatest enthusiasm wherever shown.'

Between 1897 and 1915, hundreds of suits and counter suits were filed, not just by Edison against other firms but also among firms other than Edison as well. The plaintiffs in these various suits alleged that some proprietary technologies in use by other companies infringed on patents held by the plaintiff. The defendants maintained the claim that their technology was sufficiently unique to give them the right to continue making both film equipment and the actual films without infringing on another firms patents. Although all major firms contributed to the patent wars, Edison was by far the primary driver, filing 278 suits against his competitors in this period.

The period from 1897 to 1902 represented Edison's greatest success at using litigation as a competitive weapon. He first drove a foreign competitor, Lumière, out of the film business in the United States. He then focused on his major competitor, the American Mutoscope and Biograph Company (henceforth, Biograph). In July 1901 it seemed that Edison had won the war when a federal court upheld his claim that Biograph's technological system infringed on his patents. In effect, this decision left the Edison Company as the only one in the country that legally could produce films and sell them for. All the other players in the industry other than Edison were thrown into upheaval by the decision, even though Biograph appealed and enforcement was stayed pending the outcome of that appeal. For example, Sigmund Lubin not only left the industry, he also left the country. However, Edison's legally declared monopoly was short-lived: In April 1902, a higher court reversed the decision against Biograph. This however was not the end of the patents war. Edison, Biograph and many other firms in the industry found additional bases upon which to launch new litigation. After its court victory in 1902, Biograph enhanced its legal position by purchasing additional patents to equipment. As the Edison–Biograph legal dispute dragged on for the next five years, groups of firms grew up around their rival systems for film exhibition. Although patent infringement litigation continued throughout these years, firms could ally themselves with one group or another and reduce their risk of litigation in that way. In 1907, the courts ultimately decided in favor of Biograph, granting that their technology was sufficiently different as to not represent an infringement on Edison's patents.

Biograph's 1907 court victory was a watershed event in the patent wars; although they did not end, this event marked a qualitative change in how patent infringement litigation would affect industry dynamics. In the wake of the Biograph victory, Lubin returned from Europe and reopened his business. Selig placed its polyscope projector on the market and began selling its films more aggressively. During this period Edison entered into negotiations with Biograph in hopes of combining forces to create effective industry control by wielding their patents, but he refused to give Biograph an equal share, and negotiations broke down. As a result the industry broke into two groups of licensees. The first was organized around Edison's company, referred to as the Licensed Companies and officially structured as the United Film Service Protective Association. The second was organized around Biograph's technology and was referred to as the Independents. The competition between the two sets of firms did not make for effective control of the market control, which Edison clearly wanted. At the same time, Biograph obtained the patent for the Latham Loop, making it clear that they had another important technology under their control. At this time, Edison and Biograph reentered negotiations, ultimately agreeing to be equal partners in controlling film technology. The result was the founding of the Motion Pictures Patents Company (MPPC also known as the Patents Company) on 1 January 1909.

The ostensible goal of the organization was to share income from the patents that gave members the rights to the various machine patents necessary for the production and exhibition of films. The MPPC charged exhibitors $2 a week for the right to use equipment covered by their patents. The policies of the MPPC, however, reveal that its true goal was total market control. All member companies agreed not to sell or lease to any distributor buying from any other production company. When exhibitors would not comply, the Patents Company returned to the familiar practice of filing lawsuits. When lawsuits were not enough, the MPPC would use violence against defiant filmmakers and exhibitors. Most of these tactics were exercised through the formation of a strong-arm subsidiary to oversee the distribution of the films produced by members of the trust called General Film Corporation. Aberdeen (2001) described the situation as follows: 'With coercive tactics that have become legendary, General Film confiscated unlicensed equipment, discontinued product supply to theaters which showed unlicensed films, and effectively monopolized distribution with the acquisition of all U.S. film exchanges, except for the one owned by the independent William Fox who defied the Trust even after his license was revoked.'

Although the MPPC was a tough competitor, those outside its control were able to remain credible because approximately 25% of the film exchanges did not join the MPPC. Thus, many of those who defied the MPPC represented distributors. The American Film Manufacturing Corporation was an independent distribution operation set up by members of several film exchanges because they were not happy with the policies of the MPPC. In 1909 film distributor Carl Laemmle defied the MPPC by setting up his own Independent Moving Picture Company. The challenge for these organizations was not finding someplace to show their films, but rather finding films that they could show without an MPPC license. With domestic sources of film cut off, they looked oversees. When Carl Laemmle's MPPC licenses were revoked as a result of his defiance of cartel rules, he began importing raw film stock from abroad. This triggered a series of events that ultimately proved to be the undoing of the MPPC. With its rules geared towards a per foot pricing structure that favored short films and its tight control of the production of member firms, the MPPC refused to move into the production of longer films. Foreign firms were not under the control of the MPPC and had nothing to gain from maintaining the status quo of film production that it was enforcing. At the same time, those American distributors and exhibitors outside of the MPPC were clamoring for films from outside the US. The result was the precipitous rise to dominance of the costume spectacle from Italy. *Quo Vadis*, 9 reels in length, created an international sensation, demonstrating that the public would not only sit through much longer films, but that their appetite for them was insatiable. The 12-reel *Calabria*, released in 1914, demonstrated the enormous commercial potential of the super-spectacle, making it clear that the future of cinema belonged to the feature length film.

The MPPC, focused on market control, suppressed innovation and never understood the importance of features; the stubborn refusal of the organization to embrace features led to its downfall. It also brought down the whole American film industry, ending American dominance in the industry. By the time the Wilson administration sued the MPPC for restraint of trade in 1912, the organization was already in decline. Film production by companies outside the MPPC had already grown to just about equal that of the MPPC. In 1913, D. W. Griffith secretly made a feature length film, in defiance of his bosses at Biograph, while in California for the winter. When the company tried to suppress the film because it violated MPPC rules, Griffith quit the firm. His epic, *Birth of a Nation*, debuted in 1915; the same year that the Justice Department declared the MPPC an illegal conspiracy. By the time the final appeals were exhausted, with the same verdict, in 1917, the MPPC had ceased to be an important player in the American film industry.

A second type of litigation, relating to copyright infringement, also affected the growth and evolution of the early American film industry. Before 1900 film producers relied on trademark laws to protect their intellectual property because copyright protection was much more expensive to acquire and it was not clear how or whether films could be copyrighted (Musser, 1990). Producers went so far as to have their company logo or symbol appear in each frame of a film. These logos and symbols would be attached to trees or other parts of the sets; thus, each individual frame could be protected as trademarked. As the moving picture audience became more sophisticated, producers were criticized for this practice because it undermined the illusion of a given film. Although some producers continued this practice until 1906, by 1901 most producers recognized that copyright protection was needed to protect films from the rampant piracy plaguing the industry. Not coincidentally, litigation alleging copyright infringement also began with Edison. In 1898, he filed suit against Ernst Lubin for duping (making copies from an original) one of his films. This along with patent infringement litigation was costly to Lubin. Rather than continue to contest these suits, Lubin returned to Germany, where he continued to market his films out of an office in Berlin, but with less success (Musser, 1990). When the Edison victory over Biograph in the patent wars was reversed in 1902, Lubin returned to the US and began making and distributing films again.

One of the films in his catalog at this time documented the visit of Prince Henry to the U.S., using copies of Edison footage that he had copied, or 'duped' to use the terminology of that day. Edison was quick to file suit in June 1902, but was unable to obtain an injunction stopping the duping of his films by Lubin. Worse still, in January 1903, the court ruled in favor of Lubin, who had argued that each frame had to be submitted for copyright and against Edison, who had claimed an entire film could be submitted for copyright. The judge ruled that new legislation was required for the kind of copyright protection that Edison sought; existing law only allowed for the copyrighting of individual frames as photographs. The effect of this decision on the Edison company was dramatic: Unable to protect his original films, he stopped all film production for several months early in 1903. Lubin, too, stopped all original production, preferring instead to dupe the films of other companies, foreign and domestic. However, the chilling effect of this decision went beyond the direct effect on the parties to the suit; it disrupted film production throughout the country. Musser (1990: 331) described the situation as follows: 'As a result of this decision, it became imprudent for an American producer to invest substantial sums of money in a film's negative, and the copyright issue disrupted American production for several months until the Court of Appeals found in Edison's favor.'

This occurred in April 1903, when the Court of Appeals overrode the lower court decision; ruling that Edison's method of copyrighting films was sufficient to stake sole claim to the content of a film. Edison resumed production, as did other who had curtailed it in the wake of the ruling. While the legal chaos surrounding copyrighting was reduced by the April 1903 reversal of the decision against Edison, the lower court judge's claim that new legislation was needed remained unsatisfied until 1912. There remained unresolved issues around copyrighting throughout this period, and Lubin and Edison, as well as others, continued to dupe films produced by other companies. Part of the reason for this was that companies began remaking films almost scene for scene, as this did not seem to be prohibited by the April 1903 decision in Edison's favor. For example, the enormous success of *The Great Train Robbery* directed by Edwin S. Porter for the Edison Company inspired a Lubin imitation. In very short order of the release of this film by Edison to great popular acclaim, Lubin produced *The Bold Bank Robbery* with a virtually identical story. This undercut the value of investing resources in creating effective narrative, since a competitor could see what was successful and quickly imitate it.

In addition, the proprietary alliances that dominated the industry created enormous incentives to imitate the success of those outside the alliance to which a given firm happened to be a member. In the wake of its 1902 victory over Edison in the patent wars, Biograph had gone on to become the leading producer of films in the US by the summer of 1904. It was a leader in story films, which were quickly emerging as popular with a public that had grown weary of cursory newsreels and images designed to do little more than highlight new film technology. Although narrative films were clearly a more expensive proposition, the company was turning out about one per month and achieving enormous success with some of them. When the company denied hits like *The Escaped Lunatic* and *Personal* to theaters that did not subscribe to its exhibition service, these owners looked elsewhere to obtain similar story films. An exhibition service allied with Edison, Kinetograph Company, began supplying Edison's company with the earliest prints of these story films, which it quickly imitated. Biograph executives sued Edison's company for copyright infringement, but lost because its film had been imitated rather than duped. The court did provide guidelines for the copyrighting of story films as literary properties, which Biograph followed in the future. Nonetheless, copyrighting remained an uncertain proposition until Congress passed legislation in 1912 clarifying the status of films under copyright law. Many firms, especially foreign firms, continued to have their films duped on a wide scale because they did not understand the copyright process in the U.S. or found the process of submitting to the Library of Congress too cumbersome or expensive (Musser, 1990: 364–365).

The effect of litigation on entrepreneurship

Entrepreneurship in the early American film industry was affected by this litigation in several ways. First, we believe that both types of litigation created uncertainty that made foundings less likely. Under conditions where a new firm would be taken to court or have its products stolen because it could not establish copyright protection, potential entrepreneurs will tread lightly. Thus, the first effect that we expect from litigation is that foundings will be suppressed during periods of greatest legal uncertainty. The first of these periods was created by patent infringement litigation. Based on our review of the history, we would suggest that the period where the effect of patent infringement on foundings would be most severe are the months when Biograph was found guilty of infringing on Edison's patents. This is the period between 15 July 1901, when Edison won a judgment against Biograph in the U.S. Circuit Court for the Southern District of New York, and 10 March 1902, when the Circuit Court of Appeals reversed the lower court ruling and dismissed Edison's claims. We formalize this claim as Hypothesis 1A. The second period of greatest legal uncertainty is related to copyright violation litigation. Based on our review of the history, we believe that the effect of this litigation would be most severe during the months when Edison's method of copyright for films was rejected in the courts. This period actually consists of two subperiods. The first is between June 1902, when Edison filed suit alleging copyright violation and January 1903, when his claim was rejected; its effect will be captured by Hypothesis 1B. The second period of uncertainty occurred between January 1903, when Edison's copyright claim was rejected, and April 1903, when a higher court overturned the lower court ruling and upheld Edison's claim of copyright violation; its effect will be captured by Hypothesis 1C.

Hypothesis 1A: Foundings will be suppressed between July 1901 and March 1902 because of the uncertainty created by Edison's victory in patent infringement claims.

Hypothesis 1B: Foundings will be suppressed between June 1902 and January 1903 by ongoing copyright litigation.

Hypothesis 1C: Foundings will be suppressed between January 1903 and April 1903 by the legal finding that films could not be copyrighted.

We hypothesize that a second period in which foundings were suppressed was caused by the market control that various firms and cartels of firms exercised, most successfully the Motion Pictures Patent Company (MPPC). We think that the market control exercised by these firms constrained entrepreneurship by diverting resources to member firms. Within the cartel, production rates and schedules were established so that the volume of films was limited and timed carefully. Distribution to exchanges, the spot markets set up to supply the theaters that dominated during the era of shorts: the nickelodeons, was controlled as well. Block booking was imposed, forcing exchanges that were interested in getting the more popular releases to take several other films as well. The cartel did not rely solely on litigation; it had other tactics to control competition as well. Lussier (1999) tells the story of how Lubin evaded squads sent out to disrupt his production: 'During this time, quite a few tactics were used to disrupt filming, and Edison wasn't beyond sending out thugs to bring a stop to a day's shooting. One of Lubin's favorite tricks to deal with these situations was to set up a fake film crew. While they were taking the thugs on a merry chase, the real film company would be in some other location completing their day's work.' Thus, we expect that between the formation of the cartel, in January, 1909, and the filing of the anti-trust suit by the independent companies, led by Fox, on August 15, 1912, foundings will be suppressed. Further, since many of the most anti-competitive tactics of the era only began after the formation of the General Film Distribution Company in April 1910, we expect the negative effect on foundings to be exacerbated after its formation. These claims are captured by Hypotheses 2A and 2B.

Hypothesis 2A: Foundings will be reduced between January 1909 and April 1910 by the activities of the MPPC.

Hypothesis 2B: Foundings will be reduced between April 1910 and August 1912 by the activities of both the MPPC and the General Film Distribution Company.

In addition to attempting to exercise market control, the MPPC also suppressed innovation. First, they resisted the administrative innovation of organizing film distribution by using distribution organizations rather than in spot markets, delaying the national advertising and distribution of films. Second, they actively resisted the creation of stars, preferring to leave films as a commodity product whose production and distribution were under their control. Third, they tried to prevent the emergence of feature films by not allowing members to make films over one reel in length and even opposing the creation of serial short films that carried over themes or characters. Eventually, one of the many lawsuits brought against the MPPC found the cartel to be a case of illegal collusion and it was disbanded. However, this did not occur until 1917; by that time, the building of a new order in the film industry around feature length films had rendered the MPPC irrelevant as a source of market control in the film industry. Thus, we expect to see foundings enhanced by the emergence of feature length films, which greatly undercut the power of the trust. Cones (2000) summarized the situation as follows: 'By 1915, the year that the lower court decision was handed down in the government's case against the Motion Picture Patents Company, feature producers were well entrenched in the motion picture industry; and by December 1916 feature-length pictures were predominant.' Thus, we expect to see foundings enhanced between August 1912 and December 1916.

Hypothesis 3: Foundings will be enhanced between August 1912 and December 1916.

Since much early film production took place out of doors and in natural light, filmmakers found the short days and cold weather of Midwestern and Easter winters a burden. Some began wintering in warmer locales, including the Los Angeles area and in 1910; the first studios were founded there. The increasing demand for Westerns also helped the growth of Hollywood because Southern California provided numerous convenient locales for their production. D. W. Griffith made his first feature length film while wintering in the Los Angeles area during his employment by Biograph. There, was also active lobbying by the Los Angeles Chamber of Commerce to try to attract firms involved in the production of films to move their businesses there. An additional motivation to move was supplied by the increasingly violent tactics on the streets of the East as the courts began to turn against the MPPC. To avoid MPPC enforcement, monitoring, and control, many firms chose to move west, leading to the creation of Hollywood. Thus, we believe that foundings in California would actually be enhanced by actions in the legal environment during later years.

Hypothesis 4: Foundings in the Los Angeles area will be enhanced between January 1910 and August 1912.

Implications and conclusions

In their theorizing about the creation of legitimacy for new industries, Aldrich and Fiol (1994) suggested that the creation of technological standards is an important aspect of new industry development. Thus, one answer to the critics who have noted that institutional theory has portrayed firms as passive recipients is an analysis like ours. The development of standards, including technological standards, is an obvious case where human agency and the agency of actors other than people is important. The case of the early American film industry demonstrates this by examining the legal environment and how patent infringement litigation played a role in developing technological standards for the emerging film industry. From 1895 until the emergence of feature films effectively began ending the stranglehold of the MPPC in 1912, there was significant legal uncertainty about what technologies could be legally employed in the production and exhibition of films. Active agency in the form of the patent wars repeatedly impeded production and curbed the domestic supply of films during this period. For example, in describing the decision in favor of defendant Biograph against plaintiff Edison in 1907, Musser (1990: 451) indicated its more widespread implications: 'But while freeing Biograph, the opinion offered strong support for Edison's legal position in his many other suits. ... Thus, the climate for investment in American film production grew steadily worse as the nickelodeon era began.' Though we have focused on the relationship between this climate and the founding of production companies, its effects were actually much more widespread. The growth of the film industry in the US was impeded. It was only by turning to European producers that exchanges and exhibition venues were able to continue to grow. This opened the door for European producers to make steady headway in becoming the leading producers of films at the expense of American production. It was only by dint of the ingenuity of the independents that fled to Hollywood and the extreme adverse effect of World War I on European producers that American production recovered. Absent these developments, the MPPC might have sent American film production into a long-term decline.

Perhaps most ironically, neither Edison nor Biograph was able to capitalize on the narrowing of production possibilities created by their legal battle, despite the fact that demand for films was exploding as the population of nickelodeons burgeoned. We believe this illustrates an important difference between assumptions about the role of agency from an institutional perspective as opposed to its more managerialist predecessors. As the patent wars illustrate, agency in the legal environment, and we would guess institutional environments more generally, while active is not necessarily rational. The history of the patent wars is consistent with the old adage 'Be careful what you wish for, you may get it.' We believe that by sheltering themselves from competition by using litigation, both Edison's company and the Biograph cut themselves off from the market in a way that was damaging to their long-run survival. This was only exacerbated by their eventual alliance with other firms in the MPPC. As Paramount chief Adolph Zukor said of the firms in that alliance: 'They put some brains into their mechanical devices and into their sales department, but never by any chance into their films.' As feature length films produced in Hollywood began to dominate the American film industry, the wounds that the MPPC had inflicted on itself became increasingly apparent. The firms as a group suffered from the hangover of their resistance to change during the zenith of their power. They had resisted internalization of the distribution function, leaving them ill equipped to compete with companies that released films nationally with coordinated promotion and advertisement. Related to this was the refusal of the MPPC to allow members to move into feature length films. As it became clear that audiences preferred feature lengths films and these replaced shorts, the members of the MPPC found themselves lacking in the new capabilities required. The higher costs of these films and the administrative functions required to support the production of a film that could sustain a narrative over an hour and longer were sorely lacking. In addition, the link between the longer narrative, the more sustained presence of actors on the screen, and the rise of stars gave advantage to early movers into feature films. The result of these disadvantages was a mass extinction of firms that had dominated the film industry during the shorts era; the feature length film industry came to be dominated by a set of newly founded firms.

Finally, the processes relating the legal environments and population dynamics are important even beyond the effect on the population processes directly affected. In reviewing recent developments in the global pattern of patenting, the *Economist* (April 8, 2000: 78) harkened back to the days of Edison and his fellow patent warriors. The key assertion has clear relevance to entrepreneurship and the rise of new industries: 'There is a moral in the story of the earlier patent wars. Patentholders (even Edison) abused the system. As a result, the patenting system fell out of favour. Patent protection was weakened. Business suffered. History has a habit of repeating itself.' Our conclusion form this sweeping claim is simple: Understanding how the legal environment and population dynamics are linked is an important topic, affecting the climate for business at the national and even global levels. This study is an attempt to enhance our understanding of this topic; we invite others to join us in the hard work of advancing the vast empirical work that lies ahead.

7

Industry Creation, Legitimacy and Foundings: the Case of the American Film Industry, 1896-1928

Elizabeth Boyle and Stephen J. Mezias

Introduction

One of the earliest and most consistent claims of organization theory has been that organizations face a liability of newness (Stinchcombe, 1965). This claim has obvious relevance to the study of entrepreneurship and is reflected in the emerging consensus among organizational scholars of entrepreneurship that new firms and new industries face a legitimacy challenge. As Aldrich & Fiol (1994: 645) noted: '...founders of new ventures appear to be fools, for they are navigating, at best, in an institutional vacuum of indifferent munificence and, at worst, in a hostile environment impervious to individual action.' They develop the argument that successful entrepreneurship requires the development of two types of legitimacy: cognitive and sociopolitical. Lounsbury and Glynn (2000) focused on the specific strategies that members of newly founded firms might take to use narrative to overcome the legitimacy problem by linking their enterprise with the larger social context. At the interorganizational level, specifically the population level of analysis, the field of organizational ecology has had a focus on a phenomenon of central interest to entrepreneurship: the founding of new firms. A central claim of the density dependence model (Carroll & Hannan, 1995; Hannan & Carroll, 1992; Hannan & Freeman, 1989) is that founding will increase at low levels of density, which is defined as the total number of firms in a population. This is because each incremental addition to the population at low levels of density provides additional legitimacy to the population; the argument is explicitly about how legitimacy built for a whole group of firms makes the founding of similar new firms more likely. In a similar vein, entrepreneurship scholars have begun to turn their attention to the issue of how legitimacy created for new industries (Lounsbury and Glynn (2000).

Suchman, Steward, and Westfall (2000: 352) outlined the conditions when new industry creation will occur: 'Overall, then, widespread entrepreneurship would seem to depend on a relatively rare conjunction of environmental conditions: resources must be plentiful, but at the same time, models for identifying and capturing those resources must be clear.' To understand this, they argue that a framework linking institutional and ecological perspectives will be useful. We agree: Our focus in this study will be to suggest an integration of the ecological focus on the population as the unit of analysis, specifically the rate of foundings, and research on the creation of legitimacy for a new industry. We develop an approach that emphasizes the specific legitimacy problems of a new industry and direct measurement of legitimacy related to these problems. Our central premise is straightforward: Success in dealing with legitimacy problems will enhance the foundings of new firms in the emerging industry. As our context for developing this approach, we will study the early American film industry. We proceed as follows. In the next section we review briefly the general issue of the legitimacy problems facing new industries. We then review the history of the early film industry in the United States with a special focus on the legitimacy problems faced by that industry. Following this review, we discuss how the legitimacy problems revealed by our brief history can be understood in terms of cognitive and sociopolitical legitimacy (Aldrich and Fiol, 1994). We posit some explicit hypothesis about how foundings would be related to specific activities that affect the legitimacy of the new industry. Then, we turn our attention to the task of creating direct measures of legitimacy, suggesting that categorization of popular press coverage of the industry might be a suitable. Having made this argument, we review press coverage of the early film industry, suggest some ways that it might be coded to obtain measures of legitimacy, and present some preliminary data analysis. We close with a discussion of our findings and implications for future research.

Legitimacy problems in new industries

Despite the fact that the study of entrepreneurship is not new, complaints about its lack of rigor and our lack of understanding of important processes that lead to more effective entrepreneurship are common (Thornton, 1999). According to Aldrich (1999: 256), this is especially true of the emergence of new industries: 'The period during which a new industry emerges deserves more theoretical attention, because the struggle to carve out a niche for a new industry involves such strong forces that the events of that period may be forever imprinted on the organizations that persist.' We focus on the struggle to carve out a niche for a new industry in terms of social resources. In their study of the emergence of the specialty coffee niche, Rindova and Fombrun (2001: 238) argued that success was tied to transforming perceptions of the industry. The result was '...changing perceptions of coffee, ... changes in consumer lifestyle, and ... ultimately, higher levels of industry growth.' Thus, our perspective emphasizes, as did Rao (2001: 263), that the '... the creation of new organizational forms entails an institutionalization project where in the theory and values underpinning the form are justified.' The institutionalization project that we study involves the creation of perceptions of legitimacy for a new industry. We agree with Swaminathan and Wade (2001: 286) that '... entrepreneurs in emerging industries face the key task of gaining cognitive and sociopolitical legitimacy.' Thus, we discuss the legitimacy problems faced by the emerging film industry in the United States, propose direct measures of perceptions of the legitimacy of the industry, and suggest some ways that these may be linked with the founding of new firms in the industry. Thus, our next step is to discuss the legitimacy problems faced by the film industry during the first decades of its existence.

Legitimacy problems facing the emerging film industry

The choice of the film industry as an arena to study the legitimacy problem of emerging industries is not coincidental: We chose this industry specifically because films are cultural products. As Lampel, Lant, and Shamsie (2000: 264) pointed out, cultural products '... derive their value from subjective experiences that rely heavily on using symbols in order to manipulate perception and emotion.' Thus, the producers of cultural goods depend on the (extremely subjective) experience of consumers of their products to achieve success; we believe that this makes the legitimacy problem particularly acute for producers of cultural goods. Thus, we expect the legitimacy problem for new industries that produce cultural goods to be especially acute, combining both the generic problems of new industries, with the greater ease of challenging assertions of quality when the good is cultural. Consider how producers of a non-cultural product like the automobile are able to use certification processes like races to demonstrate the utility of their product (Rao, 2001). By contrast, certification processes in film, e.g., the Academy Awards, did not occur until the industry was already established. Thus, in addition to the general question of whether film represented a new business, the emerging film industry also had to deal with two other problems. The first involved claims that film was an illicit, immoral marginal business; the second involved educating the public, including members of the industry itself, about what the product was and how it could be consumed. We discuss each of these legitimacy problems in turn.

Problem 1: is film a viable business?

First, like all new industries, the film industry had to convince multiple potential stakeholders and even society at large, that it was a viable business. The difficulty of this problem is illustrated by the fact that even pioneers in developing the technology of film projection did not believe it had a commercial future. Puttnam (1997: 9) quotes Louis Lumière, responsible for the first projection of film in Paris in 1896, as dismissing the product as an 'invention without any commercial future'. Despite his future fierceness in battling for control of the industry, Edison is also quoted by Puttnam (1997: 35) as dismissing the moving image as 'a mere toy'. Initial skepticism about whether film could ever be a viable business was muted as cinema exploded as novelty during the last years of the 19th Century. However, its incredible popularity as a novelty did not immediately translate into an effective business model for earning profits from film. For one thing, the incredible popularity of the movies led people to dismiss it as a craze, which in one sense it was. Musser (1990: 298) characterized the situation as follows: 'In Cincinnati, a long-standing critic later remarked: 'When pictures first came out people said it was only a craze – that it would not last – that the public would soon tire of it and after a few years it did seem that the public was getting tired of moving pictures ... It did seem for a while that moving pictures would go out of fashion.'

In a quick progression, the public tired of what was offered to them on film. At first it was short films of everyday occurrences such as a train pulling into a station. After that it was films of famous people, political speeches or former President Theodore Roosevelt hunting. After that they tired of novelty films that provided little or no narrative. The popularity of shock films, such as those showing scantily clad women, crimes being committed, or people being shot, was fleeting. Short films developing a brief narrative proved slightly more enduring, but ultimately they too faded from public favor. It was not until feature length films using established stars to present a sustained narrative came along that the sustained drawing power of film came to be accepted, and this did not occur until around 1916. At the same time that the public was waxing and waning over these early forms of filmed entertainment, the industry was experiencing other problems as well. Musser (1990: 297) described the situation as the industry tried to resolve technological and legal issues even as the novelty of projected images wore off and competition intensified: 'The American motion-picture industry experienced severe difficulties in the early 1900's on account of numerous factors: problems with technological standardization, patent and copyright problems, audience boredom with predictable subject matter, stagnant demand, and cutthroat competition.' None of these developments engendered much respect for the nascent film industry. Puttnam (1997: 29) provided a quote from one early industry commentator that illustrates the level of disdain heaped on early producers of film: 'All you needed was fifty dollars, a broad, and a camera.'

By 1907, however, the spectacular growth of the film industry could no longer be ignored; interestingly, however, it was exhibition rather than production that attracted much of the positive attention. For example, a *Harper's Weekly* headline from 1907, reported by Bowser (1990: 1) described nickelodeons as 'nickel madness,' reporting on the amazing spread of this new 'amusement enterprise' and how it was making a 'fortune' for exhibitors. Only the French company Pathe had developed the aspects of the business model for film production that eventually came to dominate. Musser (1990: 488) summarizes the viable business model that they had developed: '... by mid 1906 the French company had already introduced such key aspects of the studio system such as a stock company of actors and multiple production units, both of which did not become common in the United States for at least another two years.' As American producers did develop more consistent and viable business models, however, the perception of viability first accorded exhibitors became more widespread. Perceptions of film as an industry with commercial viability also became more widespread. In January 1909, *The New York Times* described a nationwide wave of moving pictures that had swept over the country. Rather than describe film as a craze, however, the article focused on investment in the industry, which was put at $40 million, and employment in the industry, which was pegged at 100000.

Nonetheless, there were still concerns about the viability of the film business. Indeed, at this time, the exhibitors, who had been leaders in creating the perception of viability, now came to represent the industry's problems as nickelodeons were attacked as unsafe and unsavory. For example, as recorded by Brown (1984: 4), *The New York Times* reported on March 8, 1908 that the mayor of New York City had revoked all of the licenses of 'picture shows,' pending an 'inquiry into the public's safety.' Fires in theaters were sensationalized, calling into question both the technology of projection and the safety of theaters. Equally lurid were reports of public violence associated with films that depicted violence or aggravated racial tensions and these reports called for the shut down of the business permanently, not just while safety inspections were conducted. In fact, nickelodeons did not survive this challenge to their viability, as the exhibition function of the industry eventually moved to the theater palace as the primary venue (Mezias and Kuperman, 2001).

The viability of film as a business also faced a challenge on another front during this time: its perception among performers. The recent organization of vaudeville performers, initially only the men, into unions strengthened them as a constituency group. Of particular importance was the White Rats union that had arisen in 1900 on the East Coast to counter the monopoly position of the Vaudeville Managers Association and the United Booking Office (Gilbert, 1940). The industry had been organized in a trust, the Motion Pictures Patents Company, which insisted on keeping actors anonymous. Performers responded by not taking the new industry seriously, a situation well summarized by Brown (1995: 7): 'It was not clear what role the performers on the screen would play in the new industry. In film, as late as 1909, they were anonymous. Stage actors called the movies "the flickers". They did not take them seriously, working in them in the summer to make ends meet when Broadway's boards got a rest.' DeCordova (2001) described how the film industry answered this challenge with the creation of the Hollywood star system. Once again, this viability challenge to a business model premised on the actor as anonymous caused upheaval in the industry before it was resolved. The firms in the trust that dominated the industry in 1910 resisted the star system, which was developed by West Coast upstarts, damaging their long run viability.

A final challenge to the viability of emerging industry is one indicator that it had progressed beyond the stage where the public did not believe it was viable: motion picture investment schemes. In 1915, Harry Aitken established Triangle pictures with financing obtained by selling shares of stock. This was the first time that a film company went public (Mendrala, 2002). Hucksters capitalized on the burgeoning interest in film as an investment opportunity, marketing all kinds of get rich schemes involving investment in motion pictures. Bowzer

(1990) related a 1915 warning in *Motion Picture World* that investors should stay away from investment schemes in motion pictures. However, despite this warning and the historical unpredictability of investments in the emerging industry, the moving picture business was now on a path of growth that removed all doubt of its long-term viability. *The New York Times*, on March 2, 1916, reported that the motion picture industry was 'fifth in importance among the industries of this country.' The viability of motion pictures as an industry ceased to be a contested perception around this time.

Problem 2: Are motion pictures an unsavory, marginal business?

Film started off as quite an unsavory business; linked with carnivals and other commercial amusements, it clearly was not a business that refined people supported. Musser (1990: 78) described how this was true from the earliest days: 'Sex and violence figured prominently in American motion pictures from the outset. In fact, such subjects were consistent with the individualized, peephole nature of the viewing experience: they showed amusements that often offended polite and/or religious Americans.' The move away from peepholes and toward projection did little to enhance the image of cinema. Describing the situation in 1905, Puttnam (1997: 36) wrote: '... the movies were neither respectable commerce nor respectable culture. They were run by what one observer called a variegated collection of former carnival men, ex-saloon keepers, medicine men, concessionaires of circus sideshows, photographers and peddlers. They were a diversion for the poor and rootless.' Communities as diverse as Asbury Park, NJ and San Francisco engaged in censorship actions against films even before they were first projected (Musser, 1990: 78). One saving grace, however, was that as motion pictures proliferated, they were used by all kinds of groups, including church groups and people presenting so-called refined entertainments. Thus, film becoming increasingly widespread, while not stopping legitimacy challenges to the nature of the business, tended to move activity towards cleaning up the industry rather than shutting it down. This seems to be how legitimacy challenges linking the content of films with their effect on culture operate even today.

Thus, Edison is quoted in *Moving Picture World* of 21 December 1907 as calling for films of good moral tone. Apparently, he had forgotten that his 1896 kintetoscope film, *The Kiss*, with its close-up shots of lips meeting, had elicited the first calls for censorship (Brown, 1995). May (1980) pointed out that the nickelodeons were seen as dens of iniquity where young people, particularly women, were led astray. Bowser

(1990: 37) quoted a colorful observation of the mood of some of the public: '... that for three or four years prior to December last the moving picture business occupied in public esteem a position so offensive, so contemptible, and in many respects so degrading, that respectable people hesitated to have their names associated with it.' A series of sensationalized fires at nickelodeons, coverage of which was fanned by Edison's sponsorship of film stock that was less flammable than the nitrous-based stock that was then common, also damaged the perception of films and especially the nickelodeons where most people viewed them. Negative perception reached a crescendo with the decision by the Mayor of New York to close all nickelodeons in the city on Christmas Eve, 1908. Although the owners were able to obtain a court order getting them reopened very quickly, the industry could no longer ignore the depth of feeling against it in some quarters.

As with church exhibition and educational shows in the previous era, there was once again a movement to use film for higher purposes, the so-called uplift movement. Educational films, story films based on classic as opposed to vulgar, popular literature, and films with religious themes set a higher moral tone for film content. Exhibitors were admonished as well to clean up their act. *Motion Picture World* in an October 1909 claimed '... the moving picture is just at that stage of its career when the support of the better classes is gradually being extended to it. Their support will come surely enough in due time if repellent influences are sternly suppressed.' When a Board of Censorship was organized in New York City in March 1909, the industry decided it need to regulate itself in order to avoid legally imposed censorship (Bowser, 1990: 48–49). At the same time, the crowd attracted by a better class of story films as well as the increasing length of the most popular story films created a need for more comfortable, better constructed venues for film exhibition, and the movie palace was born (Mezias and Kuperman, 2001).

Self-regulation and the move to more dignified theaters seem to have improved the public perception of the film industry. There were periodic fulminations about the content of particular films; for example, there was an energetic campaign against film violence. For the most part, however, the threat of legal censorship receded. Nonetheless, as there are today, there were still occasional bouts of criticism of the effects of film on larger culture. For example, when the cartel set up by Edison established its own censorship standards board, it was highly critical of the lax moral tone in European productions. There was lingering concern that film did not represent the best kind of people, and scandals involving movie stars generated intense coverage. At the same time, film came more and more to be seen as a legitimate medium of cultural expression that could be used to serve useful social purposes. This trend was accelerated by events following the entry of the United States into World War I. Puttnam (1997: 74) quoted the following depiction of film by President Woodrow Wilson, who in 1917 described film as '...the very highest medium for the dissemination of public intelligence.' As the nation mobilized for war, Puttnam (1997) provided the following description: 'The movie business was declared "an essential industry" in August 1918, enabling it to continue to operate despite a shortage of materials. It had achieved official recognition at the very highest level.'

Problem 3: What is this product, and how do I consume it?

The earliest approaches to movies as a product took as a starting point that consumers were receivers and that the purpose of film was to convey information. Often, as with early newsreels depicting the Spanish-American war that coordinated closely with newspaper coverage of the same events (Castonguay, 1999), film presented the familiar. Audience knowledge of the subject was assumed and essential to the success of the presentation. A second approach was for the producer of the film to rely on the exhibitor to provide knowledge essential to the successful consumption of the film. Often, this included the addition of live narration, music, sound effects, and spoken dialog from actors hidden out of sight. The third approach, based exclusively on the representational capability of known film techniques at the onset of the industry, did not rely on external knowledge or exhibitor embellishment. For this reason, films using this approach relied on tricks, simple sequential narrative, or the frequent imposition of written cues to guide the audience (Musser, 1990). Brown (1995: 3) summarized the approach as follows: 'Early movies were mostly slices of life. Nonfiction films constituted more than half of the titles produced until about 1908. The novelty of the new medium was itself enough to carry the day. When people could be amazed and thrilled by a shot of an approaching train or a passing parade, a story did not seem that necessary.' While this approach clearly avoided the legitimacy problem of needing to explain to the consumer what was happening on the screen, it created a perception of film as a novelty and did not sustain audience interest. This was reflected in how films were distributed at the time, with little attempt to shape the presentation or differentiate among products. Bowser (1990: 53) described how films were marketed as a commodity product, '... handed out over the counter like so many feet of sausage.'

The challenge faced by films as audiences tired of novelty subjects is summarized by Jacobs (1968). He recounted the famous description of the movies at this time by film pioneer William DeMille as 'galloping tintypes' that had no potential to develop into anything that could be described as art. The solution was the story film, which presented significant financial and technical problems to producers. Although the transition to story films, particularly crime and chase films, boosted the popularity of films, narrative techniques remained extremely circumscribed during the early years (Musser, 1990). Attempts to move beyond these extremely circumscribed narratives created problems of audience understanding. Bowser (1990: 53–54) described the problem: 'The most common criticism of specific films concerned the need for clarity. The *Moving Picture World* reviewer noted, 'The Devil, Dr. Jekyll and Mr. Hyde, etc., are clever plays but they have been presented in motion pictures in a way that the public do not understand them.' Change, spearheaded by Biograph was, however, in the offing. Musser (1990: 375) described the transition: 'By means of complex spatial and temporal constructions, camera movement, and interpolated close-ups, these Biograph films yielded accomplished examples of the representational system established in the pre-nickelodeon era.' Catalogs communicated the content of these increasingly sophisticated films, building brand image for consumers. Bowser (1990) relates the story of two ladies in front of a Herald Square theater trying to ascertain the brand of a film prior to deciding whether to see it. In addition to becoming aware of the film brands, consumers also responded to these new film techniques with curiosity and were hungry for explanations of the techniques that they saw on the screen.

At the same time, the move away from strictly representational presentation created a need to help the audience shape their expectations prior to entering the theater. The solution that developed to this problem was the creation of genres (Mezias and Mezias, 2000). Once again, Bowser (1990: 167) summarized the role of genres well: 'Genre may be considered as standardization of the film product. The audience has some idea what to expect from a comedy or a Western, just as consumers know what to expect when they order a specific kind of sausage.' The popularity of films in the Western genre at this time illustrates the interplay of audience expectations and the expanded possibilities of new film techniques. The immense popularity of this genre can be linked with the rediscovery by highly urbanized audiences of wide open spaces and days of freedom and adventure that urbanization. The fact that the majority of the audience was immigrants or city dwellers that had never experienced the life that was being 'recreated' did little to dampen enthusiasm for what was created on the screen. From this point, it was no longer really possible for the film industry to be challenged on what the product could mean to consumers: The magic of the movies had been born. The super spectacle motion pictures produced by the Italians reinforced the perception that the screen offered a form of entertainment that was distinctive and allowed the recreation of experience of historical and distant events not possible in any other medium. Later developments such as the star system (DeCordova, 2001) and creation of national campaigns for the launch of specific films deepened popular understanding of the alternative reality that could be created in the darkened theater. The idea that film offered consumers a unique and profound experience was firmly established in the public mind.

Legitimacy and foundings in new industries

The use of direct measures of legitimacy

One of the central claims of organizational ecology is that increases in density when population levels are low will enhance foundings (Carroll and Hannan, 2000). This has been linked explicitly with legitimacy, which is posited to increase with each additional founding of a firm of the new type. This argument is clearly relevant to entrepreneurship research, suggesting the claim that new industries must build legitimacy, which will enhance foundings. The use of density as a measure of this process has been called into question. Zucker (1989) was among the first researchers to take issue with the assumption that increasing density was the result of increased cognitive legitimacy. She argued that density may be a construct reflecting the effects of many other factors and suggested caution in interpreting its effect as legitimacy. Petersen and Koput (1991) demonstrated that unobserved heterogeneity might also be leading to what the density dependence model labels legitimacy. Delacroix & Rao (1994), Baum & Powell (1995) and Baum (1994), among others, have continued to raise concerns with the equivalence between density and legitimacy, suggesting that this measurement of legitimacy is too narrow and does not reflect the sociopolitical nature of legitimacy.

We believe that understanding the role of legitimacy in the emergence of new industries is a central issue for entrepreneurship research.

We also believe that improving how legitimacy is measured is an important step in our progress toward grappling with this issue. The work that has begun to emerge on aspects of this suggests some important issues for future research (Aldrich, 1999; Aldrich & Wiedenmayer, 1993; Barron, 1998; Hybels, 1994; McLaughlin & Khawaja, 2000). Barron found that credit unions acted in a social-movement-like manner to enhance their moral legitimacy, implying that the legitimation benefits the industry as a whole not just specific firms. McLaughlin & Khawaja (2000) reported a correlation between the founding rate of national environmental organizations and the number of environmental books published each year, suggesting that widely available social information may be critical to the legitimation process leading to the founding of firms. This is precisely what Hybels (2000) found: Industry level legitimacy, measured by the appearance of certain kinds of articles in the business press, was correlated with increased foundings in the emerging biotech industry. He also found, consistent with Petersen and Koput (1991), that the direct measurement of legitimacy changed the effect of density.

In attempting to move forward the measure of legitimacy, we begin with the definition crafted by Suchman (1995): 'Legitimacy is a generalized perception or assumption that the actions of an entity are desirable, proper, or appropriate within some socially constructed system of norms, beliefs, and definitions.' Our review of the history of the early film industry suggests that the main issues for the emerging film industry concerned whether its business practices were proper, whether the experience of viewing a film was desirable, and whether the its presentation and content were appropriate. These judgments were made relative to socially constructed categories: Were the finances of firms in the new industry consistent with prevailing definitions of a viable business? Was the experience of cinema consistent with beliefs about what constituted a desirable experience? Was film consistent with norms about appropriate cultural presentation? In attempting to measure legitimacy in a manner consistent with providing an answer to these questions, we follow Aldrich (1999: 230), who in his review of the role of legitimacy in the emergence of new industries, distinguished between two types, cognitive and sociopolitical. Thus, we use cognitive legitimacy to refer '...to the acceptance of a new kind of venture as a taken for granted feature of the environment.' We use sociopolitical legitimacy to refer to '... the acceptance by key stakeholders, the general public, key opinion leaders, and government officials of a new venture as appropriate and right.' We propose measures of cognitive and sociopolitical legitimacy using popular press coverage of the emerging film industry. Based on our review of the legitimacy problems faced by the early films industry, we will interpret this coverage as either enhancing or undermining the legitimacy of the industry.

Measures

We analyzed headlines and sub-headlines appearing in The New York Times between 1896 and 1928. We believe this is an appropriate choice for several reasons. First, for most of the period of our study, New York was the center of the film industry, having the most theaters in the country and serving as headquarters location for the Motion Pictures Patents Company. Second, it was by far the largest city in the U.S. in this period with a population of approximately 3.5 million and the clear cultural center of the country. The leading newspaper of the city, especially in terms of cultural developments, was *The New York Times*, which had a circulation of approximately 2.7 million (Editor & Publisher, 1902–1928). We used the *New York Times Encyclopedia of Film* (Gene Brown, 1984), which is an exhaustive compilation of all articles related to the film industry in these years. To interpret the effect of each article on legitimacy, we analyzed the content of headlines and sub-headlines, using the methods we describe below.

The first task we did was to categorize the headlines of articles as referring to either cognitive legitimacy or to sociopolitical legitimacy. A headline was coded as relating to cognitive legitimacy when it concerned the spread of knowledge about the industry and/or the spread of knowledge about how to conduct business successfully in the industry. For example, the establishment of a dominant technological design is central to the achievement of cognitive legitimacy for an industry (Aldrich & Fiol, 1994) as is the acceptance of common business practices. Other indicators of cognitive legitimacy include the establishment of trade associations and the development of educational programs that facilitate the diffusion of knowledge about the industry. Table 7.1 lists the criteria we used to code headlines as relating to cognitive legitimacy.

We divided cognitive legitimacy into nine categories: Financial Status; Bankruptcy; Investment Size; International Interest in Films; Patent Litigation; Copyright Litigation; Explanation of Film Process; and Movement of Professionals From Other Fields Into Film. Table 7.1 summarizes the criteria we used to determine whether a headline belonged in each category. For example, we coded an article as belonging in the Financial Status category if the headline mentioned box

Table 7.1   The coding of cognitive legitimacy and sample headlines

Category	Criterion	Sample headline/sub-headline
Financial Status	Mentions box office receipts, number of individuals attending; dollar losses and costs (e.g. salaries, production costs)	'Finance and Pictures – Expert Tells of Expansion of Film Industry Along Sound Business Lines'; '$50 000 000 Is Lost In Wildcat Films – Several in Bankruptcy'; 'Seek to Check Slump in Movie Patronage'
International Interest in Films	Mentions any aspect of the film industry involving a non U.S. country	e.g. 'Movies in Japan'
Bankruptcy	Mentions bankruptcy or firm failure	'$50 000 000 Is Lost In Wildcat Films – Several in Bankruptcy'
Investment Size	Mentions dollar amount of investment	'Shuberts Enter Field of Movies – Form with the World Film a $2 000 000 Corporation to Make Photo Plays'
Explanation of Film Technology	Mentions filmmaking and exhibiting technology	'Tricks of Films Explained and Method of Making Told by Those On the Inside'
Patent Litigation	Mentions patents	'Edison Controls Pictures – Court Decision Gives Him an Injunction Against Remaining Independents'
Copyright Litigation	Mentions copyrights	'Film Rights, and What They Are Worth'
Explanation of Film Process	Mentions the work of film making or sensational event related to film making (e.g. directing, acting , script writing, etc.)	'Tricks of Films Explained and Method of Making Told By Those on the Inside'; 'Amazing Developments in The Moving Picture Field'
Movement of Professionals from Other Fields	Mentions the movement of actors, directors, producers, writers, cameramen and the like to the film industry	'Daniel Frohman Gets Big Stars To Act For Movies – Famous Manager Expects to Work a Revolution in the Moving Picture Field'

office receipts, industry expansion, profits, and/or the dollar amount of a loss.

A headline was coded as relating to sociopolitical legitimacy when it referred to the industries relationships with key stakeholders – the general public, key opinion leaders, bankers, government officials and the media. An industry attains sociopolitical legitimacy when it is accepted as appropriate and right, given the existing norms and laws (Aldrich & Fiol, 1994). A key factor in attaining sociopolitical legitimacy is an industries ability to conform to the expectations of stakeholders. This will be indicated as the degree of organizational stakeholder trust in the industry, which we observed in several different kinds of headlines. We divided these sociopolitical legitimacy headlines into thirteen categories: Prominent Person; Competition with Theatres; Venue Safety; Financing Sources; Insurance; Industry Organization; Anti-trust; Government Use of Film; Scandal; Federal Government Activities; State and Local Government Activities; Novelty vs. Narrative (Quality); and Comparison to Theatre. Table 7.2 summarizes the criteria we used to determine whether a headline belonged in each category. For example, we coded an article as belonging in the Financing Sources category when the article mentions financing from private funds (e.g. the entrepreneurs own assets), or banking or Wall Street.

Having established the two categories of legitimacy and determined rules for allocating articles to the two categories, we next had to determine whether a particular discussion of legitimacy enhanced or undermined the legitimacy of the industry. To do this, we related the various kinds of headlines to the legitimacy problems of the emerging film industry. For example, articles linking prominent persons with the film industry are interpreted as enhancing the legitimacy of the industry by countering the perception that film is a marginal business. Similarly, articles that report on the growing size of the business, either financing or total employment, are interpreted as enhancing the legitimacy of the industry by countering the perception that film is not a viable business. Tables 7.3 and 7.4 summarize our criteria for assessing whether a headline indicated an event that enhanced or undermined the industry's cognitive or sociopolitical legitimacy. For example, we coded an article as reporting an event that enhanced the industry's cognitive legitimacy when the headline described increased profits and/or revenue. Improvements in the industries financial status is interpreted as indicating that successful business practices are spreading throughout the industry. A headline reporting industry contraction or losses, on the other hand, would be coded as indicating the occurrence of an event

Table 7.2   The coding of sociopolitical legitimacy and sample headlines

Category	Criterion	Sample headline/sub-headline
Prominent Person	Mentions an individual by name	'Hays Cure for Movie Evils – Recommends That Public Stay Away from Objectionable Pictures – Coming Reforms'
Competition with Theatres	Mentions effect of movie industry on the theatre industry	'Moving Pictures Sound Melodrama's Knell'
Venue Safety	Mentions fire or violence taking place during exhibition	'25 Die, 50 Hurt, in Theatre Rush'
Financing Sources	Mentions privately sourced financing or banking/Wall Street financing	'Bankers are Associates'; 'Finance and Pictures – Experts Tells of Expansion of Film Industry Along Lines of Sound Business'
Insurance	Mentions the word insurance	'Snow Before Nov. 20 Insured for $25 000 – Eighteen Companies Take Unique Griffith Risk on Filming of "The Two Orphans"'
Industry Organization	Mentions trade associations, studio formation, employee unionization, trust formation, mergers and acquisitions, firm foundings	'A. H. Woods Enters Movies – $1 000 000 Corporation Formed to Film His Plays for Tours'; 'Nations Meet Over Films – International Exhibit and Conference Opens in London'

Anti-trust	Mentions anti-trust and/or unfair business practices	'Monopoly Output and Distribution of American Pictures is Charged'
Government Use of Film	Mentions government use of film; sponsoring film production	'Film Interest Mobilized. Representatives in Each State to Promote Wartime Activities'
Scandal	Mentions the word scandal	'Arbuckle Film Withdrawn. Action Is Taken in Los Angeles Following Murder Charge'
Federal Government Activities	Mentions regulations, laws, police action, censorship	'Movie Trade is Essential – Crowder Decides Actors and Musicians are Employed Usefully'; 'To Guard American Films – State Department Agents Abroad to Aid in Barring Pirated Films'
State and Local Government Activities	Mentions regulations, laws, police action, censorship	'Movie Censorship Law Signed By Miller'
Novelty vs. Narrative (Quality)	Mentions the use of material previously portrayed on the 'legitimate stage'	'The Photoplay – It has Achieved a Distinct Technique and Appeal to the Public'
Comparison to Theatre	Compares quality of film and theatre product on any relevant dimension including--acting, writing, directing, display (e.g. referring to movies as 'the flickers')	'Says Stage Folk are Scared Off Screen'; Erlanger-Shubert From Movie Chain – Convert One Legitimate Theatre in Every City and Town for Showing of Feature Films'

Table 7.3   Coding of the effect of headlines on cognitive legitimacy

Category	Question Addressed	Enhances Legitimacy	Undermines Legitimacy
Financial Status	Viable?	Increased revenue/profits and/or industry expansion indicates that successful business practices have been developed and that these practices are shared by many firms in the industry	Losses and/or industry contraction indicates that successful business practices have not yet been identified or have not yet spread to most firms
International Interest in Films	Product Understanding?	Increased and/or broadening interest indicates that knowledge and understanding of film industry practices has increased to include citizens of countries outside the U.S.	Decreased interest that knowledge and understanding of how to consume film product
Bankruptcy	Viable?	Decreases in firm failures indicates that the successful business practices have diffused and that the industry may be stabilizing	Increases in firm failures indicates that successful business practices have not yet diffused
Investment Size	Viable?	Larger investments indicate that founders and stakeholders believe in the viability of the industry	Small investment size indicates that firms are operating on 'shoe-string' budgets that will increase firm mortality

Explanation of Film Technology	Product Understanding?	Diffusion of knowledge concerning how films are made increases the number of people aware of industry business practices thereby aiding in the establishment of dominant technological and business designs and increasing the industries access to important resources such as talented actors and financing	Lack of knowledge and general awareness of how the product is made and consumed delays the adoption of dominant technological and business designs and makes it more difficult for firms to access important resources
Patent Litigation	Viable?		All litigation is viewed as destabilizing the industry and delaying the acceptance of a dominant design
Copyright Litigation	Viable?		All litigation is viewed as destabilizing the industry and delaying the acceptance of a dominant design
Explanation of Film Process	Product Understanding?	Diffusion of knowledge concerning how films are made increases the number of people aware of industry business practices thereby 1) aiding in the establishment of dominant technological and business designs; and 2) increasing the industries access to important resources such as talented actors and financing	Articles decrying the amount of money and resources invested in film making indicate that the industry has not yet attained a 'taken for granted' status amongst all key stakeholders
Movement of Professionals from Other Fields	Viable?	Actors, producers, directors, etc. entering the industry lend their reputation to the final product and their cross-over from other entertainment vehicles indicates that a broad diffusion of film knowledge has occurred	When actors, producers, directors, etc. actively discredit film (e.g. referring to them as 'the flickers') and/or will not appear in movies this indicates a lack of knowledge and acceptance of industry business practices

Table 7.4 Coding of the effect of headlines on sociopolitical legitimacy

Category	Question Addressed	Enhances Legitimacy	Undermines Legitimacy
Prominent Person	Marginal?	Association of prominent persons with the industry enhances the reputation of the industry	Association of prominent persons with the industry enhances the reputation of the industry
Competition with Theatres	Marginal?	Reports that moving pictures are a credible threat to 'legitimate' theater enhances the industries stature	Reports that moving pictures will never replace the legitimate stage undermines the industries reputation
Venue Safety	Marginal?	Safer viewing conditions enhance public trust	Unsafe viewing conditions erodes public trust
Financing Sources	Viable?	Financing from established/previously legitimated firms indicates that those stakeholders have trust that their investment will be rewarded with an adequate return and that reliable business practices have been developed	Funding from non-traditional sources undermines the industries reputation
Insurance	Viable?	Insuring a film indicates that the risks have become more predictable and measurable which in turn indicates the establishment of reliable business practices	Unavailability of insurance or very high premiums indicates that reliable business practices have not been established and/or diffused
Industry Organization	Viable?	Adoption of practices used by legitimate businesses, those that are already 'taken for granted' indicates attempts by the members of the industry to attain legitimacy through mimetic isomorphism	Business practices that differ from those of established firms increases the uncertainty around both process and outcomes, that makes it more difficult for stakeholders to trust the entrepreneurs

Anti-trust	Viable?		All litigation is viewed as destabilizing the industry and delaying the acceptance of the industry as moral and right
Government Use of Film	Marginal?	Utilization of film by key stakeholders increases the industries reputation and indicates that the medium has achieved cultural legitimacy	When government officials eschew the use of the medium the industries reputation is undermined
Scandal	Marginal?		Reports of illegal acts and/or professional misconduct by key industry figures erodes the industries claims that their product is morally consistent with the established social order
Federal Government Activities	Marginal?	Activities such as trade protection endorses the industry and supports its right to exist and utilize important societal resources	Activities denying motion pictures advantages afforded other industries indicates a lack of trust and a low valuation of moving pictures
State and Local Government Activities	Marginal?	Activities such as permitting theaters to operate on Sunday endorses the industry and supports its claims to be morally consistent with the established social order	Activities denying motion pictures advantages afforded other industries indicates a lack of trust and a low valuation of moving pictures
Novelty vs. Narrative (Quality)	Marginal?	Movement to narrative based films was associated with greater attendance among the middle and upper classes indicating that the repugnant nature of films had abated.	Characterizing motion pictures as a novelty or fad undermines the industries reliability as a source of profitable investment
Comparison to Theatre	Marginal?	Favorable comparisons to established theater enhances the reputation of the industry	Unfavorable comparisons to established theater undermines the reputation of the industry

that undermined the film industry's cognitive legitimacy. When firms lose money and/or movie attendance decreases it is an indication that successful business practices have not been identified or that those practices have not been accepted amongst all industry participants. Patent infringement litigation is another example of a subject interpreted as undermining the legitimacy of the industry by feeding into the perception that film is not a viable business. Tables 7.3 and 7.4 report on how we interpreted the content of the cognitive and sociopolitical legitimacy articles, respectively.

What pattern should we expect to observe in the data on legitimacy? The first answer we would give to this question is based on the fact that the industry rapidly achieved legitimacy; thus, we would expect that articles that enhance legitimacy to outnumber those that undermine legitimacy for both types of legitimacy, especially in later years of the data:

Hypothesis 1: The success of the film industry will be reflected by a greater number of articles that enhance legitimacy as opposed to undermine legitimacy.

Second, our analysis of events showed that film achieved status as an important industry fairly quickly. At this point, statements that undermine the cognitive legitimacy of the industry themselves cease to be legitimate:

Hypothesis 2: Articles that undermine the cognitive legitimacy of the film industry will be infrequent relative to other kinds of articles.

Third, since film is a cultural industry (Lampel, Lant, and Shamsie, 2000; Hirsch, 2000), we expect the sociopolitical problems to be more ongoing. Even after gaining the status of being taken-for-granted, the unique role of movies and their effect on culture will lead to film being subjected to questioning of its effect on culture. We see this even today, with violence and sex in Hollywood being a staple of political and cultural discourse. As a result, we expect that the quantity of sociopolitical discourse will remain high with articles that undermine the sociopolitical legitimacy of the industry continuing even after it has achieved status as a major industry. These ideas are summarized in the following hypotheses:

Hypothesis 3a: The quantity of headlines addressing sociopolitical legitimacy will be greater than the quantity addressing cognitive legitimacy.

Hypothesis 3b: The ratio of headlines undermining as opposed to enhancing sociopolitical legitimacy will be greater than the same ratio for cognitive legitimacy.

In essence then, the exploratory analyses presented here test three ideas about legitimacy in the early film industry. The first is the industry success hypothesis; to test it we investigate whether the emergence of film and Hollywood is reflected in a concomitant shift in tone. We expect a surplus of articles that enhance legitimacy as opposed to articles that undermine it. The second hypothesis is the taken-for-grantedness hypothesis. While we have predicted a general shift away from articles that undermine legitimacy as a result of the success of the industry, we also predict that the shift away from articles that undermine legitimacy should be especially marked for cognitive legitimacy. The two final hypotheses are meant to capture the idea that film will be at the center of a culture war, which we would argue continues even to today. Since discourse about sociopolitical legitimacy is the battleground for these cultural wars, we expect that the quantity of articles addressing that form of legitimacy will be higher than the quantity addressing cognitive legitimacy. In addition, because the cultural effect of the industry can remain contested even after its taken-for-granted status has been accepted, we expect the ratio of articles that undermine as opposed to enhance the legitimacy to be greater for sociopolitical discourse as opposed to cognitive discourse.

Data analysis

To do a preliminary exploration of these hypotheses about legitimacy, we selected a random sample of 10% of the 1047 articles that appeared in the *The New York Times* between 1896 and 1928. We did this by assigning sequence numbers to the articles and then choosing those that matched a list of 105 random numbers generated in Excel. We coded headlines and sub-headlines of these articles using the methods described above. Not surprisingly, articles did not fall exclusively into categories; some articles discussed multiple aspects of legitimacy, sometimes including both cognitive and sociopolitical aspects of the construct. The maximum number of categories coded from a single article headline was 5, the minimum was 1; the mean was 1.7. Table 7.5 summarizes the results of the coding of these articles. 54 of the headlines were coded as referring to cognitive legitimacy; of these, 48 were coded as enhancing the cognitive legitimacy of the industry, while only 6 were coded as undermining the cognitive legitimacy of the industry. 74

of the headlines were coded as referring to sociopolitical legitimacy; of these, 50 were coded as enhancing the sociopolitical legitimacy of the industry, while 24 were coded as undermining it. We also plot the cumulative distribution of the data in Figure 7.1.

Table 7.5   Distribution of *New York Times* articles

	Cognitive	Sociopolitical
Enhances	48	50
Undermines	6	24

It is obvious from inspection that Hypothesis 1, the industry success hypothesis, is supported. The proportion of legitimacy enhancing articles is 76.6%, over three quarters, while the proportion of legitimacy undermining articles is 23.4%, less than one quarter. The null hypothesis that the proportions are equal is rejected in favor of the alternative hypothesis that the proportion of enhancing articles is greater, $p < 0.001$, regardless of whether we use parametric or non-parametric tests. It is also obvious from inspection that Hypothesis 2, the taken-for-grantedness hypothesis, is supported: Only 4.7% of the articles were coded as undermining the cognitive legitimacy of the film industry. Once again, the null hypothesis that this proportion is equal to the others can be rejected against the alternative hypothesis that it is lower, $p < 0.01$, for all four comparisons. In addition, our data support Hypotheses 3, the culture wars hypothesis, which suggested that sociopolitical discourse would be more contested than cognitive discourse. Hypothesis 3a suggested that sociopolitical discourse will be more frequent and is supported. The null hypothesis that the proportion of headlines coded as addressing cognitive legitimacy, 42.2%, is equal to the proportion of headlines coded as addressing sociopolitical legitimacy, 57.8%, is rejected in favor the null hypothesis that the latter proportion is larger, $p < 0.01$. Once again, this is true regardless of whether parametric or non-parametric tests are used. The final hypothesis, 3b, suggested that the ratio of legitimacy undermining headlines will be greater for sociopolitical legitimacy than for cognitive legitimacy. The null hypothesis that the undermining proportion for sociopolitical, 24 of 74 or 32.4%, is equal to the undermining proportion for cognitive, 6 of 54 or 11.1%, is rejected in favor of the alternative hypothesis that the former proportion is larger, $p < 0.01$.

Discussion and conclusions

The statistical evidence in support of our hypotheses is borne out by visual inspection of the time pattern of the cumulative distribution of the coding of headlines presented in Figure 7.1. The extent to which our measures of legitimacy bear out the success of the industry is clearly shown. Headlines coded as legitimacy enhancing pull ahead of those coded as undermining legitimacy almost from the beginning. This lead also seems set to increase over time, with the increase in undermining articles flattening in later years even as the increase in enhancing headlines continues to increase. With regard to Hypothesis 2, claiming taken-for-grantedness, the figure suggests a more nuanced interpretation than the statistical results. Specifically, it is clear that the decrease in the relative proportion of headlines coded as addressing cognitive legitimacy is driven almost entirely by a decline in headlines coded as undermining cognitive legitimacy. Headlines coded as enhancing cognitive legitimacy do not decline. Two explanations are possible. The first is related to the fact that we are still looking at a relatively early portion of the history of the film industry. There was still a need to build public understanding of the industry, especially in terms of explaining changes that occur in the normal course of maturing. The second is related to the nature of cultural industries, which present considerable difficulties of market understanding as well as an ongoing need to be fresh and new (Lampel, et al., 2000; Mezias and Mezias, 2000). In this instance, the continuing attention to enhancing cognitive legitimacy is driven by events like the emergence of feature films, the star system, Hollywood, the Academy Awards, and the introduction of sound technology. A more complete coding of article content, which is beyond the scope of this chapter, might be sufficient to sort out these different possible explanations.

Ultimately, we believe one the most important goals of the analysis of legitimacy in the early American feature film industry must be to link changes with the legitimacy of the industry with foundings of firms in that industry. This is related to our fundamental belief that the understanding of the emergence of new industries, which many students of entrepreneurship now agree is a key issue for research, will be enhanced by better articulation of how legitimacy and the emergence of new industries are related. Towards that end, we suggest the following propositions, based on the results of our preliminary exploration of legitimacy, as a starting point for future research. These propositions link measures of legitimacy with foundings in the early film industry.

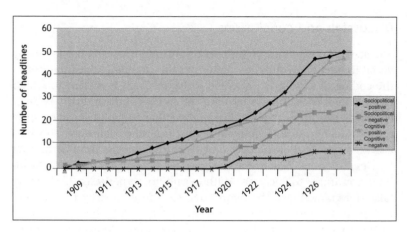

Figure 7.1   Cumulative headline count

Based on our results, we expect separate effects for cognitive and sociopolitical legitimacy. Also based on our results, we expect articles that undermine legitimacy to have a separate effect from articles that enhance legitimacy. These distinctions result in four propositions:

Proposition 1: The appearance of articles that enhance cognitive legitimacy will have a positive effect on foundings.

Proposition 2: The appearance of articles that undermine cognitive legitimacy will have a negative effect on foundings.

Proposition 3: The appearance of articles that enhance sociopolitical legitimacy will have a positive effect on foundings.

Proposition 4: The appearance of articles that undermine sociopolitical legitimacy will have a negative effect on foundings.

Of course, future research should also address some shortcomings in our preliminary analysis. First, we only looked at headlines from one newspaper; we believe a more complete analysis of how the popular press affects perceptions of legitimacy would likely encompass a broader collection of relevant media outlets. Second, we only looked at statements in published media as a source of perceptions of the legitimacy of the new industry. Clearly, expanding the focus of study to include additional sources of social information that affects perceptions of the industry might be a worthwhile goal. Third, we did not examine directly the active agency that was involved in the creation of this attention to the legitimacy of the new industry nor did we examine how particular participants in the industry may have benefited from or been damaged by this attention (Rindova and Fombrun, 2001). For example, we know that Thomas Edison actively encouraged attacks on European films as immoral as they encroached on his market share. These limitations, notwithstanding, we believe that our analyses and study of the early American film industry have made a contribution to the understanding of entrepreneurship. We plan to address important issues concerning the role of legitimacy in new industry creation and invite others to join us in tackling these difficult issues.

Part IV
Conclusion

8
Organizational Dynamics of Creative Destruction: Entrepreneurship and the Emergence of New Industries

Throughout this book our focus has been on developing the contribution of organization theory to the study of entrepreneurship. We have done this in terms of four primary ideas; we will review each of these and suggest some implications for future research from each as a way of concluding our book. The first idea is that demand side perspectives on entrepreneurship have been prominently featured in refereed journal articles in the recent past. Much of this work is derived from the subfield of sociology known as organizational theory. Of most direct relevance to students of entrepreneurship, we have argued that applying perspectives from organization theory to understand entrepreneurship expands the definition and the scope of the phenomenon. In terms of definitions, we suggest, following Mezias and Kuperman (2000) that both innovative and imitative behaviors by both newly founded and existing firms are essential to understanding the emergence of new industries. In terms of level of analysis, we interpret perspectives from organization theory as suggesting that levels of analysis higher than the individual founder or even the individual founded firm are necessary to fully comprehend entrepreneurship.

This first idea has several implications for future research. As a start, we would suggest that the issue of level of analysis in entrepreneurship research might be the subject of a methodological analysis. What can be learned at what levels of analysis? What phenomena or questions are highlighted at each level of analysis? How can insights at one level of analysis be applied to other levels of analysis? The burgeoning of entrepreneurship and the increasing important of a demand side perspective deserve more rigorous analysis. While we provided a cursory and somewhat exploratory look at how the literature of entrepreneurship is shifting, a more complete analysis is obviously merited.

The second idea is based directly on the notion that behavior by existing firms is relevant to understanding entrepreneurship and that an effective lens for studying these behaviors is provided by the organizational learning literature. In terms of empirical work, we pointed to the dynamics of learning in the emerging biotechnology industry revealed by Powell, Koput, Smith-Doerr (1996). However, in our chapters, we concentrated on the theoretical aspect of how to understand the role of existing firms, focusing on the notion of ecologies of learning. We presented research that has used ecologies of learning to explore some key ideas. Mezias and Lant (1994) examined the strong form of the structural inertia argument (Freeman and Hannan, 1984). Using the ecology of learning framework, they examined the boundary conditions under which organization level change will be selected out of a population of firms. Their conclusion is that mimetic change can survive under a broad range of conditions, calling into question the strong form of the structural inertia argument. Mezias and Glynn (1993) used the ecology of learning argument to examine the issue of why firms subject to selection pressures and learning from experience often fail to innovate. They revealed the paradoxes of innovation and revolution, which help to explain why the intention to innovate more may not have the effect of producing more innovation.

We also believe this second idea has several implications for future research. Applying the ecology of learning idea to further theoretical development is one of them. For example, Mezias and Eisner (1997) added imitability and competitive impact to an ecology that is essentially the same as the one developed by Mezias and Glynn (1993). Their results revealed that imitability was the more important aspect of the ecology in reducing innovation. At the same, time we also believe it is important for this work to move toward more direct empirical measurement of ecologies of learning. While existing work incorporating learning concepts has begun to make some progress on this difficult issue, there is still a long way to go. We would urge direct examination of the different sources of variance within ecologies of learning. Work should focus on the various roles of firm level change, interaction between firms, the founding of new firms, and events in the cultural environment affecting legitimacy, legal, and general societal norms and values.

The third idea that animated our book was the integration of the study of population dynamics, particularly the study of foundings, with the study of entrepreneurship. The dominant ecological paradigm, density dependence tends to focus on mature populations and long time spans. The questions that motivate much entrepreneurial research tend to be more about the creation of new industries and shorter times spans, especially those that are characterized by the rapid founding of large numbers of firms in a fairly short period of time, such as during the rapid emergence of a new industry. In fact, the predictions from population ecology discussed so far depend on the size of the population hitting the carrying capacity in order to hold. Yet, many of the populations most appropriate for the study of questions of interest to students of entrepreneurship may not reach carrying capacity during the period of their emergence. Thus, Mezias and Mezias (2000) used the resource partitioning argument, which was applicable because of the rapid speed with which the early film industry became concentrated. They linked their study of foundings directly with the emergence of the new film industry by showing that small specialist firms were more likely to engage in the creation of new film genres. Mezias and Kuperman (2000) used a community dynamics model to argue that the relevance of an ecological perspective goes beyond merely illuminating the vital rates of a single population. Using the social context perspective suggested by Van de Ven (1993b), they argued that the vital rates of several populations can be interdependent in the emergence of a new industry.

Once again we see several implications for future research arising from these ideas. First, we would urge direct study of the how populations in communities may affect each other's vital rates. In other words, does the increasing density of a population in the production portion of the value chain imply increased competition if the density of firms in the distribution portion increases commensurately? Related to this is direct empirical examination of the propositions from Mezias and Kuperman (2000) regarding second sourcing and related sourcing. Second sourcing claims that increased foundings do more than just legitimate a form; they may actually facilitate joint action such as the founding of exchanges by nickelodeon owners. They may also create a context where members of a community that is interdependent with the growing population, e.g., producers depending on nickelodeon owners, are willing to invest in growth or product innovation. Finally, we would like to see an ecological perspective brought directly to bear on the issue of how an emerging industry grows and matures. Again returning to the case of the American film industry, we would urge careful study of the population processes that led to the emergence and stabilization of a highly concentrated set of studios in the Los Angeles warren of Hollywood.

The fourth and set of ideas that animated our book were related to the institutional perspective. Specifically, we were interested in the issue of how cultural environments affected the emergence and development of new industries. Following the lead of Aldrich and Fiol (1994), we turned our attention first to the issues of how legitimacy can be affected by the emergence of standards. Thus, in Chapter 6 we examined how litigation became a key part of how standards were mediated in the early film industry. The patent wars involved litigation over who controlled key patents for technology of film production and projection. We highlighted periods where we believe there was significant legal uncertainty around patenting issues and predicted that this would have a negative impact on foundings. The copyright wars were somewhat briefer but of a similar nature, highlighting the issue of whether films were intellectual property that could be protected by law. Once again we highlighted periods where we believed the legal uncertainty was highest and predicted a negative impact on foundings. Finally, we discussed how litigation and the legal environment became a competitive tool, particularly during the MPPC period. We linked this both with a decrease in foundings and migration to Hollywood where the MPPC was not as strong. In Chapter 7, we turned our attention to the issue of legitimacy problems that faced the industry. We examined three distinct legitimacy challenges and provided some exploratory evidence regarding their resolution.

Once again we believe there are implications for future research arising from the ideas we developed in this section. Of key importance for us will be further development of the empirical evidence presented in these chapters. Designing rigorous empirical tests of the hypotheses linking the legal environment and foundings will be one avenue of research that we will pursue. We would urge others to examine the links between legal environments and the emergence of new industries as well. Further developing the direct measures of legitimacy that we explored in Chapter 7 will also be an important avenue for our continuing work. Again, we see the issue as quite general: Improved measures of legitimacy, especially in terms of how it impacts, foundings, growth, and death are key issues for a better understanding of new industry emergence and growth.

Finally, we believe that the institutional perspective highlights issues that might be missed from a more rational or materialist perspective. As an example, we would call attention to the burgeoning demand of nickelodeons for more product during the years from 1905 to 1907. American firms, which were preoccupied with issues in the legal environment and attempting to exercise market control, could not deliver and European firms benefited. Again in 1912, we see the MPPC focusing on market control and ignoring audience preference for feature length films. They did not build the production, e.g., the star system, or distribution capabilities, e.g., coordinated national release and promotion for films, that were necessary to succeed with more expensive feature length films. As a result, they did not survive: Not a single MPPC firm went on to become a major Hollywood studio. That is an extraordinary outcome of extinction and rebirth that will likely have many lessons for our understanding of the creation of new industries. Understanding the institutional dynamics of how it happened is a worthwhile avenue for future work.

We will close with an observation that we hope has become clear in the course of reading the many parts of this study. We are excited about entrepreneurship research, study of the emergence of new industries, and believe that perspectives from organization theory have much promise for more complete understanding. In many ways, the issues we have raised here may represent more questions than answers. Nonetheless, we remain steadfast in the belief that broader definitions of entrepreneurship and higher levels of analysis for comprehending the phenomenon are important avenues for future research. In this conclusion, we have highlighted some routes for that future research. We close on that note in the belief that pursuit of knowledge often depends at least as much on asking the right questions as it does on finding satisfactory answers.

Notes

Chapter 2

1. Population ecologists have argued that the structural inertia of organizations brought about by selection pressure is so great that most significant change and renewal comes about at the population level through the birth and death of new organizations (Hannan and Freeman, 1997; 1984). We agree with these analysts that a certain degree of structural inertia may be favored by selection pressures; however, we explicitly reject the proposition that this inertia is so high as to render fundamental change by existing organizations impossible, insignificant, or uninteresting. This will be especially true for organizations whose large size buffers them from selection pressures (Levinthal, 1990).

2. As we detail in the Appendix, the pool of refinement possibilities is replenished each time there is an innovation. Than the whole process of decreasing returns to refinements of current technology begins anew.

3. Standard practice in learning curve discussions is to talk about the reduction in unit costs associated with experience; thus, organizations move down the learning curve. For analytical convenience in this study, units move toward a maximum potential level of performance with a technology as they gain experience with it; hence, we describe units as moving up the learning curve.

4. The operationalizations of these conditions is described in greater detail in the Appendix.

5. All of the comparisons we report below as not significant using the nonparametric tests are also not significant using t-tests.

6. Recall that simulation was initialized as if all units had made an innovation in period 0 and we assumed that the value of innovation increases with the time since last innovation. This combination yields a period of no innovation following initialization of the simulation.

7. It is notable, however, that the gap in resources depicted in Figure 6 was not altered greatly in the sensitivity analysis where we ran six variations on the baseline model that varied the parameters and structural equations.

8. Copies can be obtained by writing to the first author.

9. The variance of a uniform distribution is equal to the square of the range of the distribution divided by twelve. Since the range increases with the square of time since the last innovation, so does the variance.

10. Initial values of the minimum cost of search are less than one resource unit. For values of cost of search less than one resource unit, the cost of search is multiplied by ten, raised to the exponent appropriate to their experience, and then deflated. This avoids the problem that squaring quantities less than one would have the opposite effect of that intended.

Chapter 3

1. The size of the organization does not affect the likelihood of organizational change in this simulation; thus, the implications of the results are limited by this assumption.

2. Both fixed and mimetic firms draw on the same resources in the environment and thus are affected by the same carrying capacity.

195

3. All firms engage in founding search at the initialization of the simulation. After initialization all firms that replace bankrupt firms also engage in founding search to determine which firm type they will become. As discussed previously, however, whether firms are fixed or mimetic is a property inherited from a firm randomly drawn from among all those with positive performance in the period of replacement.

4. This negative selection process results in the birth of new firms only after another firm has exited the population. We do not include elements of mass or concentration in our operationalization of competition.

5. We have talked about organizational change in terms of core dimensions of the organization. Thus, the type of change we are interested in modeling results in significant changes to the characteristics of an organization. Some institutional theorists (Meyer and Rowan, 1977) have suggested that organizations change peripheral features while buffering their core characteristics. Under the assumption that core changes are more costly than peripheral changes, the continuum from core to peripheral changes can be represented by the distribution of the cost of change across populations in the simulation. Thus, the implications of this simulation are not necessarily limited to a discussion of changes to core dimensions.

Bibliography

Aberdeen J.A. 2001. *Hollywood Renegades: The Society of Independent Motion Picture Producers*. (http://www.cobbles.com/sim;_archive/bibliography.htm).

Abernathy W.J, Clark K.B. 1900. Innovation: Mapping the winds of creative destruction. *Readings in the Management of Innovation* 2: 25–36.Tushman M.L., More W.L. (eds). Ballinger: Cambridge, MA.

Abrahamson E., Rosenkopf L. 1997. Social network effects on the extent of innovation diffusion. *Organization Science* 8: 289–309.

Aiken M., Hage J. 1971. The organic organization and innovation. *Sociology* 5: 63–82.

Aldrich H.E. 1990. Using an ecological perspective to study organizational founding rates. *Entrepreneurship Theory and Practice* 15: 7–24.

Aldrich H.E. 1999. *Organizations Evolving*. Sage Publications Inc: Thousand Oaks, CA.

Aldrich H.E., Fiol C.M. 1994. Fools rush in? The institutional context of industry creation. *Academy of Management Review* 19: 645–670.

Aldrich H.E., Wiedenmayer G. 1993. From traits to rates: An ecological perspective on organizational foundings. In *Advances in entrepreneurship, firm emergence, and growth*, Vol. 1, Katz J.A., Brockhaus R.H. (eds). JAI Press: Greenwich, CT.

Allen R.C., Gomery D. 1985. *Film History Theory and Practice*. Alfred A. Knopf: New York, NY.

Amabile T.M. 1988. A model of creativity and innovation in organizations. In *Research in Organizational Behavior*, Vol.10, Staw B, Cummings LL (eds). JAI Press: Greenwich, CT.

Amburgey T., Kelly D., Barnett W. 1990. Resetting the clock: The dynamics of organizational change and failure. In *Best Paper Proceedings of the Academy of Management Meetings*, Jauch L.R., Wall J.L. (eds).

Amit R., Glosten L., Muller E. 1993. Challenges to theory development in entrepreneurship research. *Journal of Management Studies* 30: 815–834.

Anderson P., Tushman M.L. 1990. Technological discontinuities and dominant designs: A cyclical model of technological change. *Administrative Science Quarterly* 35: 604–633.

Angle H.L., Van de Ven A.H. 1989. Suggestions for managing the innovation journey. In *Research on the Management of Innovation*, Van de Ven A.H., Angle H.L., Poole M.S. (eds). Ballinger/Harper Row: New York, NY.

Argote L., Beckman S.L., Epple D. 1990. The persistence and transfer of learning in industrial settings. *Management Science* 36: 140–154.

Argote L., Epple D. 1990. Learning curves in manufacturing. *Science* 247: 920–924.

Argyris C., Schon D. 1978. *Organizational Learning*. Addison-Wesley: Reading, MA.

Arrow K.J. 1969. The organization of economic activity. *The analysis and evaluation of public expenditure*, Joint Economic Committee, 91st Congress; 59–73.

Astley W.G. 1985. The two ecologies: Population and community perspectives on organizational evolution. *Administrative Science Quarterly* 30: 224–241.

Balio T. 1976. United Artists: *The Company Built By The Stars*. University of Wisconsin Press: Madison WI.

Barnett W.P. 1991. Strategic deterrence among multipoint competitors. In *Academy of Management Best Papers Proceedings*, Wall J.L., Jauch L.R. (eds).

Barnett W.P., Carroll G.R. 1987. Competition and commensalism among early telephone companies. *Administrative Science Quarterly* 20: 400–21.

Barron D.N. 1998. Pathways to legitimacy among consumer loan providers in New York City, 1914–1934. *Organization Studies* 19(2): 207–233.

Baron J.N., Dobbing F.R., Jennings P.D. 1986. War and Peace: The evolution of modern personnel administration in U.S. industry. *American Journal of Sociology* 92(2): 350–383.

Baum J.A.C. 1996. Organizational ecology. In *Handbook of Organization Studies*, Clegg S., Hardy C., Nord W. (eds). Sage: London.

Baum J.A.C., Mezias S.J. 1992. Localized competition and organizational failure in the Manhattan hotel industry, 1898–1990. *Administrative Science Quarterly* 37: 580–604.

Baum J.A.C., Powell W.W. 1995. Cultivating an institutional ecology of organizations: Comment on Hannan, Carroll, Dundon, and Torres. *American Sociological Review* 60: 529–38.

Baum J.A.C., Singh J.V. 1994a. Organization–Environment coevolution. In *Evolutionary Dynamics of Organizations*, Baum J.A.C., Singh J.V. (eds). Oxford University Press: New York, NY.

Baum J.A.C., Singh J.V. 1994b. Organizational niches and the dynamics of organizational founding. *Organization Science* 5: 483–501.

Barnouw E. 1978. *The Sponsor: Notes on a Modern Potentate*. Oxford University Press: New York, NY.

Beck M., Smith S.J. 1996. *Hollywoods's wakeup call*. New York Daily News (March 26) Movie Section: 1.

Berg A.S. 1989. *Goldwyn: A Biography. New York*: Alfred A. Knopf.

Biggadike R. 1979. The risky business of diversification. *Harvard Business Review* May–June: 103–111.

Blanchard K. 1989. Innovation. *Journal for Quality and Participation* 12: 38–39.

Block Z., MacMillan I.C. 1993. *Corporate Venturing: Creating New Business Within The Firm*. Harvard Business School Press: Boston, MA.

Boone C., Brocheler V., and Carroll G.R. 1998. Custom service: Application and tests of resource partitioning theory among Dutch auditing firms from 1980 to 1982. Paper presented at the 14th Meeting of the European Group of Organization Studies, Maastricht, Netherlands.

Bourgeois L.J. 1981. On the measurement of organizational slack. *Academy of Management Review* 6: 29–39.

Brewer G. 1980. On the theory and practice of innovation. *Technology in Society* 2: 337–363.

Brown G. 1984. *The New York Times Encyclopedia of Film, 1896–1928*. Times Books: New York, NY.

Brown G. 1995. *Movie Time*. MacMillan: New York, N.Y.

Brown J.S. 1991. Research that reinvents the corporation. *Harvard Business Review* Jan–Feb: 102–111.

Brown R.H. 1978. Bureaucracy as praxis: Toward a political phenomenology of formal organizations. *Administrative Science Quarterly* 23: 365–382.

Bowser E. 1990. *The Transformation of Cinema: 1907–1915* Charles Scribner's Sons: New York, NY.

Bruno A.V, McQuarrie EF, Torgrimson CG. 1992. The evolution of new technology ventures over 20 years: Patterns of failure, merger, and survival. *Journal of Business Venturing* 7:291–302.

Burgelman R.A. 1983a. A process model of internal corporate venturing in the major diversified firm. *Administrative Science Quarterly* 28: 223–244.

Burgelman R.A. 1983b. Corporate entrepreneurship and strategic management: Insights from a process study. *Management Science* 29: 1349–1364.

Burgelman R.A. 1985. Managing the new venture division: Research finding and implications for strategic management. *Strategic Management Journal* 6: 39–54.

Burns T., Stalker G. 1961. *The Management of Innovation*. Tavistock: London.

Burt R.S. 1980. Autonomy in a social topology. *American Journal of Sociology* 85: 892–925.

Bygrave W.D., Hofer C.W. 1991. Theorizing and entrepreneurship. *Entrepreneurship Theory and Practice* 16: 13–22.

Cable D.M., Shane S. 1997. A prisoner's dilemma approach to entrepreneur-venture capitalist relationships. *Academy of Management Review* 22: 142–176.

Carroll G.R. 1984. Organizational ecology. *Annual Review of Sociology* 10: 71–93.

Carroll G.R. 1985. Concentration and specialization: Dynamics of niche width in populations of organizations. *American Journal of Sociology* 90: 1263–1283.

Carroll G.R., Hannan M.T. 1989a. Density dependence in the evolution of populations of newspaper organizations. *American Sociological Review* 54: 524–541.

Carroll G.R., Hannan M.T. (eds). 1995. *Organizations In Industry: Strategy, Structure, And Selection*. Oxford University Press: New York, NY.

Carroll G.R., Hannan M.T. 2000. Why Corporate Demography Matters: Policy Implications of Organizational Diversity. *California Management Review* 42: 148–164.

Carroll G.R., Swaminathan A. 1992. The organizational ecology of strategic groups in the American beer brewing industry from 1975–1990. *Industrial and Corporate Change* 1: 65–97.

Carroll G.R., Swaminathan A. 1993. On theory, breweries, and strategic groups. *Industrial and Corporate Change* 1: 65–97.

Carroll G.R., Wade J.B. 1991. Density dependence in the evolution of the American brewing industry across different levels of analysis. *Social Science Research* 20: 271–302.

Carter N.M., Williams M., Reynolds P.D. 1997. Discontinuance among new firms in retail: The influence of initial resources, strategy and gender. *Journal of Business Venturing* 12: 125–145.

Castonguay J. 1999. Hypertext scholarship and media studies. *American Film Quarterly* 51(2): 247–249

Chandler, Jr A.D. 1977. *The Visible Hand: The Managerial Revolution in American Business*. Harvard University Press: Cambridge, MA.

Child J. 1972. Organizational structure, environment, and performance: The role of strategic choice. *Sociology* 6: 2–22.

Cohen W.M., Levinthal DA. 1990. Absorptive capacity: A new perspective on learning and innovation. *Administrative Science Quarterly* 35: 128–152.

Cole A.H. 1968. The entrepreneur: Introductory remarks. *American Economic Review* 63: 60–63.

Cones J.W. 2000. *Politics, Movies and the Role of Government.* (http://www.homevideo.net/FIRM/antitrst.htm)

Cook D.A. 1981. *A Narrative History of Film.* W. W. Norton & Company: New York.

Cooper A.C., Smith C.G. 1992. How Established Firms Respond to Threatening Technologies. *Academy of Management Executive* 6: 55–70.

Cooper R.G. 1979. The dimensions of industrial new product success and failure. *Journal of Marketing* 43: 91–103.

Covin J.G., Slevin D.P. 1994. Corporate entrepreneurship in high and low technology industries: A comparison of strategic variables, strategy patterns and performance in global markets. *Journal of Euromarketing* 3: 99–127.

Covin J.G., Miles M.P. 1999. Corporate entrepreneurship and the pursuit of competitive advantage. Entrepreneurship Theory & Practice Spring: 47–63.

Cyert R.M., March J.G. 1963. *A Behavioral Theory of the Firm.* Prentice-Hall: Englewood Cliffs, NJ.

Dacin M.T. 1997. Isomorphism in context: the power and prescription of institutional norms. *Academy of Management Journal* 40: 46–81.

Damanpour F. 1991. Organizational innovation: A meta-analysis of effects of determinants and moderators. *Academy of Management Journal* 34: 555–590.

DeCordova R. 2001. *Picture Personalities: The Emergence of the Star System in America.* Urbana University of Illinois Press: Chicago, IL.

Delacroix J., Carroll G.R. 1983. Organizational foundings: an ecological study of the newspaper industries of Argentina and Ireland. *Administrative Science Quarterly* 28: 74–91.

Delacroix J., Rao H. 1994. Externalities and ecological theory: unbundling density dependence. In *Evolutionary Dynamics of Organization,* Baum JAC, Singh J.V. (eds). Oxford University Press: New York.

Delacroix J., Solt M.E. 1988. Niche formation and foundings in the California wine industry 1941–1984. In *Ecological Models of Organization,* Carroll GR (ed). Ballinger Publishing Company: Cambridge, MA.

Delacroix J., Swaminathan A., Solt M. 1989. Density dependence versus population dynamics: An ecological study of failings in the California wine industry.*American Sociological Review* 54: 245–262.

Delbecq A.L., Mills .PK. 1985. Managerial practices that enhance innovation. *Organizational Dynamics* 14: 24–34.

Dewar R.D., Dutton J.E. 1986. The adoption of radical and incremental innovations: An empirical analysis. *Management Science* 32: 1422–33.

DiMaggio P.J., Powell W.W. 1983. The iron cage revisited: institutional isomorphism and collective rationality in organizational fields. *American Sociological Review* 48: 147–160.

DiMaggio P.J., Powell W.W. 1991.The New Institutionalism in Organizational Analysis, Powell W.W., Dimaggio P.J. (eds). The University of Chicago Press: Chicago.

Dobbin F., Sutton J.R. 1998. The strength of a weak state: The rights revolution and the rise of human resources management divisions. *American Journal of Sociology* 104(2): 441–476.

Dobbin F., Sutton J.R., Meyer J.W., Scott R. 1993. Equal opportunity law and the construction of internal labor markets. *American Journal of Sociology* 99(2): 396–427.

Dobrev S. 2001. Revisiting Organizational legitimation: cognitive diffusion and sociopolitical factors in the evolution of Bulgarian newspaper enterprises, 1846–1992. *Organization Studies* 22 (3): 419–444.

Dorfman R. 1980. A Formula for the GINI Coefficient. *Review of Economic Statistics* 28: 146–149.

Dosi G. 1984. *Technological Change and Industrial Transformation.* St. Martin's: New York, NY.

Dougherty D., Hardy C. 1996. Sustained product innovation in large, mature organizations: Overcoming innovation-to-organization problems. *Academy of Management Journal* 39:1120–1153.

Downs G.W. 1976. *Bureaucracy, Innovation, and Public Policy.* D.C. Health: Lexington, MA.

Drucker P.F. 1985.Innovation and Entrepreneurship: Practice and Principles. Harper Row: New York, NY.

Edelman L.B. 1990. Legal Environments and Organizational Governance: The Expansion of Due Process in the American Workplace. *American Journal of Sociology* 95(6): 1401–1440.

Edelman L.B. 1992. Legal Ambiguity and Symbolic Structures: Organizational Mediation of Civil Rights Law. *American Journal of Sociology* 97(6): 1531–1576.

Edelman L.B, Suchman M.C. 1997. The legal environment of an organization. *Annual Review of Sociology* 23: 479–515.

Edelman L.B, Uggen C., Erlanger H.S. 1999. The endogeneity of legal regulation: Grievance procedures as rational myth. *American Journal of Sociology* 105(2): 406–454.

Editor & Publisher. 1902–1928. Series. Editor & Publisher Co.: New York, NY.

Eisenhardt K.M, Schoonhoven C.B. 1996. Resource-based view of strategic alliance formation: Strategic and social effects in entrepreneurial firms. *Organization Science* 7: 136–150.

Epple D., Argote L., Devadas R. 1991. Organizational learning curves: A method for investigating intra-plant transfer of knowledge acquired through learning by doing. *Organization Science* 2: 58–70.

Ettlie J.E., Bridges W.P., O'Keefe R.D. 1984. Organization strategy and structural differences for radical versus incremental innovation. *Management Science* 30: 682–695.

Eyman S. 1990. *Mary Pickford: America's sweetheart.* Donald I. Fine: New York.

Fast N.D., Pratt S.E. 1981. Individual entrepreneurship and the large corporation. In *Frontiers of entrepreneurship research*, Vesper K. (ed.). Babson Center for Entrepreneurial Studies: Wellesley, MA.

Fombrun C. 1988. Crafting an institutionally informed ecology of organizations. In *Ecological Models of Organizations*, Carroll G. (ed). Ballinger Publishing Company: Cambridge, MA.

Foster R.N. 1986. *Innovation.* Summit Books: New York, NY.

Freeman J., Lomi A. 1994. Resource partitioning and founding of banking cooperatives in Italy. In *Evolutionary Dynamics of Organizations*, Baum J., Singh J., (eds). Oxford University Press: New York.

Freeman J., Hannan M. 1983. Niche width and the dynamics of organizational populations. American Journal of Sociology 88: 1116–45.

Galbraith J.R. 1973. *Designing Complex Organizations*. Addison-Wesley: Reading, MA.

Galbraith J.R. 1982. Designing the innovating organization. *Organizational Dynamics* 11: 5–25.

Gartner W.B. 1989. Some Suggestions For Research On Entrepreneurial Traits And Characteristics. *Entrepreneurship Theory and Practice* 14: 27–39.

Gartner W.B. 1990. What are we talking about when we talk about entrepreneurship. *Journal of Business Venturing* 5: 15–28.

Ginsberg A., Guth W.D. 1990. Guest editors' introduction: Corporate entrepreneurship. *Strategic Management Journal* (11): 5–15.

Glynn M.A. 1996. Innovative genius: A framework for relating individual and organizational intelligences to innovation. *Academy of Management Review* 21: 1081–1111.

Glynn M.A., Lant T., Mezias S.J. 1991. Incrementalism, learning, and ambiguity: An experimental study of aspiration level updating. In *Best Paper Proceedings of the Academy of Management Meetings*, Wall J.L., Jauch L.R. (eds). Omnipress: Madison, WI.

Glynn M.A., Webster J. 1992. The Adult Playfulness Scale: An Initial Assessment. *Psychological Reports* 71: 83–103.

Granovetter M. 1985. Economic action and social structure: A problem of embeddedness. *American Journal of Sociology* 91: 481–510.

Greene W.H. 1989. Limdep. Econometrics Software, New York.

Hampton B. 1931. *A History Of The Movies*. Harper & Row, New York.

Hannan M.T., Carroll G.R. 1992. *Dynamics of organizational populations: Density, legitimation, and competition*. Oxford University Press: New York.

Hannan M.T., Freeman J.H. 1977. The population ecology of organizations. *American Journal of Sociology* 82: 929–964.

Hannan M.T., Freeman J.H. 1984. Structural inertia and organizational change. *American Sociological Review* 49: 149–164.

Hannan M.T., Freeman J.H. 1987. The ecology of organizational founding: American labor unions, 1836–1985. *American Journal of Sociology* 92: 910–943.

Hannan M.T., Freeman J.H. 1989. *Organizational Ecology*. Harvard University Press: Cambridge, MA.

Hardy C., Dougherty D. 1997. Powering product innovation. *European Management Journal* 15: 16–27.

Harmon B., Ardishvili A., Cardozo R., Elder T., Leuthold J., Parshall J., Raghian M., Smith D. 1997. Mapping the university technology transfer process. *Journal of Business Venturing* 12: 423–434.

Harrison R., March J.G. 1984. Decision making and postdecision surprises. *Administrative Science Quarterly* 35: 26–42.

Haveman H., Nonnemaker L. 1998. Competition in multiple geographic markets: The impact on growth and market entry. Unpublished manuscript, Cornell University, Ithaca, NY.

Henderson R.M., Clark K.B. 1990. Architectural innovation: The reconfiguration of Existing product technologies and the failure of established firms. *Administrative Science Quarterly* 35(1): 9–30.

Herriott S.R., Levinthal D., March J.G. 1988. Learning from experience in organizations. *Decisions and Organizations*: 219–227. Basil Blackwell: New York, NY.

Highan C. 1973. *Cecil B. DeMille*. Charles Scribner's Sons, New York.

Hirsch P.M. 1969. *The Structure of the Popular Music Industry*. University of Michigan Research Center, Ann Arbor, MI.

Hirsch P.M. 1972. Processing fads and fashions: An organizational-set analysis of cultural industry systems. *American Journal of Sociology* 77: 639–659.

Hirsch P.M. 2000. Cultural industries revisited. *Organization Science* 11: 356–361.

Hitt M.A., Ireland R.D., Camp S.M., Sexton D.L. 2001. Guest Editors' Introduction to the Special Issue Strategic Entrepreneurship: Entrepreneurial Strategies for Wealth Creation. *Strategic Management Journal* 22: 479–491.

Hofer C.W., Bygrave W.D. 1992. Researching entrepreneurship. *Entrepreneurship: Theory and Practice* 16: 91–100.

Hornaday R.W. 1992. Thinking about entrepreneurship: A fuzzy set approach. *Journal of Small Business Management* 30: 12–23.

Howell J.M., Higgins C.A. 1990. Champions of change: Identifying, understanding, and supporting champions of technological innovations. *Organizational Dynamics* 19: 40–55.

Hull F.M., Hage J., Azumi K. 1985. R D management strategies: American versus Japan. *IEEE Transactions on Engineering Management* 32: 78–83.

Hybels R.C. 1994. Legitimation, population density, and founding rates: The institutionalization of commercial biotechnology in the U.S., 1971–1989. PhD dissertation, Cornell University.

Hybels R.C. 2000. Interorganizational endorsements and the performance of entrepreneurial venture. *Administrative Science Quarterly* 44(2): 315–349.

Jacobs L. 1967. *The Rise Of The American Film*. Teachers College Press: New York.

Jelinek M., Schoonhoven, C.D. 1990. *The Innovation Marathon*. Basil Blackwell: Cambridge, MA.

Jewell R.B., Harbin V. 1982. *The RKO Story*. Octopus Books Ltd.: London, UK.

Kanter R.M. 1983. *The Change Masters*. Simon and Schuster: New York, NY.

Kelly E., Dobbin F. 1999. Civil rights law at work: Sex discrimination and the rise of maternity leave policies. *The American Journal of Sociology* 105(2): 455–492.

Kidder T. 1981. *The Soul of a New Machine*. Little Brown: Boston, MA.

Kimberly J. 1981. Managerial innovation. In *Handbook of Organizational Design* Vol. 1, Nystrom P, Starbuck W (eds).

Kirzner I.M. 1979. *Perception, Opportunity, And Profit*. University of Chicago Press: Chicago, IL.

Kohn M.G., Shavell S. 1974. Optimal adaptive search. *Journal of Economic Theory* 9: 93–124.

Koszarski R. 1990. *An Evening's Entertainment: The Age of the Silent Feature Picture 1915–1928*. Charles Scribner's Sons: New York.

Kotter J.P., Schlesinger L.A. 1979. Choosing strategies for change. *Harvard Business Review* March–April: 106–114.

Lahue K.C. 1971. *Dreams for sale: The Rise and fall of the triangle film corporation*. A. S. Barns & Co: New York.

Landstrom H., and Sexton D. 2000. Remaining issues and suggestions for further research. In *Handbook of Entrepreneurship*, Sexton D. & Landstrom H. (eds). Blackwell: Oxford, England.

Lant T.K. 1992. Aspiration level updating: An empirical exploration. *Management Science* 38: 623–644.

Lant T.K., Mezias S.J. 1990. Managing discontinuous change: A simulation study of organizational learning and entrepreneurship. *Strategic Management Journal* 11: 147–179.

Lant T.K., Mezias S.J. 1992. An organizational learning model of convergence and reorientation. *Organization Science* 3: 47–71.

Lant T.K., Montgomery D.B. 1987. Learning from Strategic Success and Failure. *Journal of Business Research* 15(6): 503–518.

Lave C.A., March J.G. 1975. *An Introduction to Models in the Social Sciences*. Harper & Row: New York, NY.

Lawless M.W., and Price L.L. 1992. An agency perspective on technological champions. *Organization Science* 3: 342–355.

Leavitt H.J. 1965. Applied organizational change in industry: Structural, technological, and humanistic approaches. *Handbook of Organizations*, March J (ed.). Chicago: Rand McNally.

Levitas E., Hitt M.A., Dacin M.T. 1997. Competitive intelligence and tacit knowledge development in strategic alliances. *Competitive Intelligence Review* 8: 20–27.

Levinthal D.A. 1990. Organizational adaptation, environmental selection, and random walks. *Organizational Evolution: New Directions*, Singh J.V. (ed.). Sage: Newbury Park, CA.

Levinthal D.A., March J.G. 1981. A model of adaptive organizational search. *Journal of Economic Behavior and Organization* 2: 307–333.

Levitt B., March J.G. 1988. Organizational learning. *Annual Review of Sociology* 14: 319–340.

Lieberman J.K. 1983. *The Litigious Society*. Basic Books: New York.

Lippman S.A., Rumelt R.P. 1982. Uncertain Imitability: An Analysis of Interfirm Differences in Efficiency Under Competition. *Bell Journal of Economics* 13: 418–438.

Lounsbury M., Glynn M.A. 2001. Cultural entrepreneurship: Stories, legitimacy, and the acquisition of resources. *Strategic Management Journal* 22: 545–564.

Lussier T. 1999. http:// www.silentsaregolden.com/articles/lubinfilmarticle.html.

MacMillan I.C. 1986. Progress in research on corporate venturing. In *The art and science of entrepreneurship*, Sexton D.L., Smilor R.W. (eds). Ballinger: Cambridge, MA.

MacMillan I.C, Block Z., Narasimha PNS. 1986. Corporate venturing: Alternatives,obstacles encountered, and experience effects. *Journal of Business Venturing* 1: 177–192.

MacMillan I.C., Katz J.A. 1992. Idiosyncratic milieus of entrepreneurial research: The need for comprehensive theories. *Journal of Business Venturing* 7:1–8.

Maddala G.S. 1984. *Limited Dependent And Qualitative Variables In Econometrics*. Cambridge University Press: Cambridge, UK.

March J.G. 1976. The technology of foolishness. In *Ambiguity and Choice in Organizations*: *Universitetsforlaget*. March J.G. Olsen JP (eds). Bergen, Norway.

March J.G. 1981. Footnotes to organizational change. *Administrative Science Quarterly* 26: 563–577.

March J.G. 1988. Variable risk preferences and adaptive aspirations. *Journal of Economic Behavior and Organization* 9: 5–24.

March J.G. 1991. Exploration and exploitation in organizational learning. *Organization Science* 2: 71–87.

March J.G., Olsen J.P. 1976. Ambiguity and Choice in Organizations. Universitetsforlaget: Bergen, Norway.

March J.G., Simon H.A. 1958. *Organizations*. Wiley: New York, NY.

Marcus A.A. 1988. Implementing externally induced innovations: A comparison of rule-bound and autonomous approaches. *Academy of Management Journal* 31: 235–256.

May, L.L. 1980. *Screening the Past: The Birth of Mass Culture Industry*. New York: Oxford University Press.

McClave J.T., Benson P.G. 1988. *Statistics for Business Economics*, 4th Ed. Dellen Publishing Company: San Francisco, CA.

McClelland D.C. 1975. *Power: The Inner Experience*. Irvington/Halstead: New York.

McKelvey B., Aldrich H. 1983. Populations, natural selection, and applied organizational science (in The Utilization of Organizational Research, Part 2). *Administrative Science Quarterly* 28(1): 101–128.

McLaughlin P., Khawaja M. 2000. The organizational dynamics of the U.S. environmental movement: Legitimation, resource mobilization, and political opportunity. *Rural Sociology* 65: 422–439.

Mendrala J. 2002. A brief history of film and digital cinema. (http:// www.tech-notes.net/Dig-Cine/Digitalcinema.html).

Meyer J.W., Rowan B. 1977. Institutionalized Organizations: Formal Structure as Myth & Ceremony. *American Journal of Sociology* 83(2): 340–363.

Meyer J.W., Scott R.B. 1983. Centralization and the legitimacy problems of local government. In *Organizational environments: Ritual and Rationality*. Meyer J., Scott W.R. (eds). Sage Publications: Beverly Hills, CA.

Meyer J., Scott W., Deal T. 1983. Institutional and technical sources of organizational structure: Explaining the structure of educational organizations. Reprinted in Meyer J., Scott W. (eds). Organizational Environments: Ritual and Rationality. Sage: Beverly Hills, CA.

Meyer M.H., Utterback J.M. 1993. The product family and the dynamics of core capability. *Sloan Management Review* 34: 29–47.

Mezias J.M. 2001. Identifying liabilities of foreignness and strategies to minimize their effects: The case of labor lawsuit judgments in the United States. *Strategic Management Journal* 23 (3): 229–244.

Mezias J.M., Mezias S.J. 2000. Resource Partitioning, the founding of specialist firms, and innovation: The American feature film industry, 1912–1929. *Organization Science* 11(3): 306–322.

Mezias S.J. 1988. Aspiration level effects: An empirical study. Journal of Economic Behavior and Organization 10: 389–400.

Mezias S.J. 1990. An institutional model of organizational practice: Financial reporting at the fortune 200. *Administrative Science Quarterly* 35(3): 431–457.

Mezias S.J., Eisner A.B., Mezias J.M., Kuperman J.C. 1996. Competition, mutualism and strategic change: The American film industry, 1912–1929. Presented at the Academy of Management meeting, Cincinnati, OH.

Mezias S.J., Glynn M.A. 1993. The three faces of corporate renewal: Institution, revolution, and evolution. *Strategic Management Journal* 14: 77–101.

Mezias S.J, Kuperman J.C. 2001. The community dynamics of entrepreneurship: The birth of the American film industry, 1895–1929. *Journal of Business Venturing* 16: 209.

Mezias S.J., Lant T.K. 1994. Mimetic learning and the evolution of organizational populations. In *Evolutionary Dynamics of Organizations*, Baum J.A.C., Singh J.V. (eds). Oxford University Press: New York, NY.

Morecroft J.D. 1984. Strategy support models. *Strategic Management Journal* 5: 215–29.

Mitchell W. 1994. The dynamic model of evolving markets: The effect of business sales and age on dissolutions and divestitures. *Administrative Science Quarterly* 39: 575–602.

Musser C. 1990. *The Emergence of Cinema: The American Screen to 1907*. Charles Scribner's Sons: New York, NY.

Nadler D.A., Tushman M.T. 1989. Organizational frame bending: Principles for managing reorientation. *Academy of Management Executive* 3: 194–204.

Nelson R., Winter S. 1982. *An Evolutionary Theory of Economic Change*. Harvard University Press: Cambridge, MA.

Nord W.R., Tucker S. 1987. Implementing Routine and Radical Innovation. Lexington Books: Boston, MA.

Nodoushani O., Nodoushani P.A. 1999. A deconstructionist theory of entrepreneurship: A note. *American Business Review* January: 45–49.

Oliver C. 1990. Determinants of Interorganizational Relationships: Integration and future directions. *Academy of Management Review* 15(2): 241–266.

Ostgaard T.A., Birley S. 1996. New venture growth and personal networks. *Journal of Business Research* 36: 37–50.

Payne J.W., Laughhunn D.J., Crum R. 1980.Translation of gambles and aspiration level effects on risky choice behavior. *Management Science* 26: 1039–1060.

Perrow C. 1986. *Complex Organizations: A Critical Essay*. 3rd Ed. Scott-Foresman: Glenview, IL.

Petersen T., Koput K.W. 1991. Density dependence in organizational mortality: Legitimacy or unobserved heterogeneity? *American Sociological Review* 56:399–410.

Peterson R.A., Berger D.G. 1971. Entrepreneurship in organizations: Evidence from the popular music industry. *Administrative Science Quarterly* 16: 97–106.

Peterson R.A., Berger D.G. 1975. Cycles in symbol production: The case of popular music. *American Sociological Review* 40: 158–173.

Pfeffer J. 1981. Management as symbolic action: The creation and maintenance of organizational paradigms. In *Research in Organizational Behavior Vol. 3*, Cummings L.L., Staw B.M. (eds). JAI Press: Greenwich, CT.

Pfeffer J., Salancik G.R. 1978. *The External Control of Organizations*. Harper and Row: New York, NY.

Pierce J.L., Delbecq A.L. 1977. Organizational structure, individual attitudes, and innovation. *Academy of Management Review* 2: 26–37.

Pinchot G. 1985. *Intrapreneuring*. Harper & Row: New York, NY.

Powell W.W., Koput K.W., Smith-Doerr L. 1996. Interorganizational Collaboration and the Locus of Innovation: Networks of Learning in Biotechnology. Administrative Science Quarterly 41(1): 116–145.

Puttnam D. 1997. *The Undeclared War: The struggle for control of the world's film industry*. HarperCollins Publishers: London, England.

Quinn J.B. 1985. Managing innovation: Controlled chaos. *Harvard Business Review* May–June: 73–84.

Radner R. 1975. A behavioral model of cost reduction. *Bell Journal of Economics* 6: 196–215.

Ranger-Moore J., Banaszak-Holl J., Hannan MT. 1991. Density-dependent dynamics in regulated industries: Founding rates of banks and life insurance companies. *Administrative Science Quarterly* 36: 36–65.

Rao H. 1994. The social construction of reputation: Certification contests, legitimation, and the survival of organizations in the American automobile industry. *Strategic Management Journal* 15: 29–44.

Rao H. 2001. The power of public competition: Promoting cognitive legitimacy through certification contests. In *The Entrepreneurship Dynamic*, Schoonhoven C.B., Romanelli E. (eds). Stanford University Press: Stanford, CA.

Reynolds P.D. 1991. Sociology and entrepreneurship: Concepts and contributions. *Entrepreneurship Theory and Practice* 16: 47–70.

Rhode E. 1976. *A History Of The Cinema: From Its Origins To 1970*. Hill and Wang: New York, NY.

Rindova V.P., Fombrun C.J. 2001. Entrepreneurial Action in the Creation of the Specialty Coffee Niche. In *The Entrepreneurship Dynamic*, Schoonhoven CB, Romanelli E. (eds). Stanford University Press: Stanford, CA.

Rogers E.M. 1983. *Diffusion of Innovation*. Free Press: New York, NY.

Rogers E.M, Shoemaker F.F. 1971. *Communication of Innovation*. Free Press: New York, NY.

Romanelli E. 1989. Organization birth and population variety: a community perspective on origins. In *Research in Organizational Behavior*, Cummings L.L., Staw B. (eds). JAI Press: Greenwich, CT.

Sahal D. 1981. *Patterns of Technological Innovation*. Addison-Wesley: Reading, MA.

Schumpeter J.A. 1934. *The Theory of Economic Development*. Harvard University Press: Cambridge, MA.

Schumpeter J.A. 1942. *The Process of Creative Destruction, in Capitalism, Socialism, and Democracy*. Harper & Brothers Publishers: New York, NY.

Schumpeter J.A. 1950. *Can Capitalism Survive?* Harper & Row: New York, NY.

Scott WR. 1998. *Organizations: rational, natural, and open systems*. Prentice Hall: New Jersey.

Seidel M.D. 1997. Competitive realignment in the airline industry: A dynamic analysis of generalist versus specialist organizations under different network structures. Unpublished thesis. University of California at Berkeley, Haas School of Business.

Senge P.M. 1990a. *The Fifth Discipline*. Doubleday Currency: New York, NY.

Senge P.M. 1990b. *The Leader's New Work: Building Learning Organizations*. Doubleday Currency: New York, NY.

Shane S.A. 1992. Why Do Some Societies Invent More than Others? *Journal of Business Venturing* 7: 29–46.

Shane S.A. 1996. Explaining variation in rates of entrepreneurship in the U.S.: 1899–1988. *Journal of Management* 2: 747–781.

Shane S.A. 1997. Who is publishing entrepreneurship research? *Journal of Management* 23: 83–95.

Shane S.A., Kolvereid L. 1995. National environment, strategy, and new venture performance: A three-country study. *Journal of Small Business Management* 33: 37–50.

Shane S.A., Venkataraman S. 1996. Renegade and rational championing strategies. *Organization Studies* 17: 751–771.

Shapiro C., Varian H.R. 1999. The art of standard wars. *California Management Review* 41(2): 8–32.

Simon H.A. 1947. *Administrative Behavior*. MacMillan: New York.

Simon H.A. 1957. *Models of Man*. Wiley: New York, NY.

Singh J.V., House R.J., Tucker D.J. 1986. Organizational change and organizational mortality. *Administrative Science Quarterly* 31: 587–611.

Singh J.V., Lumsden C.J. 1990. Theory and research in organizational ecology. *Annual Review of Sociology* 16: 161–195.

Singh J.V., Tucker D.J., House R.J. 1986. Organizational legitimacy and the liability of newness. *Administrative Science Quarterly* 31: 171–193.

Singh J.V., Tucker D., Meinhard A. 1988. Are voluntary social service organizations structurally inert? *Paper presented at the Academy of Management*, Anaheim, CA.

Sitkin S.B., Bies R.J. 1993. Focused issue: The legalistic organization. *Organization Science* 4(3): 345–351.

Slide A. 1986. *The American Film Industry: A Historical Dictionary*. Greenwoodpress, Westport, CT.

Slide A., Gevinson A. 1987. *The Big V: A History of the Vitagraph Company*. The Scarecrow Press, Metuchen, NJ.

Smith A.E. 1952. *Two Reels and a Crank*. Doubleday: New York, NY.

Stata R. 1989. Organizational learning – The key to management innovation. *Sloan Management Review* Spring: 63–74.

Stearns T.M., Carter N.M., Reynolds P.D., Williams M.L. 1995. New firm survival: Industry, strategy, and location. *Journal of Business Venturing* 10: 23–42.

Stearns T.M,. Hills G.E. 1996. Entrepreneurship and new firm development: A definitional introduction. *Journal of Business Research* 36:1–4.

Sterman J. 1987. Testing behavioral simulation models by direct experiment. *Management Science* 33:1572–1592.

Sterman J. 1989. Modeling managerial behavior: Misperceptions of feedback in a dynamic decision making experiment. *Management Science* 35: 321–339.

Stewart T.A. 1991. GE keeps those ideas coming. *Fortune* August 12: 41–49.

Stinchcombe A.L. 1965. Social structure and organizations. In *Handbook of organizations*, March J.G. (ed.). Rand-McNally: Chicago, IL.

Suchman M.C. 1995. Managing legitimacy: Strategic and institutional approaches. *Academy of Management Review* 20(3): 571–610.

Suchman M.C., Steward D.J., Westfall CA. 2001. The legal environment of entrepreneurship: Observations on the legitimation of venture finance in Silicon Valley. In *The Entrepreneurship Dynamic*, Schoonhoven CB, Romanelli E (eds). Stanford University Press: Stanford, CA.

Sutton J.R., Dobbin F. 1996. The two faces of governance: Responses to legal uncertainty in U.S. firms, 1955 to 1985. *American Sociological Review* 61(5): 794–811.

Sutton J.R., Dobbin F., Meyer J.W., Scott W.R. 1994. The Legalization of the workplace. *American Journal of Sociology* 99(4): 944–971.

Swaminathan A. 1995. The proliferation of specialist organizations in the American wine industry. *Administrative Science Quarterly* 40: 653–680.

Swaminathan A. 1998. The impact of resource partitioning and mobility barriers on the evolution of specialist organizations in the American wine industry. Paper presented at the Stanford Conference on Strategic Management, Stanford, CA.

Swaminathan A., Wade J.B. 2001. Social Movement Theory and the Evolution of New Organizational Forms. In *The Entrepreneurship Dynamic*, Schoonhoven C.B., Romanelli E. (eds). Stanford University Press: Stanford, CA.

Swaminathan A., Wiedenmayer G. 1991. Does the pattern of density dependence in organizational mortality rates vary across levels of analysis? Evidence from the German brewing industry. *Social Science Research* 20: 45–73.

Swann G.M.P. 1987. Industry standard microprocessors and the strategy of second source production. In *Product Standardization and Competitive Strategy*, Gabel H.L. (ed). Elsevier: Amsterdam.

Thompson J.D. 1967. *Organizations in Action*. McGraw-Hill: New York, NY.

Thompson V.A. 1965. Bureaucracy and innovation. *Administrative Science Quarterly* 10: 1–20.

Thornton P.H. 1999. The Sociology of Entrepreneurship. *Annual Review of Sociology* 25: 19–47.

Tucker D., Singh J.V., Meinhard A. 1990. Organizational form, population dynamics, and institutional change: The founding patterns of voluntary organizations. *Academy of Management Journal* (33) 1: 151–179.

Tushman M.T. 1977. Special boundary roles in the innovation process. *Administrative Science Quarterly* 22: 587–605.

Tushman M.T., Anderson P. 1986. Technological Discontinuities and Organizational Environments. *Administrative Science Quarterly* 31: 439–465.

Tushman M.T., Nadler D. 1986. Organizing for innovation. *California Management Review* 28: 74–92.

Tushman M.T., Nelson R.R. 1990. Introduction: Technology, organizations, and innovation. *Administrative Science Quarterly* 35: 1–8.

Tushman M.T., Newman W.H., Romanelli E. 1986. Convergence and upheaval: Managing the unsteady pace of organizational evolution. *California Management Review* 29: 29–44.

Tushman M.T., Romanelli E. 1985. Organizational evolution: A metamorphosis model of convergence and reorientation. In *Research in organizational Behavior* Vol. 7, Cummings L.L., Staw B.M. (eds). JAI Press: Greenwich, CT.

Tushman M.T., O'Reilly C.A. 1996. Ambidextrous organizations: Managing evolutionary and revolutionary change. *California Management Review* 38: 8–30.

Tushman M.T., Rosenkopf L. 1996. Executive succession, strategic reorientation and performance growth: A longitudinal study in the U.S. cement industry. *Management Science* 42: 939–953.

Tjosvold D., Weicker D. 1993. Cooperative and competitive networking by entrepreneurs: A critical incident study. *Journal of Small Business Management* 31: 11–21.

Utterback J.M., Abernathy W. 1975. A dynamic model of process and product innovation. *Omega* 33: 639–656.

Utterback J.M., Suárez F.F. 1993. Innovation, competition, and industry structure. *Research Policy* 1993: 1–21.

Van Gelder L. 1996. Worldwide echoes of independents' Oscar joy. *New York Times* (March 26).

Vandermerwe S., Birley S. 1997. The corporate entrepreneur: Leading organizational transformation. *Long Range Planning* 30:345–352.

Van de Ven A.H. 1986. Central problems in the management of innovation. In *Readings in the Management of Innovation,* 2nd edition, Tushman M.L., Moore W.L. (eds). Cambridge, MA: Ballinger.

Van de Ven A.H. 1993a. A community perspective on the emergence of innovations. *Journal of Engineering & Technology Management* 10: 23–51.

Van de Ven A.H. 1993b. The development of an infrastructure for entrepreneurship. *Journal of Business Venturing* 8: 211–230.

Van de Ven A.H., Garud R. 1989. A framework for understanding the emergence of new industries. *Research on Technological Innovation Management and Policy* 4: 195–225.

Varian H.R. 1978. *Microeconomic Analysis.* Norton Company: New York, NY.

Wade J.B. 1995. Dynamics of organizational communities and technological bandwagons: An empirical investigation of community evolution in the microprocessor market. *Strategic Management Journal* 16: 111–133.

Wade J.B. 1996. A community-level analysis of sources and rates of technological variation in the microprocessor market. *Academy of Management Journal* 39: 1218–1244.

Wade J.B., Swaminathan A., Saxon M.S. 1998. Normative and resource flow consequences of local regulations in the American brewing industry, 1845–1918. *Administrative Science Quarterly* 43 (4): 905–935.

Weber M. 1904. *The Protestant Ethic and the Spirit of Capitalism.* Routledge: New York.

Weick K. 1979. *The Social Psychology of Organizing.* Addison-Wesley: Reading, MA.

Weinraub B. 1997. Independent award ceremony seems to rival Academy's. *New York Times* (March 24).

Wid's Film Daily. 1926. Tremendous strides. July 26: 1,3.

Wid's Film Daily. 1924. Holds seventh place. April 15: 7.

Williamson O.E. 1983. Organizational innovation: The transaction-cost approach to entrepreneurship. In *Entrepreneurship,* Ronen J (ed.). Lexington Books: Lexington, MA.

Winter S.G. 1990. Survival, selection, and inheritance in evolutionary theories of organization. In *Organizational Evolution: New Directions,* Singh J.V. (ed). Sage: Newbury Park, CA.

Woo C.Y., Daellenbach U., Nicholls-Nixon C. 1994. Theory building in the presence of 'randomness': The case of venture creation and performance. *Journal of Management Studies* 31: 507–524.

Writers' Program – New York. 1985. *The Film Index: A Bibliography* 2. Kraus International Publications: White Plains, NY.

Yelle L.E. 1979. The learning curve: Historical review and comprehensive survey. *Decision Sciences* 10: 302–328.

Zucker L.G. 1989. Combining institutional theory and population ecology: No legitimacy, no history. *American Sociological Review* 54: 542–545.

Index

American film industry 10, 13, 81,
88, 114, 115, 116, 117, 126, 127,
128, 140, 143, 146, 150, 153, 156,
157, 160, 185, 191
American Film Manufacturing
Company 149
American motion-picture industry
163

Biograph 11, 117, 118, 121, 134,
136, 148, 149, 150, 151, 152, 153,
155, 156, 157, 168

Censorship 166
Competence 20, 27, 28, 71
Competency trap 29
Copyright 92, 146, 147, 150, 151,
152, 153, 154, 163, 192
Creative destruction 1, 7
Cultural industry 85, 88, 109, 110,
180

Demille 168
Dominant design 28, 116, 117, 129
dominant technology 84, 90

Ecological perspective 8, 9, 16, 84,
113, 191
Ecologies of learning 5, 16
Edison 11, 117, 121, 134, 136, 147,
148, 149, 151, 152, 153, 154, 156,
157, 158, 162, 165, 166, 185
Entrepreneurship 2
community dynamics 6, 9, 13,
81, 112, 113, 114, 115, 126, 129,
130, 132, 133, 134, 135, 139,
140, 141, 191
definition 2
demand side perspectives 3, 15,
189
related sourcing 10, 12, 81, 112,
114, 129, 135, 136, 137, 141, 191

search 6
second sourcing 10, 112, 114,
129, 135, 138, 191
supply side perspective 3, 5
trend 5
Environment 5, 8, 10, 11, 20, 31,
46, 55, 58, 59, 60, 61, 62, 63, 64,
65, 66, 68, 71, 73, 74, 77, 78, 84,
106, 113, 115, 137, 138, 143, 145,
146, 156, 157, 158, 159, 170, 190,
192, 193
ambiguous 20, 26, 43, 63, 71
munificent 84, 138
Experiential learning systems 8, 19,
26, 46, 56

Film
distribution 84, 86, 87, 89, 91,
92, 93, 94, 97, 100, 101, 104,
105, 107, 108, 116, 120, 121,
122, 123, 125, 126, 128, 129,
132, 133, 136, 137, 140, 149,
150, 155, 157, 182, 191, 193
duping 151
exhibition 10, 81, 85, 86, 91,
116, 117, 118, 119, 120, 121,
124, 126, 127, 128, 136, 137,
138, 147, 148, 149, 152, 156,
163, 164, 166
feature 5, 7, 9, 62, 81, 84, 85, 86,
87, 89, 90, 91, 93, 95, 97, 101,
102, 104, 108, 109, 113, 123,
124, 126, 128, 129, 133, 134,
137, 150, 155, 156, 157, 162,
170, 183, 193
investment 44, 156, 163, 164,
165
pricing 122, 150
production 11, 12, 23, 42, 81, 83,
84, 86, 87, 89, 91, 92, 93, 94, 97,
101, 104, 105, 107, 108, 116,
119, 120, 121, 122, 123, 124,

125, 126, 127, 128, 130, 133,
134, 136, 137, 138, 147, 149,
150, 151, 152, 154, 155, 156,
157, 163, 191, 192, 193
public perception   166
scandals   167
star system   12, 164, 169, 183, 193
Founding   83, 93, 134
innovative   32, 48, 49, 57, 75,
124, 132, 134

General Film Distribution Company
154
Griffith, D.W.   150, 155

Hollywood   11, 12, 83, 84, 87, 116,
133, 155, 156, 157, 164, 180, 181,
183, 192, 193

Independent Moving Picture
Company   150
Industry emergence   3, 13, 81, 82,
112, 116, 143, 144, 192
Innovation   4, 6, 7, 8, 16, 17, 18,
19, 20, 21, 22, 23, 24, 25, 27, 28,
29, 30, 31, 33, 34, 36, 37, 38, 39,
40, 41, 42, 43, 44, 45, 46, 47, 48,
50, 81, 83, 88, 90, 97, 107, 108,
109, 110, 112, 114, 117, 124,
130, 131, 132, 133, 134, 135,
136, 138, 139, 140, 141, 150,
155, 190, 191
administrative   6, 18, 31, 124,
132, 155, 157
bureaucratic   8, 17, 18, 19, 22, 23,
38, 43, 45, 109, 146
evolutional   19, 21, 22, 25, 30, 39,
43, 45
institutional   5, 7, 10, 13, 19, 21,
22, 24, 28, 39, 42, 43, 44, 45, 53,
54, 55, 57, 62, 63, 72, 73, 74, 76,
77, 78, 114, 115, 127, 128, 143,
145, 156, 157, 159, 160, 192, 193
radical   8, 17, 18, 20, 22, 24, 44
revolutionarl   19, 21, 22, 23, 24,
29, 39, 42, 43, 44, 45
Intrapreneuring   6, 7, 8, 15

Laemmle, Carl   150

Legitimacy   8, 10, 11, 12, 13, 77, 78,
94, 108, 116, 143, 144, 146, 156,
159, 160, 161, 162, 165, 167, 169,
170, 171, 173, 180, 181, 182, 183,
184, 185, 190, 192
Cognitive   11
Levels of analysis   1, 2, 3, 15, 78,
111, 113, 189, 193
Litigation   10, 11, 121, 143, 146,
147, 148, 150, 151, 153, 154, 156,
157, 180, 192
Lubin   148, 151, 152, 154

Motion Picture Patents Corporation
market control   11, 84, 147, 149,
150, 154, 155, 193
Motion Pictures Patents Company
11, 149, 164, 171
Moving Picture World   119, 165, 168
MPPC   *See* Motion Pictures Patent
Corporation

New industry   3, 7, 9, 10, 13, 81, 82,
86, 89, 108, 112, 114, 116, 131,
133, 136, 138, 140, 141, 143, 144,
146, 147, 156, 160, 161, 164, 170,
184, 185, 191, 192
New York Times   144, 163, 165, 171,
181

Organization theory   1, 5, 7, 8, 11,
13, 22, 53, 159, 189, 193
Organizational change   17, 18, 19,
25, 26, 54, 55, 56, 58, 62, 63, 64
Organizational learning   7, 16, 19,
23, 24, 26, 27, 43, 54, 55, 56, 64,
71, 74, 78, 190
Organizational myopia   27
Organizational theory
See organization theory

Patent   11, 121, 129, 146, 147, 148,
149, 151, 152, 153, 156, 157, 158,
163, 192
Population dynamics   8, 9, 13, 55,
61, 62, 72, 78, 81, 82, 87, 93, 113,
147, 157, 158, 190
Population ecology   7, 8, 9, 113,
140, 146, 191

carrying capacity   9, 59, 62, 67,
    68, 72, 73, 77, 191
  density dependence   8, 94, 95,
    108, 159, 169, 191
  mass dependence   9

Resource-partitioning model   9, 81,
    84, 85, 89, 90, 93, 106, 109
Routines   18, 25, 26, 27, 28, 32, 33,
    35, 36, 43, 45, 46, 47, 49, 50, 51

Search   4, 6, 7, 8, 26, 27, 28, 29, 30,
    32, 33, 35, 36, 37, 38, 39, 40, 41,
    42, 43, 44, 45, 47, 48, 49, 50, 51,
    52, 54, 55, 56, 57, 58, 59, 60, 62,
    63, 64, 65, 66, 67, 68, 69, 71, 72,
    73, 74, 75, 76, 77, 78, 130, 141, 15

fixed   57, 58, 59, 60, 61, 62, 63,
    66, 67, 68, 69, 71, 72
  mimetic   54, 55, 57, 58, 60, 61,
    62, 63, 64, 65, 66, 67, 68, 69, 70,
    71, 72, 73, 74, 75, 76, 77, 190
Self-regulation   166
Selig   148
Simulation   19, 20, 21, 31, 32, 33,
    38, 39, 40, 41, 42, 43, 44, 45, 46,
    47, 48, 51, 54, 59, 60, 62, 63, 64,
    66, 71, 72, 73, 76
Sociopolitical   11, 12, 116, 143, 144,
    159, 160, 161, 169, 170, 171, 173,
    180, 181, 182, 184
Stakeholders   11, 162, 170, 173

Typologies   6, 7, 21, 132, 139